More Praise for *Applying AI in Learning and*

"*Applying AI in Learning and Development* is a comprehensive and in-depth discussion of the exciting new world of AI in L&D. This book will give you the background and road map you need to launch ahead in this critical new era in corporate learning."
—**Josh Bersin**, Global Industry Analyst and CEO, The Josh Bersin Company

"This book offers a wide-ranging and practical view of how AI is poised to transform our field. Josh Cavalier maps out not just what's emerging, but how these technologies are already reshaping the work of learning professionals—a future that's arriving faster than many might expect. This is not a speculative vision; it's a grounded tour through the tools, platforms, and strategies that will soon become, as Josh so aptly puts it, 'just another Tuesday in L&D.'"
—**Megan Torrance**, CEO, TorranceLearning; Author, *Agile for Instructional Designers* and *Data and Analytics for Instructional Designers*

"In a time when AI is both transforming and challenging the landscape of L&D, Josh Cavalier offers clarity, strategy, and heart. This book isn't just about AI technology; it's also about how we design for people working alongside AI. It provides practical and actionable pathways for L&D professionals ready to embrace and work in a world we share with AI. Of course, this is a must-read for anyone who is serious about the future of workplace learning."
—**Karl M. Kapp, EdD,** Author, *The Gamification of Learning and Instruction* and *Action-First Learning*

"This book is an invaluable primer that provides a practical guide to using AI. From basics such as prompting and governance, Cavalier explores what is possible today and the implications for tomorrow. It's essential reading for the L&D professional looking to prepare for the future."
—**Donald H. Taylor,** Lead Researcher, The L&D Global Sentiment Survey

"This book is the guide our industry has been waiting for. Josh Cavalier doesn't just explain what AI can do; he shows L&D professionals how to thoughtfully and responsibly apply it to improve performance."
—**David Kelly,** Former Chairman and CEO, Learning Guild

"Josh Cavalier has written a practical, forward-looking guide for HR and L&D professionals who know AI isn't just today's buzzword—it's a wholesale workforce transformation. He makes a compelling case for why embedding AI into our daily workflow isn't optional if we want to stay competitive and drive real impact across the business and for the future-ready workforce. This is a must-read for all HR and L&D professionals."
—**Brandon Carson,** Chief Learning Officer, Docebo

"This book is a blueprint for the future of learning—where machines accelerate potential and humans remain the architects of meaning."
—**Abhijit Bhaduri,** Former Partner and GM Global L&D, Microsoft

"Josh's book is *the* blueprint for AI-enabled learning. Things will never be the same; L&D will be able to work with more ingenuity, creativity, and influence to create a better future. A must-use (not just read) for anyone committed to learning, which is everyone."
—**Dave Ulrich,** Rensis Likert Professor Emeritus, University of Michigan; Partner, the RBL Group

"Frankly, in a domain so often obscured by speculation and hype, this book offers L&D professionals the precise, hands-on blueprint they need to genuinely harness AI for impactful organizational transformation. He distills complex AI capabilities into the actionable strategies and practical steps essential for building robust, future-ready capabilities from within."
—**Markus Bernhardt, PhD,** AI Strategist, Endeavor Intelligence

Applying AI
in Learning & Development

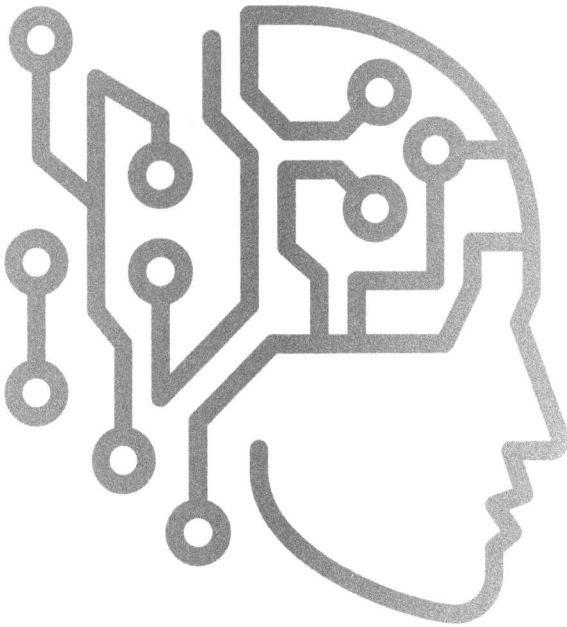

Josh Cavalier

atd
PRESS
Alexandria, VA

ATD Press is an internationally renowned source of insightful and practical information on talent development, training, and professional development.

ATD Press
1640 King Street
Alexandria, VA 22314 USA

Ordering information: Books published by ATD Press can be purchased by visiting ATD's website at td.org/books or by calling 800.628.2783 or 703.683.8100.

Library of Congress Control Number: 2025938446

ISBN-10: 1-96023-152-9
ISBN-13: 978-1-960231-52-9
e-ISBN: 978-1-96023-153-6

ATD Press Editorial Staff
Director: Sarah Halgas
Manager: Melissa Jones
Content Manager: Alexandria Clapp
Developmental Editor: Jack Harlow
Production Editor: Katy Wiley Stewts
Text Designer: Shirley E.M. Raybuck
Cover Designer: Brandon Rush

Text Layout: Kathleen Dyson

Contents

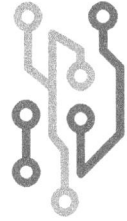

Introduction

The Day AI Decided to Crash My Morning Coffee (and My Career)

The aroma of freshly brewed coffee filled my home office as I settled into my worn Herman Miller Aeron chair, a silent witness to three decades of technological revolutions in L&D. It was December 5, 2022, and little did I know that this day would kick off yet another paradigm shift in my career.

A *New York Times* headline caught my eye as I scrolled through my morning news feed: "The Brilliance and Weirdness of ChatGPT." Fascinated, I immersed myself in every paragraph, disclosing the remarkable potential of this emerging type of artificial intelligence.

The article referenced a post on Twitter (now X) by Thomas H. Ptacek (@tqbf) that captured my imagination.

> **Prompt:** Write a biblical verse in the style of the King James Bible explaining how to remove a peanut butter sandwich from a VCR.
>
> **ChatGPT:** And it came to pass that a man was troubled by a peanut butter sandwich, for it had been placed within his VCR, and he knew not how to remove it.
>
> And he cried out to the Lord, saying, "Oh, Lord, how can I remove this sandwich from my VCR, for it is stuck fast and will not budge?"
>
> And the Lord spoke unto him, saying "Fear not, my child, for I shall guide thy hand and show thee the way. Take thy butter knife, and carefully insert it between the sandwich and the VCR, and gently pry them apart. And with patience and perseverance, the sandwich shall be removed, and thy VCR shall be saved."

And the man did as the Lord commanded, and lo and behold, the sandwich was removed from the VCR, and the man was saved.

And the Lord said, "Verily I say unto thee, seek not to put thy peanut butter sandwiches in thy VCR, for it is not a suitable place for such things. Rather, keep thy sandwiches in thy refrigerator or on thy plate, where they belong."

And the man heeded the Lord's words, and from that day forth, he kept his sandwiches in their proper place, and was saved from trouble and woe. Amen.

I found myself chuckling at the absurdity and marveling at the implications. If ChatGPT could seamlessly blend an ancient literary style with technical instructions for removing a sandwich from a VCR, what else could it do?

This moment reminded me of the early 1990s when, as an art director, I helped create e-learning courses for CD-ROMs. Delivering interactive multimedia instruction to desktops was revolutionary then. We transitioned from overhead projectors to digital learning with text, images, sound, video, and interactions, and I was fully engaged.

Curiosity piqued, and my coffee cup refilled, I signed up for an OpenAI account. As the website loaded, I had no idea what to type in. The *New York Times* article mentioned poems and limericks, so I went in that direction.

I started with a playful test. I typed in the ChatGPT message box:

Write a limerick about drinking beer with friends.

It was sophomoric but a good first test. The response appeared almost instantly:

Gathered with friends in good cheer,
We raised up our glasses of beer.
With laughter and jest,
We enjoyed the best,
In camaraderie, we held dear.

I leaned back, impressed. ChatGPT had nailed the limerick structure and captured the essence of friendship and celebration. It was wild to see this application seemingly understand the nuances of human interaction.

As I experimented with more prompts, a thought struck me. During the COVID-19 pandemic, I discovered a new passion: smoking food. Suddenly, these seemingly unrelated threads—AI, learning, and smoked cuisine—intertwined in my mind. Because nothing says "experiential learning" quite like a well-crafted side dish at a BBQ, right?

With a mix of curiosity and skepticism, I typed:

Write learning objectives for cooking a smoked potato salad.

(It was initially phrased, "Write learning objectives for smoking a potato," but ChatGPT said that it couldn't complete the task and smoking a potato—like a cigarette—would be dangerous!)

If ChatGPT could handle this culinary curveball, I figured, it could potentially handle anything—even the most complex training needs analysis. ChatGPT generated learning objectives that were accurate, nuanced, comprehensive, and exceptionally well-crafted. They accounted for food safety, flavor profiles, and even presentation—aspects that spoke to the science and art of cooking.

It was a moment that made me pause and consider how this technology would affect L&D. I realized we were on the cusp of a massive technological shift. Just as CD-ROMs and e-learning had revolutionized corporate training, AI was poised to transform how we approach knowledge sharing and skills development.

But this realization also brought a wave of questions. How does ChatGPT work? How would this technology affect instructional designers? And, most importantly, could it explain why learners never remember to click the "next" button in an e-learning course?

As I pondered these questions, I couldn't help but think of how far we've come in L&D. From the behaviorist approaches of the mid-20th century to the cognitive revolution, personal computers, the internet, mobile phones, and now to the dawn of AI-assisted learning, our field has always been at the forefront of adopting new technologies and methodologies. Yet, the core principles that have guided our work for decades remain relevant. The challenge is to apply these time-tested principles to the brave new world of AI.

This book is born out of a moment of reflection, as a guide for navigating the AI revolution in L&D. It is more than just a technical manual on generative AI or a collection of best prompt practices. It explores how AI is reshaping jobs, skills, and human performance, as well as what that means for us as L&D professionals and, more fundamentally, as humans in an increasingly AI-augmented world.

The central thesis of this book is simple yet profound: No matter how advanced AI becomes, our focus must remain on performance of both humans and machines.

As L&D professionals, we are evolving into human-machine performance analysts. We orchestrate learning journeys for humans, coordinate with AI agents, and dig deep into data analytics to ensure we are moving the needle.

Whether you're on the front line of training design and delivery or behind the scenes shaping strategy—whether you're a hesitant skeptic with little experience testing AI capabilities or an early adopter with several years of trial-and-error experience—we need to embrace this evolution to control our future. This future will be one in which we will deliver high-quality, effective training and boost organizational results, all aided by this latest technological tool.

But how do we navigate this evolution?

Why You Need This Book

I wrote this book to equip L&D professionals with insights on integrating AI into their workflows, training modules, and learning strategies. I want it to:

- Inspire, guide, and empower you in leveraging the potential of generative AI for continuous self-improvement and upskilling.
- Help you navigate the nuanced ethical considerations, ensuring the responsible adoption of AI in learning environments.
- Stimulate and spark new ideas for building the next generation of AI-enhanced learning platforms.
- Enable you to make more informed, strategic decisions about implementing and optimizing AI-driven learning initiatives.

Figure I-1 guides you through how this book will prepare you for our AI-enabled future.

Figure I-1. How to Read This Book

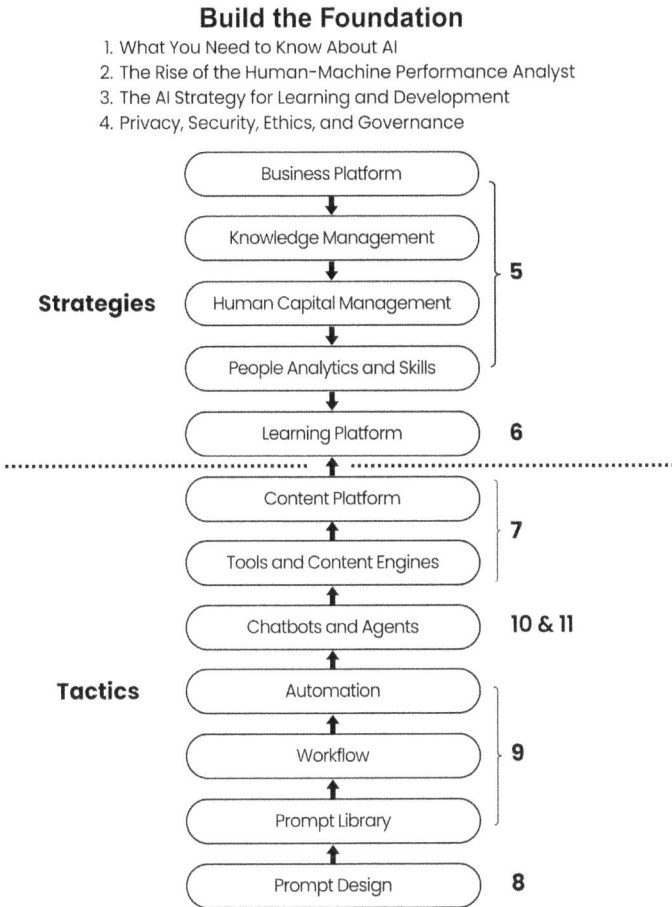

Build the Foundation

1. What You Need to Know About AI
2. The Rise of the Human-Machine Performance Analyst
3. The AI Strategy for Learning and Development
4. Privacy, Security, Ethics, and Governance

Strategies

Business Platform

Knowledge Management

Human Capital Management — 5

People Analytics and Skills

Learning Platform — 6

Content Platform

Tools and Content Engines — 7

Chatbots and Agents — 10 & 11

Tactics

Automation

Workflow — 9

Prompt Library

Prompt Design — 8

The first four chapters build our foundation. Consider them your compass for understanding and implementing AI in the L&D landscape and how AI affects the learning profession. These chapters offer essential insights for everyone involved in L&D:

- **Chapter 1** introduces you to what you need to know about AI and generative AI. We map how generative AI transforms manual curation into sophisticated automation.

- **Chapter 2** explores the transformation of our profession. AI amplifies our capabilities as L&D professionals. Watch our roles evolve from content creators into human-machine performance analysts.

- **Chapter 3** wades into the kind of AI strategy you need to implement AI seamlessly within your organization and the L&D function.
- **Chapter 4** addresses our crucial responsibilities with privacy, security, and ethics when using AI. We navigate data governance, bias prevention, and trust building, which form the bedrock of sustainable AI policy within any organization.
- **Chapters 5 and 6** provide a strategic road map for navigating your organization's path through technological advancement. Chapter 5 reveals how AI transforms your core business platforms, while chapter 6 focuses on learning platforms and their AI functions, including learning paths and content personalization.

If you want to roll up your sleeves and get right into designing content with AI, then you can jump to chapter 7. This is when we start to explore content development powered by AI. We'll keep building on these concepts through chapter 11. In addition:

- **Chapter 7** transforms our approach to content development with generative AI. We explore techniques for content creation, curation, and adaptation. We also look at how to use an AI avatar.
- **Chapter 8** goes into how to master generative AI prompting. This includes prompting techniques you can use immediately for better results and example prompts.
- **Chapter 9** discusses how to create a prompt library and reclaim your time through automation. You've likely spent hours updating course materials. We can use AI to transform them into efficient, AI-driven workflows, which frees you up for strategic work.
- **Chapters 10 and 11** introduce you to AI agents and chatbots. Chapter 10 advances to creating agents who work behind the scenes, providing learning organizations with deep, automated tasks, and chapter 11 concludes the tactical chapters with ways to map a chatbot's planning, creation, and implementation.

The conclusion wraps up the book with a quick call to action. Throughout, I've drawn on my experiences teaching L&D organizations how to use large language models and generative AI as well as my experiences in workshops and speaking engagements hearing how real L&D professionals are ideating, testing, and refining their approaches to AI. I've woven in exercises to get you thinking and playing on your own and with your team.

The Future Is Here

Applying AI in L&D presents both significant challenges and transformative opportunities that will test our assumptions and expand our capabilities. I designed the road map in this book to help you navigate AI's technical and human aspects in learning. Together, we will explore how to harness the power of AI while keeping our focus on what matters most: creating meaningful learning experiences that drive real organizational impact.

After all, in the age of AI, there's still room for a dash of human creativity—whether crafting the perfect learning module or the perfect side dish.

The future of learning is here, and it's more exciting than ever.

So, let's dream boldly, experiment fearlessly, and embrace the unknown. The Age of AI is more than technology; it's about us—our ingenuity, resilience, and power to shape a future where learning knows no bounds.

Additional Resources

By the way, if you're curious about the smoked potato salad that inspired this journey, you can find the recipe on my website, joshcavalier.ai/Applying AIBook.

You'll also find:
- A video introduction to each chapter
- Exercise files
- AI implementation checklists
- Access to my prompt library
- Customizable templates
- A comprehensive sample AI policy

These resources are regularly updated to reflect emerging best practices and regulatory changes in the rapidly evolving AI landscape.

CHAPTER 1

What You Need to Know About AI

In This Chapter

- A (very) brief history of artificial intelligence
- How today's AI stands on yesterday's breakthroughs
- Generative AI and its implications for L&D

What if the next breakthrough in L&D isn't a new methodology or platform but an intelligent partner that can help us reimagine how we approach human performance?

I'm an education technology specialist. I've spent my career exploring technology like personal computers, the internet, and mobile phones and how they influence human performance. Little did I know that I would be swept up in one of our era's most significant tipping points: the rise of generative artificial intelligence (GenAI).

My first exposure to AI actually didn't begin with GenAI but with video. Between 2015 and 2020, I spoke about using video across the entire learning journey—specifically short-form or micro video. To prepare for my speaking sessions, I dissected the anatomy of short-form videos, seeking the perfect formula to captivate and educate. I also reviewed the latest research on using video.

I learned in 2015 that Google, IBM, and numerous research universities were pushing the boundaries of computer vision technology, employing deep neural networks to decipher what was happening in moving images. Imagine a machine that could watch a video and understand it much like we do—grasping context, identifying actions, and piecing together narratives.

I envisioned a future in which vision technology would reshape the education landscape: personalized video recommendations curated by AI, content analysis that could pinpoint the most effective teaching moments, and even bespoke videos tailored to fill each learner's unique knowledge gaps. But technology, like water, does not always flow where we expect.

While AI's potential in video analysis and personalized content creation still simmers with promise, the absolute deluge of AI would come from an unexpected source. On November 30, 2022, a chatbot named ChatGPT burst onto the scene, suddenly creating song lyrics, poems, and even jokes.

Prompt: Tell me a joke about the sun.

Response: Why doesn't the sun go to college?
Because it already has a million degrees!

This moment was a technological breakthrough that started a cultural awakening. Within five days, more than one million people signed up for an OpenAI account to access ChatGPT, easily eclipsing the adoption rate of the iPhone and Instagram (Figure 1-1).

Figure 1-1. Time to One Million Users

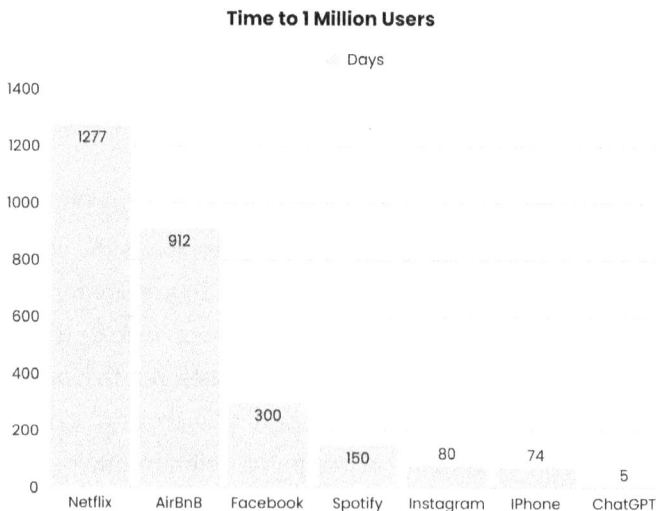

Time to 1 Million Users

Days

	Netflix	AirBnB	Facebook	Spotify	Instagram	IPhone	ChatGPT
	1277	912	300	150	80	74	5

GenAI had stepped out of the labs and into our lives, sparking a conversation far beyond tech circles. It was as if we'd all been watching a slowly filling bathtub, only to turn around and face a tidal wave.

Technology has always been a dance of disruption and adaptation in L&D. I've witnessed this firsthand through waves of innovation, from CD-ROMs to the internet, social media, and mobile learning. But artificial intelligence? This is more than another step in our digital evolution. AI will fundamentally reimagine how we approach human learning and performance.

The *how* of this transformation lies in understanding the critical interplay between human and machine capabilities, which we'll explore throughout this book. But first, let's begin by defining what GenAI is and differentiating it from other forms of AI, such as traditional AI, machine learning, and deep learning. I'll highlight its unique capabilities and relevance to L&D professionals, including its potential for personalized content, automation, and scalability. By the end, you'll understand what makes GenAI different from previous technologies and be ready to apply it in your daily work.

How Did We Get Here?

Here's the thing about overnight sensations: They usually have a fascinating backstory. While this sudden surge might seem unprecedented, AI has been evolving and finding applications in various fields since the 1950s. The history of AI is a mix of innovation, setbacks, and breakthroughs spanning more than seven decades.

You don't need to be an AI historian to begin applying AI in L&D, but it helps to have a light grasp on how AI arrived in its current iteration. Figure 1-2 shows an evolution of AI technology.

Figure 1-2. The Evolution of AI Technology

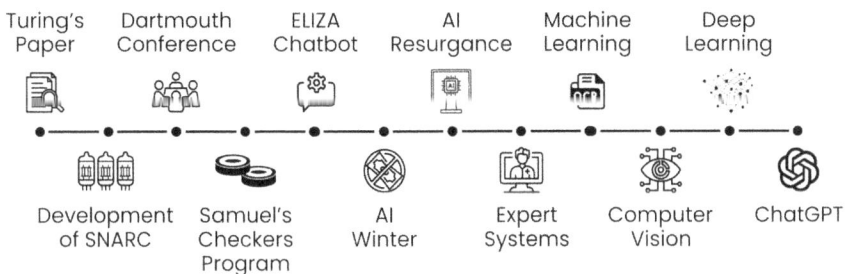

Here are the highlights:

- In 1950, Alan Turing published his seminal paper "Computing Machinery and Intelligence," which introduced the Turing test and laid the groundwork for AI research. In 1951, Marvin Minsky and Dean Edmonds developed SNARC—the first artificial neural network—using 3,000 vacuum tubes. But it wasn't until 1956 at the Dartmouth Conference that the term artificial intelligence was coined.
- Two early prototypes in the 1950s and 1960s include Arthur Samuel's checkers program (which demonstrated machine learning capabilities) and ELIZA, a chatbot with cognitive capabilities (which marked a significant milestone in natural language processing or NLP). But, in the 1970s, as early promises met technical limitations—namely, needing more computing power, better algorithms, and vast amounts of data (which is still true today!)—the first AI "winter" hit, and AI research funding dwindled.
- The fundamental AI transformation began in the 1990s and continued through the early 2000s. Suddenly, we had faster computers and the internet could generate unprecedented amounts of data. AI has found practical applications in healthcare, manufacturing, and education.

And here are some notable examples of how AI is used:

- **Expert systems for medical diagnosis.** GIDEON (Global Infectious Diseases and Epidemiology Network) was designed to diagnose infectious diseases worldwide based on symptoms, signs, and laboratory tests.
- **Machine learning algorithms for pattern recognition.** These were successfully used to recognize handwritten characters, leading to advancements in the optical character recognition (OCR) systems used by banks and postal services.
- **Natural language processing (NLP) for language translation.** Services like Google Translate have made communication easier across language barriers by providing instant text and speech translations.
- **Computer vision for image and facial recognition.** Advanced computer vision algorithms have been incorporated into medical imaging technologies, such as MRI and CT scanners, for more accurate diagnostics.

- **Robotics for industrial automation.** Computer-controlled robots have become the standard in industrial settings and other industries to perform repetitive, dangerous tasks or ones that require precision and consistency.

These real-world applications were early indicators of AI's deeper potential. Each breakthrough showed us glimpses of what machines could accomplish in specific domains.

The 2010s witnessed the early sparks of GenAI's potential, including the generative adversarial network (GAN), which is one of the technologies used for GenAI image creation. However, November 2022 marked a watershed moment—OpenAI's release of ChatGPT changed everything. Suddenly, anyone could converse with an AI product that could write poetry, explain quantum physics, or help plan a birthday party.

The public response was electric. ChatGPT reached 100 million users in just two months. Tech giants and startups alike raced to release their own GenAI models, each pushing the boundaries of what's possible. From DALL-E's artistic creations to Claude's analytical and coding prowess, these tools redefined our expectations of machine intelligence.

The Different Types of AI

To truly grasp where we're heading with GenAI, you need to understand how different types of AI build on one another (Figure 1-3).

Figure 1-3. The AI Landscape

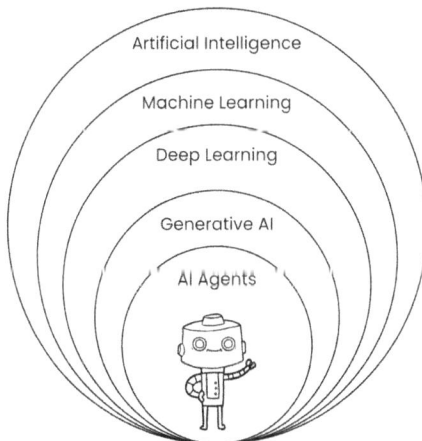

Artificial Intelligence

Machine Learning

Deep Learning

Generative AI

AI Agents

Let's discuss each one in more detail:

- **Traditional AI** focuses on rule-based systems and predefined logic to solve specific problems.

- **Machine learning** is a subset of AI that focuses on building systems that learn—or improve performance—based on the data they consume. It involves algorithms that can automatically learn patterns from data and make predictions or decisions without being explicitly programmed. Netflix's recommendation system is a prime example. It analyzes your viewing history, ratings, and preferences to suggest movies and TV shows you might enjoy. It uses algorithms that learn from user behavior patterns to make increasingly accurate predictions about what content will appeal to each user.

- **Deep learning** is a more advanced subset of machine learning that uses artificial neural networks with multiple layers to learn from large amounts of data. The human brain inspired these neural networks, which can automatically learn hierarchical representations of features from raw data, making them particularly effective for complex tasks like image and speech recognition. Google's voice recognition technology, used in products like Google's Gemini, is a real-world application of deep learning. This system leverages deep neural networks to process and understand human speech, converting it into text and interpreting commands. It can handle different accents and background noise and even improve its accuracy over time as it's exposed to more data.

- **GenAI** is a type of AI that can create new content and ideas, including conversations, stories, images, videos, and music. It is built on deep learning models and large datasets, allowing it to learn patterns and relationships in existing data and then generate novel outputs similar in structure and style to the training data. Unlike traditional AI systems that focus on analysis or prediction, generative AI has the unique ability to produce original content, making it a powerful tool for creative and problem-solving applications across various industries. DALL-E, created by OpenAI, is a powerful example of generative AI. It can create original, realistic images and art from text descriptions. For instance, if you input "an astronaut riding a horse on Mars," DALL-E will generate a unique image matching that description (Figure 1-4).

- **AI agents** are autonomous systems that can perceive their environment, make decisions, and take action to achieve specific goals. They often use machine learning and deep learning techniques to improve their performance over time. GenAI enhances AI agents by enabling them to create original content, generate human-like responses, and adapt dynamically to complex scenarios.

Figure 1-4. AI-Generated Image From DALL-E

The GenAI landscape itself is primarily divided into two categories:

- **Closed systems** offered by companies like OpenAI, Microsoft, Google, and Anthropic prioritize security and governance. These systems often provide more controlled and refined outputs, but the training data and exact methodologies are usually not publicly available. This can raise concerns about transparency and potential biases.
- **Open systems,** like those developed by Meta, offer world-class models with extensive customization options. While this provides flexibility and transparency, it also opens up the potential for misuse.

What Is Generative AI?

GenAI is already influencing various industries. In healthcare, GenAI can transcribe patient consultations and summarize clinical notes; it can also help radiologists detect patterns and anomalies in medical imaging. In marketing, it can generate personalized marketing emails, create eye-catching visuals, and even produce dynamic video content. In retail, it can enhance the shopping experience by providing personalized recommendations, creating interactive shopping interfaces, and assisting with virtual interior design.

It's also a game-changer for L&D. GenAI offers the potential to automate content creation and design a more personalized, adaptive, and engaging learning environment for employees. By automating tasks, personalizing content, and scaling content creation, GenAI empowers L&D professionals to focus on what they do best: designing and delivering effective learning experiences.

The GenAI revolution is distinct for several reasons:

- **Access.** For the first time, powerful AI tools like ChatGPT are freely available to the public and businesses of all sizes.
- **User-friendly interfaces.** Modern AI systems have intuitive interfaces that don't require specialized technical knowledge.
- **Cloud computing.** The availability of vast computational resources via cloud services has enabled more complex AI models to be deployed at scale.
- **Big data.** The explosion of digital data has provided AI systems with enormous training datasets, improving their performance and capabilities.
- **Advancements in deep learning.** Recent breakthroughs in neural network architectures have dramatically improved AI performance in tasks like NLP and image generation.
- **Integration with everyday tools.** AI is now being seamlessly integrated into common software and devices, making it a part of our daily lives.

Before exploring the different dimensions of the exciting possibilities generative AI offers for L&D, it's essential to acknowledge its limitations and potential challenges (which we'll tackle in greater depth in chapter 3 and the rest of the book):

- **Data bias.** GenAI models are trained on vast amounts of data, and if this data reflects existing biases, the AI-generated content may perpetuate them. This can lead to unfair or inaccurate representations, potentially hindering the learning experience.
- **Lack of originality.** GenAI models often rely on existing data to generate new content, sometimes resulting in a lack of originality or creativity. L&D professionals must ensure that AI-generated content is carefully reviewed and adapted to maintain quality and relevance.
- **Need for human oversight.** While GenAI can automate many tasks, it's crucial to maintain human oversight in the L&D process. AI should be seen as a tool to enhance, not replace, the role of L&D professionals. Human expertise is still essential for designing effective learning experiences, providing guidance and support, and ensuring that AI-generated content aligns with learning objectives.
- **Hallucination (or fabricated information).** GenAI can sometimes produce information that sounds plausible but is entirely made up. These "hallucinations" can mislead learners if not properly vetted, so fact-checking should be a critical part of any AI-integrated workflow.

On the cutting edge of these applications is *multimodal generative AI*, which works by processing and generating different types of content—like text, images, audio, video, code, and 3D models—using advanced AI models (Figure 1-5). Multimodal AI works because it learns to combine data in a way that mimics how humans think: We understand words, images, and sounds together to make sense of the world, and pure multimodal systems (like Google's Gemini) are trained to process these inputs the same way, creating more accurate and natural results.

Figure 1-5. Multimodal Generative AI

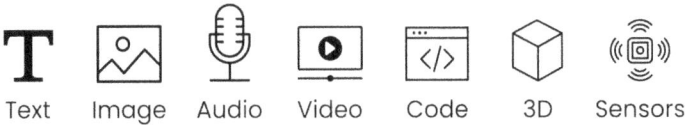

| Text | Image | Audio | Video | Code | 3D | Sensors |

Multimodal generative AI is a good test case for explaining at a high level how GenAI works in practice and how you interact with it to achieve your desired outcomes (Figure 1-6). In simple terms, AI collects and learns from massive amounts of data. It processes the input—like text, images, or audio—into something it can understand and then predicts and generates new content based on what it has learned. Then, AI refines the output and delivers it—whether it's text, an image, a video, or a combination of these formats.

Figure 1-6. Multimodal AI Content Generation

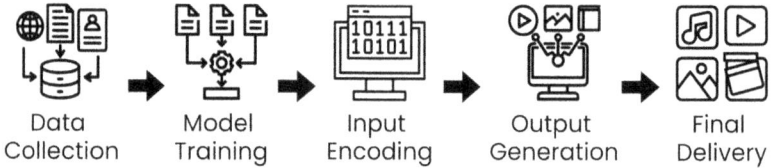

The illustration in Figure 1-6 shows how AI transforms raw data into polished, deliverable content. This five-stage process represents the backbone of modern AI content generation systems.

When you work with AI content tools, you tap into this powerful pipeline. Your prompts activate a system built on massive datasets, trained through complex algorithms, and designed to produce content that meets your needs.

Let's explore how this process works in practice.

Step 1. Collect and Prepare the Data

Multimodal AI needs examples of different types of data to learn from. For example, this could include:

- **Text**—books, articles, and conversations
- **Images**—photos, graphics, or digital artwork
- **Audio**—music, speeches, or recorded sounds
- **Video**—movies, animations, or short clips
- **Code**—programming scripts or entire projects
- **Sensor data**—measurements like temperature, motion, or environmental readings

The data is cleaned and labeled to help the AI model understand each piece's representation.

Step 2. Train the AI Model

The AI model learns by finding patterns in the data. Depending on the type of model, the process works in one of two ways:

- **A unified training model** like Google's Gemini uses a single model (pure multimodal transformer) to simultaneously process all types of inputs. For example, if you show it a photo of a dog and ask, "What is this?" it learns to connect the image (dog) with the question (text). Training involves showing the AI millions of examples that include related text, images, or other inputs.
- **Multiple models** like OpenAI's GPT-4o (text), DALL-E (images), Whisper (audio), and Sora (video) are traditional systems that use separate models for each type of data. For instance, one model handles text, while another handles images. They work together but don't process all the inputs simultaneously.

Step 3. Encode the Input

When you give the AI model a task (like asking it to create an image from a description), it encodes the input into a format it understands:

- Text becomes numerical data (tokens).
- Images become grids of pixels or patterns.
- Audio is broken into sound waves and frequency patterns.
- Video is split into frames and analyzed for motion.

This encoding helps the AI model convert real-world inputs into something it can process mathematically.

Step 4. Generate the Output

The AI model uses its training data to create new content. First, it analyzes the input—whether it's text, images, or other types of data. Multimodal systems like Google's Gemini combine all the inputs at once. For example, if you provide an image of a beach and ask, "What's a good caption?" it understands the visual and the question together.

Then, the model predicts what the output should look or sound like based on patterns it has learned. If the input is text, it predicts the next word. If it's an image, it predicts what pixels come next. For audio, it predicts sound waves.

Finally, the model improves the output by checking how realistic or relevant it is. Models like GANs have a built-in checker that improves the output.

Diffusion models gradually refine an image or sound from random noise into something clear and high quality.

Step 5. Deliver the Final Content

Once the AI model finishes generating the content, it presents the final result, which could be a story written from a text prompt, an image created from a description, a video generated to explain a concept, or code written to solve a problem.

Pure multimodal AI models combine multiple outputs seamlessly. For example, Figure 1-7 shows the process of using an input ("Create a presentation about climate change with visuals and a voice-over.") to create the output, which includes text for slides, images for visuals, and audio for the voice-over—all generated together.

Figure 1-7. Multiple Outputs

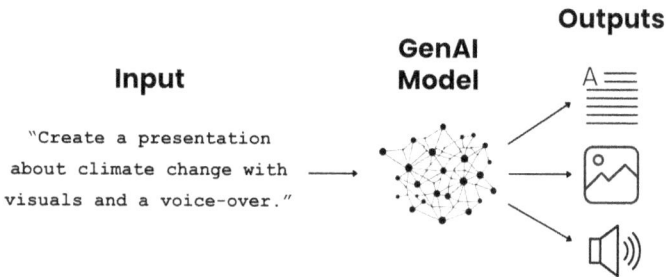

Input

"Create a presentation
about climate change with
visuals and a voice-over."

**GenAI
Model**

Outputs

The steps outlined here map out the technical architecture behind AI content systems, but what does this mean for you as a content creator? While the backend processes are fascinating, understanding the practical workflow will help you leverage these tools effectively.

At its core, AI content generation is a collaborative dance between human expertise and AI capabilities. The process transforms your ideas into polished content through a series of well-defined steps that maximize both efficiency and quality.

So, how does this AI content magic work? Let's break it down:

1. **Input and prompting.** You provide the AI with a brief, the learning objectives, and any specific requirements. The more specific your prompt, the better the output. It's like teaching a new employee—the clearer your instructions, the better the result.

2. **Generation.** The AI model generates a draft based on your input. This could be anything from a course outline to full-fledged content. It's like having a super intern who can produce a first draft at lightning speed.

3. **Human review and editing.** This is crucial. You review the AI-generated content, fact-check it, refine the tone, and ensure it meets your standards. Think of it as a collaboration—the AI brings speed and data, and you bring nuance and expertise.

4. **Iteration.** You can ask the AI model to regenerate or refine specific sections based on your edits. It's like having a tireless co-writer who's always ready for another draft.

5. **Finalization.** After several rounds of human–AI collaboration, you have your final content. The result? Content that combines AI's efficiency with human expertise, nuance, and creativity.

EXERCISE

Getting Started

Ready to dip your toes into the AI content creation pool? Here's how to get started:

1. **Choose your AI with care.** Start with a GenAI tool that gives you secure, private access—ideally one that is built for professionals, trusted with enterprise-level data, and can handle a range of content formats (including text, images, audio, and video).

2. **Master the art of prompting.** Your output's quality depends heavily on your input's quality. Learn to write clear, detailed prompts that specify not just the topic, but the tone, style, and learning approach you want. (More on this in chapter 8.)

3. **Start small.** Begin by using AI for parts of your content process—maybe generating outlines or creating knowledge check questions. As you get comfortable, you can expand its role.

4. **Always keep humans in the loop.** Remember, AI is a tool, not a replacement. Your expertise in learning design, the subject matter, understanding your audience, and creativity are still crucial.

5. **Iterate and refine.** Use AI as a starting point, then iterate. Often, the magic happens in the back-and-forth between humans and AI.

GenAI Model Dimensions

While you're only in chapter 1, the potential GenAI has to revolutionize the L&D space should already be clear. By understanding the four dimensions of GenAI, you can unlock opportunities to create personalized, engaging, and immersive learning experiences. Each dimension represents a leap in the capabilities of AI, moving from foundational text-based tools to real-time interactive systems. Figure 1-8 provides a breakdown of how they apply to the future of workplace learning.

Figure 1-8. GenAI Model Dimensions

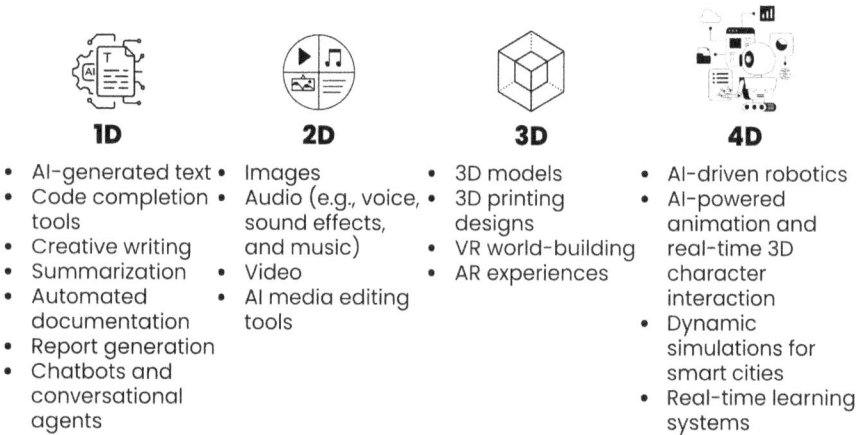

1D	**2D**	**3D**	**4D**
• AI-generated text • Code completion tools • Creative writing • Summarization • Automated documentation • Report generation • Chatbots and conversational agents	• Images • Audio (e.g., voice, sound effects, and music) • Video • AI media editing tools	• 3D models • 3D printing designs • VR world-building • AR experiences	• AI-driven robotics • AI-powered animation and real-time 3D character interaction • Dynamic simulations for smart cities • Real-time learning systems

1D: AI-Generated Text for Content Creation

At the 1D foundational level, GenAI produces and enhances text-based learning content quickly, accurately, and at scale. You can use this dimension to automate mundane tasks, speed up content creation, and ensure consistency.

Applications for L&D include:

- **Automated documentation.** Streamline the creation of training manuals, policies, and procedures.
- **Microlearning content.** Generate bite-sized, targeted lessons tailored to learners' needs.
- **Chatbots and conversational agents.** AI-powered chatbots can support learners with 24/7 assistance, answering FAQs, and delivering learning nudges.

- **Summarization.** Quickly turn lengthy reports, courses, or transcripts into concise takeaways for easy learning.
- **Creative writing.** Draft engaging scenarios, case studies, and storytelling elements for learning modules.

For example, you use tools like ChatGPT to develop course scripts, summarize complex content, or generate quizzes and knowledge checks in minutes.

2D: Multimedia AI for Engaging Learning Experiences

The second dimension takes learning beyond text, empowering L&D professionals to create visual and auditory content that drives engagement and retention.

Applications for L&D include:

- **Custom graphics and images.** AI-generated visuals enhance e-learning modules, making content visually appealing and aligned with branding.
- **AI-generated audio.** Tools like text-to-speech platforms can create natural-sounding narrations for video courses and podcasts, improving accessibility.
- **Video production.** AI tools simplify video creation by generating explainer videos, animations, and simulations without requiring complex tools or teams.
- **AI media editing tools.** Enhance and automate editing tasks—from trimming videos to improving sound quality.

For example, you can use AI to produce scenario-based videos with auto-generated voice-overs and AI avatars for compliance or soft skills training.

3D: Immersive Learning With AI Models and Simulations

At the 3D level, GenAI enables the creation of interactive and immersive environments, which is perfect for experiential learning. This dimension transforms learners' engagement with content by providing hands-on, lifelike simulations.

Applications for L&D include:

- **3D models.** Develop 3D models for technical training (like engineering, manufacturing, or healthcare scenarios).

- **Virtual reality (VR) simulations.** Create VR environments for learners to practice real-world skills in a risk-free setting (for example, leadership simulations or safety drills).
- **Augmented reality (AR).** Overlay digital learning content in real-world contexts for interactive on-the-job training.
- **3D printing designs.** AI aids in rapid prototyping for technical and vocational training applications.

For example, you can use VR simulations to train employees to handle hazardous machinery, which improves safety outcomes and learner confidence.

4D: Real-Time, Adaptive Learning Systems

4D represents the cutting edge of L&D, in which GenAI interacts with learners in real time to deliver highly adaptive, personalized, and dynamic learning experiences.

Applications for L&D include:
- **Real-time feedback.** AI tools analyze learner performance and provide instant, personalized feedback during training sessions.
- **AI-powered animation.** Create real-time, interactive 3D characters or simulations for role-playing and decision-making experiences.
- **Dynamic simulations.** Develop AI-driven systems for leadership development, sales simulations, or smart performance coaching.
- **Real-time learning systems.** Adaptive platforms adjust learning content and pacing based on learner progress and preferences.

For example, imagine an AI-driven coaching tool that observes learners' interactions in a simulation, providing on-the-spot feedback and guidance to improve communication skills.

Why This Matters for L&D

GenAI's four dimensions align perfectly with the evolving needs of learning professionals:
- **1D**—automate content development and streamline workflows.
- **2D**—design engaging, visually compelling learning experiences.

- **3D**—build immersive, hands-on simulations that enhance skill application.
- **4D**—deliver adaptive, real-time learning tailored to each individual.

By strategically leveraging these dimensions, you can reduce content development time, scale personalized learning experiences for global teams, and deliver measurable, interactive learning outcomes that drive real performance improvement.

Consider your current approach to content creation and delivery in your learning programs. How might GenAI augment or transform these processes? What opportunities and challenges do you foresee in integrating this technology into your work?

Bringing It Back to Reality: Actionable Steps for Today

AI adoption doesn't require a complete overhaul of L&D in your organization. Incremental steps drive measurable impact while building confidence and capability. For L&D professionals ready to integrate AI into their workflows, here are some immediate steps you can take:

1. **Audit your current approach.** Assess where your organization is currently—from creation to automation.
2. **Identify repetitive tasks.** Automate content delivery, reporting, and assessment.
3. **Experiment with GenAI tools.** Use tools like ChatGPT for content drafts, Descript for video, and Canva for visuals.
4. **Train your team.** Build AI literacy and foster a culture of experimentation. Ensure your L&D team understands the capabilities and limitations of AI in learning contexts.
5. **Start small.** Begin with AI-generated content or automated learning processes. Plan for the future; consider how you might integrate more advanced AI automation into your learning ecosystem over time.
6. **Measure impact.** Track time saved, learner satisfaction, and content effectiveness.

7. **Identify opportunities.** Look for areas where GenAI could enhance your current processes, whether in content creation, curation, or delivery.

EXERCISE

The AI Landscape and Its Impact

How familiar are you with the key players and recent breakthroughs in GenAI, and how might this knowledge influence your L&D strategy?

- Which GenAI tools or platforms have you experimented with in your work? What were your impressions?
- How do you stay informed about new developments in AI and their potential applications in L&D?
- What concerns do you have about the rapid advancement of AI in the learning field?
- How might the differences between open and closed AI systems affect your choice of tools for learning projects?

Now, research one GenAI tool you haven't used before. Spend 30 minutes exploring its capabilities and considering how it might be applied in your work. Share your findings with a colleague or in a professional network.

EXERCISE

How Will GenAI Affect Your Approach to L&D?

GenAI will fundamentally change L&D's approach to creating and delivering learning experiences. How might it affect you? Reflect on these questions:

- What aspects of your current work in L&D could be enhanced by GenAI?
- How do you envision the role of human expertise evolving alongside AI-generated content?
- What ethical considerations do you need to address when implementing GenAI in your learning programs?
- How might GenAI change the expectations of learners in your organization?

Now, choose one upcoming learning project or course. Spend 15 minutes brainstorming how you could incorporate GenAI into its design, development, or delivery. Consider both the potential benefits and challenges.

Conclusion

In this chapter, we've explored the transformative potential of GenAI in L&D. We've discussed how AI is not just a tool for content creation but a paradigm shift in how we approach learning design, delivery, and assessment. From tracing its historical context to understanding the nature of GenAI, we've built a detailed picture of this technology and its implications for L&D professionals.

In the next chapter, we'll shift from theory to practice. You'll explore not only the tools and techniques that bring GenAI to life in learning programs, but also how these advancements are reshaping the very identity of L&D professionals. The emergence of AI in learning isn't just about faster course creation; it's about reimagining our roles.

We'll meet the new hybrid archetype—the human-machine performance analyst—an evolved instructional designer who blends creativity, data fluency, and AI collaboration to drive meaningful performance outcomes. Let's begin that journey.

CHAPTER 2

The Rise of the Human-Machine Performance Analyst

In This Chapter

- How to become a human-machine performance analyst
- The evolution of L&D content development from manual creation to AI-driven automation
- How to get started with real-time skills gap analysis using AI
- What AI brings to the leadership table

I recently watched a demo challenging everything I knew about course development. The online learning vendor rep casually imported a standard operating procedure document into their authoring tool. He explained how "AI will convert the SOP into a course in less than a minute." My skepticism peaked. I'd seen plenty of these "revolutionary" features fall flat. But 60 seconds later, a fully structured course appeared on screen—clean slides, logical knowledge checks, and even scenario-based activities that made sense.

My 30 years of instructional design experience told me this shouldn't be possible. Yet, the first draft was completed in less time than it takes to explain ADDIE. In that moment, I knew my days of authoring custom learning experiences were numbered.

This evolution is about more than faster content creation or automated assessments. Integrating AI into L&D marks a fundamental shift in how we approach organizational performance. For example, a client of mine reduced their training development time by 60 percent using generative AI tools. But the real breakthrough was that their L&D function could now spend less time building courses and more time analyzing data, predicting skills gaps, and crafting learning strategies that directly affect business outcomes.

We're witnessing the transformation of L&D professionals from training creators to human-machine performance analysts (HMPAs)—blending human insight with machine intelligence.

The stakes are higher than ever. In a world where skills become obsolete faster than we can develop training programs, our organizations need more than just better content delivery. They need predictive insights, adaptive learning systems, and scalable personalized learning experiences across entire workforces. GenAI provides these capabilities while also raising important questions about the future of learning design, the role of human expertise, and the ethical implications of AI-driven development decisions.

The near-term future of L&D isn't about replacing our human expertise with artificial intelligence. Instead, it's about amplifying our capabilities, freeing us from routine tasks to focus on what matters most: understanding human potential and creating environments where people and machines can thrive.

This chapter explores your transformation from an L&D professional to an HMPA. This new role represents the sweet spot where data analytics and the art of learning design come together to create something truly powerful. We'll explore the skills you need to thrive in this emerging space.

We'll also look at how GenAI revolutionizes content creation with the shift toward scalable, personalized learning experiences. The discussion will then turn to real-time skills gap analysis, demonstrating how AI enables proactive identification and remediation of capability needs before they negatively affect business outcomes.

Finally, we'll examine how AI reshapes learning leadership, moving beyond traditional training management to data-driven, strategic partnerships that directly influence the organization's bottom line.

Let's begin this exploration where many of us started our L&D journeys: the fundamentals of performance, now reimagined for the age of artificial intelligence.

The Evolution of Learning and Performance

My first exposure to the importance of organizational performance was in 1997. I had the opportunity to participate in a week-long training program on performance consulting delivered by Jim Robinson. For some of you, that may not be a familiar name. Jim and his wife, Dana, founded Partners in Change and penned a few pivotal books, including *Performance Consulting: Moving Beyond Training* (1996), *Moving From Training to Performance: A Practical Guidebook* (1998), and *Strategic Business Partner: Aligning People Strategies With Business Goals* (2005). Jim and Dana considerably affected the transformation of countless training professionals into performance consultants.

As a very young art director focused on content creation, I'll admit that spending a week learning how to interview leaders and project managers to get to the root cause of organizational issues (which they often thought were training issues) was as exciting as watching paint dry. My typical workday was filled with working in Photoshop, recording audio and video, and creating animations to support e-learning development. During the workshop, I learned about a needs hierarchy (business, performance, work environment, and capabilities) and how to identify gaps and causes (not symptoms) of on-the-job performance issues and select the appropriate solutions.

As I look back on this performance consulting training experience, I realize it was one of the most essential weeks of my young career. These concepts keep coming up in various permeations from other professionals in our field; for example, Cathy Moore's Action Mapping (with a measurable business goal in the center and actions to reach it, including knowledge, skills, motivation, and environment) and Bob Mosher and Conrad Gottfredson's Five Moments of Need (when you learn something for the first time, when you want to learn more, when you try to apply or remember what you learned, when something goes wrong, and when things change).

So, what does this have to do with AI? While AI will touch every aspect of L&D, the principles of performance consulting I learned in that classroom have proven remarkably resilient (Figure 2-1). Today, as I work with AI systems that can process performance data in seconds, I find myself returning to those fundamental questions about business impact and root causes. Technology has evolved dramatically, but the core challenge remains unchanged: connecting learning to measurable business outcomes.

Figure 2-1. AI's Influence on L&D

| Performance Consulting | Performance Gap Analysis | Training Identification | Training Awareness | Outcome Analysis | Training and Performance Experiences |

This intersection of AI and performance consulting creates fascinating synergies. Traditional performance frameworks provide the essential business context for AI to deliver meaningful insights. Without this foundation, AI becomes another sophisticated tool that generates interesting but ultimately disconnected data points. Clean data is the source of truth, and when we align AI capabilities with proven performance consulting methods, we can unlock the true potential of both approaches.

AI tools have become the performance consultant's dream come true. They can spot patterns in organizational data that would take humans months to uncover, simulate the impact of different initiatives before we invest resources, and help us deliver personalized support at scale.

What Jim Robinson and others pioneered with careful observation and structured interviews, we can now enhance through AI-powered data analysis. But here's the key: Technology only works if we apply it with the same rigorous focus on business results that performance consulting taught us.

Let's explore what this means for learning professionals who find themselves at the intersection of timeless performance principles and transformative AI capabilities.

The Rise of the Human-Machine Performance Analyst

Remember when the most technical skill an L&D professional needed was being able to wrangle PowerPoint into submission? Those days are gone, my friends. Say hello to the newest role in L&D: the human-machine performance analyst. Part data wizard, part business analyst, and part L&D guru, this hybrid role is quickly becoming the linchpin of AI-powered learning organizations.

So, why do we need human-machine performance analysts? It's simple: As L&D becomes increasingly data-driven and AI-enhanced, we need professionals who can partner with the business and bridge the gap between the technical aspect of data analytics and the human art and science of learning design. These folks are translators and sense-makers who can take a sea of data and AI insights and turn it into actionable learning strategies. They're the secret sauce that makes AI-powered L&D truly effective.

Let me introduce you to Maria, a human-machine performance analyst at a large financial services firm. Maria started her career as an instructional designer but had a knack for numbers. When her company implemented an AI-powered learning platform, she became the go-to person for making sense of the flood of data they were suddenly swimming in.

One day, the AI platform flagged an unusual pattern: Completion rates for compliance training were high, but actual compliance incidents weren't decreasing. Maria dug into the data, combining AI insights with good old-fashioned interviews. She discovered that while employees were completing compliance training, they weren't applying the knowledge on the job because they didn't see its relevance to their daily work.

Armed with this insight, Maria partnered with an AI-enabled learning tool to redesign the compliance training program that included role-specific scenarios and real-time practice opportunities. The result? Compliance incidents dropped by 40 percent in the next quarter. Maria turned AI insights into real business impact, showcasing the true value of the human-machine performance analyst role.

So, what exactly does a human-machine performance analyst do? Let's break it down:

- **Data analysis and interpretation.** They're the Sherlock Holmes of learning data, sifting through information from LMSs, performance management systems, knowledge management systems, and AI-driven analytics platforms to uncover meaningful patterns and insights.

- **AI system management.** They oversee the implementation, operation, and performance of AI-driven learning systems, workflows, automations, and agents, ensuring they're used effectively and ethically.
- **Strategic alignment.** They connect the dots between learning initiatives and broader business goals. They speak the languages of both L&D and the C-suite, translating learning results into business outcomes.
- **Return on investment (ROI) measurement.** They're the value architects, developing metrics that demonstrate the tangible impact of learning on the bottom line. (No more crossed fingers when asked about ROI!)
- **Continuous improvement.** They use data and AI insights to constantly refine and improve learning programs. In their world, good enough is never good enough.

Does this role sound interesting?

Now, I'm sure you're wondering how you can start transforming yourself into a human-machine performance analyst. Figure 2-2 presents a guide.

Figure 2-2. Transforming Into a Human-Machine Performance Analyst

Upskill on Data
and Analytics

Become Proficient
in AI Literacy

Develop Business
Acumen

Hone Communication
Skills

Stay Curious About
AI Advancements

Let's discuss each task in more detail:

- **Upskill on data and analytics.** AI agents can now automatically generate learning analytics dashboards and perform initial competency mapping. However, the human touch remains essential for interpreting these analyses within organizational contexts. While AI handles the repetitive aspects of data processing, human analysts provide the critical thinking necessary to connect metrics to meaningful learning strategies. The automation of these tasks actually elevates the strategic importance of understanding how these systems work. Even as AI tools democratize data analysis, the human–AI partnership makes understanding the foundations more valuable, not less.

- **Learn about AI.** The very AI systems that have simplified learning design are built on foundational concepts like machine learning and natural language processing. Understanding these concepts doesn't mean you need to be able to build an AI model from scratch, but it does enable you to be an informed consumer and customizer of AI tools.

- **Develop business acumen.** The value of business acumen has shifted from calculation to contextualization. AI can suggest metrics, but humans determine which ones matter to the organization's unique situation and culture. Understanding business fundamentals allows you to effectively translate between AI outputs and stakeholder concerns.

- **Hone your communication skills.** AI can generate initial data narratives and visualization drafts, but compelling storytelling that resonates with audiences still requires human creativity and emotional intelligence. While AI can suggest presentation structures, humans excel at reading the room and adapting messages in real-time based on audience reactions.

- **Stay curious.** The increasing pace of innovation makes curiosity extremely valuable. You must constantly evaluate which new AI tools and models deserve attention. Give yourself time for exploration.

Think about your current skill set:

- How close are you to the outlined human-machine performance analyst?
- What skills do you need to develop to advance to this emerging role?
- How might your organization benefit from having this type of role?

Success as a human-machine performance analyst comes from recognizing three distinct modes of work:

- Tasks that humans must perform (such as a police officer making a traffic stop or an air traffic controller talking to an inbound flight crew)
- Tasks best handled by machines (such as data processing and running code)
- The growing middle ground where humans and machines collaborate

Through this lens, L&D professionals can make informed decisions about when to leverage AI, when to rely on human expertise, and how to create effective partnerships between the two. This spectrum of work can be visualized through what I call "The Human–AI Task Scale," which helps identify the varying levels of collaboration between humans and machines (Figure 2-3).

Figure 2-3. The Human–AI Task Scale

Looking at the scale, we can see seven distinct levels of human-machine interaction, ranging from fully manual human work to completely autonomous AI systems. As L&D professionals, understanding where your learning initiatives fall on this spectrum is crucial for developing effective training programs and performance support.

At levels 1 and 2, humans are the primary drivers, either working completely independently or with AI to provide targeted support for specific subtasks. Level 1 features tasks requiring deep expertise, creativity, and hands-on execution. At level 2, AI provides suggestions and information, but humans make all decisions using critical thinking and judgment.

Levels 3 and 4 represent the collaborative middle ground where humans and AI actively work together—humans guiding AI execution or engaging in true joint collaboration. At level 3, AI might generate outputs that humans then edit and refine using their domain expertise and analytical skills. Level 4 is where true partnership emerges and both contribute equally, with humans providing ethical considerations and high-level reasoning.

As we move to levels 5, 6, and 7, AI takes on increasingly autonomous roles, with humans transitioning to quality assurance and monitoring or completely stepping back from direct involvement. At level 5, AI performs most of the work, while humans provide quality control, oversight, and risk assessment. At level 6, AI manages the entire process with humans intervening only when the AI signals it needs help or to perform strategic spot checks. Finally, at level 7, AI handles everything independently, while humans focus on governance and meta-level decision making.

As a human-machine performance analyst, your role will involve monitoring these workflows across the spectrum and ensuring optimal performance at each level. This often requires a partnership with IT functions, especially as organizations implement more advanced AI-driven solutions at levels 5, 6, and 7. The technical infrastructure supporting these AI systems must be monitored alongside the human performance elements.

What's critical to understand is that human and machine performance are now fundamentally intertwined. Poor AI system design affects human performance, while human errors or inefficiencies can compromise the effectiveness of AI implementations. Success requires analyzing both components as part of a unified system, rather than as separate entities. L&D professionals must design training experiences that acknowledge this interconnection and help workers develop the specific skills needed to thrive at each level of the Human–AI Task Scale.

What happens beyond level 7—when AI begins to manage not just tasks, but other agents? When it adapts without waiting for a prompt? That future is coming into view, and we'll explore it more fully in chapter 10. For now, we'll continue with human hands on the wheel, and AI as an increasingly indispensable co-pilot.

Machine or AI?

While I use *human-machine performance analyst* for the role, I call the framework the Human–AI Task Scale because there's a meaningful difference that relates to robotics. The term *machine* encompasses a broader category that includes both physical robots and software-based AI systems.

A human-machine performance analyst monitors and optimizes interactions across this entire spectrum—from physical robots in manufacturing or warehouse settings to purely digital AI systems handling knowledge work. On the other hand, the Human–AI Task Scale specifically addresses the collaboration continuum with AI systems, which represent just one subset of machines. While all AI systems are machines, not all machines are AI systems. Many robots operate on predetermined programming without the learning or adaptive qualities of AI.

This distinction allows the role to maintain appropriate scope when dealing with traditional robotics, physical-digital hybrid systems, and purely digital AI implementations. It acknowledges that performance analysis methodologies might differ when examining a factory robot versus an AI agent, while still recognizing they exist on the same fundamental spectrum of human-machine collaboration.

EXERCISE

You as a Human-Machine Performance Analyst

Imagine how the emergence of the human-machine performance analyst role might change how your organization approaches L&D strategy and decision making.

- Consider your own expertise. How might it be augmented or challenged by AI?
- What skills do you need to develop to thrive in an AI-augmented future?
- What aspects of your current L&D processes could benefit most from the analytical skills of a human-machine performance analyst?

- How comfortable are you with data-driven decision making in L&D? What concerns or reservations do you have?
- What ethical considerations do you think are most important for a human-machine performance analyst to keep in mind?
- How might a human-machine performance analyst's insights change the conversation about L&D's value in your organization?

Now, spend some time (maybe 30 minutes) sketching a day in the life of a human-machine performance analyst in your organization.
- What data would they analyze?
- What stakeholders would they interact with?
- What decisions would they influence?

Share this vision with your team and discuss how it might change your L&D processes.

Content Creation With Generative AI

Picture this: It's 9 a.m., and you've just been tasked with creating a comprehensive training program on cybersecurity. Your deadline? Yesterday, of course. You organization was recently hit by a phishing scam, and leadership has its mandate.

Before panicking, remember you've got a new colleague to help you. Sure, it's made of algorithms and neural networks rather than flesh and blood, but it's always ready to lend a hand (or a processor). Welcome to the brave new world of content creation with generative AI.

Why is AI-assisted content creation such a game changer for L&D? Simply put, it allows us to create more content more quickly and with a level of personalization that would be impossible to achieve manually. This partnership transforms the human-machine performance analyst's role from content producer to strategic orchestrator, enabling them to focus on higher-level design and measurement while AI handles the heavy lifting of content generation. In a world where skills are evolving at breakneck speed, and learners expect Netflix-level personalization in their learning experiences, GenAI allows us to keep pace with demand without sacrificing quality or relevance.

I want to tell you about Alex, an instructional designer at a global tech company. She used to spend weeks creating e-learning modules, painstakingly crafting every screen and interaction, until she implemented a GenAI content creation system. For her latest product training, Alex input the learning objectives and some key content points. Within minutes, the AI tool generated a full draft of the module—complete with knowledge checks, scenarios, and even suggestions for interactive elements.

Alex still needs to review and refine the content, but what used to take weeks now takes days. The best part? She can easily generate content variations for different roles and skill levels. Alex went from feeling like a content-creating hamster on a wheel to shifting her role into a human-performance business analyst. Instead of just creating learning experiences, Alex now orchestrates and evaluates them.

From Creation to Automation

But how did we get here? The evolution of content creation in L&D has been a journey from manual creation to AI-driven automation. This progression reflects broader technological advancements and changing approaches to knowledge management and dissemination. Tracing this evolution helps us understand the context in which GenAI has emerged. It also highlights the ongoing quest for efficiency and effectiveness in L&D, and how each stage has built upon the last. This historical perspective is essential for making informed decisions about integrating new technologies and for anticipating future trends in the field.

In the early 1990s, I began my career in e-learning by creating content for mainframe computers. This era marked the beginning of custom e-learning development, which (while expensive) was groundbreaking in its use of gamification and multimedia. We created interactive media that included audio, video, text, interactions, and animations. The creation era was characterized by highly customized content tailored to specific organizational needs. While this approach ensured relevance, it was time consuming and often resulted in one-size-fits-all content that became outdated quickly.

Fast forward to the 2000s, and we saw a shift toward content curation. The proliferation of easily accessible creation tools led to an abundance of content. Organizations began investing in platforms with extensive content libraries covering areas like leadership development and communication, rather than creating everything from scratch. The curation era addressed some of the creation era's challenges by leveraging existing content, which allowed for more agility in responding to learning needs but sometimes sacrificed specificity for breadth.

Now, we've entered the era of AI-generated content. Multimodal GenAI can create diverse media types, which is transforming how we approach content creation in L&D. This era promises to combine the best of both worlds: customized content that can be created quickly and updated easily. However, it also brings new challenges, such as ensuring the accuracy and appropriateness of AI-generated content.

The next frontier is automation. We'll see AI systems generate content and manage the entire learning process—from needs assessment to content delivery and performance evaluation.

The Creation-Curation-Generation-Automation framework represents distinct but interconnected phases in leveraging technology for L&D (Figure 2-4). By understanding the principles behind each phase, you can unlock their full potential and align them with broader organizational goals.

Figure 2-4. The Creation-Curation-Generation-Automation Framework

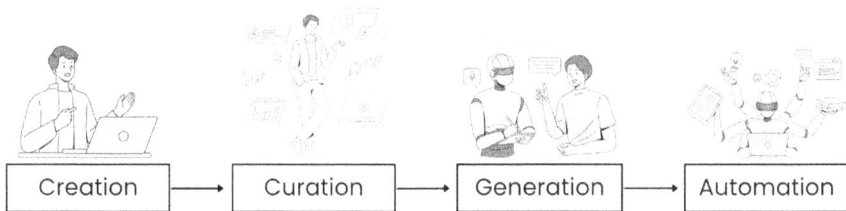

Creation → Curation → Generation → Automation

Creation: Developing Original Learning

Content creation represents the foundation of learning design—developing original content to meet specific learning objectives. This phase involves subject matter experts and instructional designers collaborating to produce tailored learning materials from scratch. Effective creation depends on:

- **Instructional design**—following sound pedagogical principles to ensure knowledge transfer

- **Subject matter expertise**—drawing on specialized knowledge to ensure accuracy and depth
- **Learner-centered design**—focusing on the needs, preferences, and contexts of the target audience

The creation phase establishes the baseline content that you can later organize and contextualize (curation). It provides the original material that you can enhance (generation) and distribute (automation)—forming the basis for all subsequent phases in the learning development life cycle.

Curation: Organizing and Contextualizing Knowledge Resources

Curation involves strategically selecting, organizing, and contextualizing existing knowledge resources to create meaningful learning experiences. It's not about creating content from scratch; instead, it's about finding, vetting, and arranging valuable resources from internal and external sources.

Effective curation relies on:

- **Relevance**—aligning content with learner goals and business priorities
- **Contextualization**—tailoring raw knowledge to meet organizational nuances
- **Access**—ensuring knowledge is easy to find, share, and apply

The curation phase bridges the gap between creation and generation by transforming content into structured learning assets. It provides the organized knowledge foundation that GenAI can later enhance, while setting the stage for automation to streamline delivery and measurement.

Generation: Using GenAI Tools for Content Creation and Enhancement

Generation marks a shift from manual processes to AI-driven content creation. GenAI tools—like GPT models and image and audio generators—can produce engaging, high-quality content at scale. This enables instructional designers to focus on strategy and learner engagement rather than getting bogged down in content production.

GenAI succeeds because it leverages:

- **Scalability**—generating content at a pace and volume humans cannot match
- **Personalization**—adapting learning materials to fit diverse audiences
- **Efficiency**—reducing time spent on mundane tasks and increasing productivity

During generation, you feed high-quality source content into an AI tool; then, you can use automation to distribute and track the effectiveness of the AI-generated materials.

Automation: Streamlining Repetitive Tasks

Automation involves applying AI to repetitive tasks, freeing up time for L&D teams to focus on strategic priorities. AI tools can streamline administrative and operational tasks to improve efficiency and learner experiences.

Effective automation focuses on:

- **Consistency**—ensuring uniform learner experiences
- **Efficiency**—optimizing tasks related to feedback, reporting, and assessments
- **Scalability**—handling tasks across large, diverse learner groups

Automation ensures curated and AI-generated content is efficiently deployed, assessed, and analyzed. However, an over-reliance on automation can depersonalize learning experiences, so you must balance it with human touchpoints to maintain learner engagement.

The evolution from creation to curation to generation and automation represents a transformative shift for L&D and has led to the need for human-machine performance analysts. AI tools empower L&D professionals to create personalized, scalable learning experiences while freeing up time for strategic initiatives. By embracing AI as a collaborator in content creation, L&D teams can drive innovation and deliver learning experiences that meet the demands of a rapidly changing workforce.

The Creativity Conundrum in AI-Assisted Content Creation

As we increasingly rely on AI for content creation, are we at risk of losing the unique spark of human creativity that can make learning truly transformative?

While AI can generate content at incredible speed and scale, it fundamentally works by recombining and repurposing existing information. The truly novel and genuinely creative content still comes from human minds. As we integrate AI into our content creation processes, we must intentionally preserve and nurture human creativity. For example, using AI to handle routine content creation can free up human creators to focus on big-picture thinking, unique connections, and empathetic, learner-centered design.

I recently worked with a leadership development team that had started using AI to generate their program content. Even though they were producing more content than ever, they noticed participant engagement was dropping. The problem? While technically correct, the AI-generated content lacked the inspirational stories and novel perspectives that the human facilitators used to bring. They corrected course by using AI for research and initial drafts but reserving the final content shaping—especially the storytelling and connecting concepts to real-world challenges—for human experts.

How can you design your AI-assisted content creation processes to enhance, rather than replace, human creativity? What aspects of content creation should you intentionally reserve for human minds?

EXERCISE

GenAI as a Content Enhancer

Think about your current content creation process. Where are the bottlenecks? The repetitive tasks? The areas where you wish you could offer more personalization? Now, imagine how AI could help in these areas. How might AI-assisted content creation change your role as an L&D professional, and how can you prepare for this shift?

Here are some targeted questions to ask yourself (and your team):
- What aspects of your current content creation process do you find most creatively fulfilling? How can you ensure these aren't lost in an AI-assisted process?
- How might access to AI-generated content change how you approach instructional design?
- What new skills might you need to develop to effectively collaborate with AI in content creation?

- How could AI-assisted content creation free you up to focus on the more strategic aspects of your role?

Now, take an existing piece of learning content. Spend some time (around 20 minutes) outlining how you might use AI to enhance or expand this content.
- How could you use AI to create variations for different levels of experience or expertise or job roles?
- How could AI help you update this content more efficiently in the future?

Real-Time Skills Gap Analysis

Remember the days of annual skills inventories? Those lovely spreadsheets were about as current as last year's fashion trends. Well, it's time to toss them in the digital dustbin. GenAI can help you turn a skills gap analysis from a point-in-time snapshot into a real-time, dynamic process.

So, why is a real-time skills gap analysis with AI so crucial? In today's rapidly evolving business landscape, skills can become obsolete faster than you can say "digital transformation." As a human-machine performance analyst, you must help your organization identify and address skills gaps as they emerge, not six months later.

As organizations increasingly deploy AI agents and automations, the human-machine performance analyst's role will become critical in orchestrating effective human-machine collaboration. Through detailed task analysis, you map the intricate relationships between human capabilities and technological processes, identifying precisely which activities should remain human-driven and which can be augmented or automated.

This granular understanding of task components enables organizations to design workflows that allow humans and AI systems to complement one another's strengths, rather than compete or duplicate efforts. The human-machine performance analyst must continuously gather and interpret skills data that reflects both the evolving capabilities of AI systems and the uniquely human competencies of the workforce—such as emotional intelligence, ethical judgment, creative problem solving, and contextual awareness.

By maintaining a comprehensive skills inventory, analysts can pinpoint emerging collaboration gaps, recommend targeted training initiatives, and help design interfaces that facilitate seamless human-machine teaming. In essence, they become the architects of hybrid workforces in which humans and digital agents function as cohesive, high-performing teams rather than disconnected entities pursuing parallel objectives.

Against the backdrop of AI agents completing tasks, real-time skills gap analysis allows you to be proactive, rather than reactive, ensuring your workforce is always equipped with the skills needed to drive business success.

So, how does this AI-powered skills gap analysis work? Figure 2-5 outlines the process.

Figure 2-5. AI-Powered Skills Gap Analysis

5. Predictive Analytics

1. Data Integration

4. Real-Time Analysis

2. Natural Language Processing

3. Continuous Learning

Let's break down each step:

1. **Data integration.** The GenAI system pulls data from multiple sources, including employee profiles, performance reviews, project management systems, LMSs, and even external job market data.
2. **Natural language processing (NLP).** The AI model can understand and categorize skills from unstructured text using advanced NLP. It can interpret job descriptions, project reports, and even Teams or Slack chats.
3. **Continuous learning.** AI doesn't just rely on preprogrammed skills categories. It continuously learns and updates its understanding of skills based on new data.
4. **Real-time analysis.** The AI model continuously updates its analysis as new data comes in. It can spot when a team struggles with a

particular task—indicating a potential skills gap—faster than you can say "needs improvement."

5. **Predictive analytics.** By analyzing trends in your industry and your organization's strategic plans, the AI model can predict what skills will be needed. It's like having a time machine for your workforce planning.

I have a word of caution, however, before you rush to embrace the AI-powered skills gap analysis. While AI is mighty at analyzing known skills and patterns, it may struggle to identify genuinely novel skills or competencies that don't exist yet in its dataset. This could lead to a situation in which you're always playing catch-up, optimizing for yesterday's skills rather than tomorrow's. Moreover, if you rely too heavily on AI recommendations, you might miss out on the creative skills combinations that often drive innovation.

For example, there was a tech company that religiously followed its AI tool's skills gap recommendations. The company efficiently filled all its identified gaps but was still falling behind its competitors. Why? The AI tool was analyzing historical data, which meant it wasn't identifying emerging skills in quantum computing and ethical AI development. Once it began to complement its AI system with human-led horizon scanning, the company was better able to prepare for future skills needs before they become critical gaps.

With that in mind, here are some ways to get started with a real-time skills gap analysis:

1. **Audit your data sources.** What systems contain information about your employees' skills and performance? The more sources you can connect, the more accurate your analysis will be.

2. **Choose the right AI platform.** Look for a system that integrates with your existing HR and L&D tech stack and offers real-time analysis and predictive capabilities.

3. **Start with a pilot test.** Choose a department or job family. This will allow you to fine-tune your approach before rolling it out company wide.

4. **Involve human experts.** While AI is powerful, it's not infallible. Have subject matter experts regularly review and validate the AI tool's findings.

5. **Close the loop.** Don't just identify gaps. Create a systematic way to address them, whether through training, hiring, or reskilling initiatives.

When selecting an AI platform for real-time skills gap analysis, you'll find numerous options in today's market. Many offer comprehensive capabilities with personalized growth plans and instant visualization through skills matrices. Specialized platforms provide real-time insights for resource allocation and analyze live job market data to benchmark skills objectively.

As you implement your chosen system, remember that the most successful organizations blend AI-driven insights with human expertise. While these platforms excel at analyzing known skills, they may struggle to identify truly novel competencies—which are exactly what your organization might need most in the future. (We'll explore the full landscape of skills gap analysis platforms and integration strategies in chapter 5.)

EXERCISE

Solving Skills Gaps With AI

Think about your organization's current approach to skills gap analysis. Do you have one? How timely is it? How accurate? How actionable? Now, imagine being able to spot and address skills gaps in real time. How would that change your L&D strategy and approach to workforce development? What about your hiring practices? Your ability to respond to market changes?

How can you balance the efficiency of AI-driven skills gap analysis with the need for human intuition and foresight in identifying emerging skills?

Here are some targeted questions to ask yourself:
- What are the pain points in your skills assessment process that real-time analysis could address?
- How might access to real-time skills data change how you design learning experiences?
- What are your concerns about using AI for skills gap analysis? How might you address them?

Now, take some time (around 15 minutes) to list all your organization's data sources that could inform a real-time skills gap analysis. Then, identify any gaps. Are there areas where you're not collecting data that could be valuable? Discuss this with your team and brainstorm ways to fill these data gaps.

Leading in the Age of AI

Even as an instructional designer or other L&D professional, being good at creating PowerPoint presentations and facilitating ice-breaker activities will only get you so far. But stepping into the role of a human-machine performance analyst? Forget about it. Those skills are as outdated as my collection of VHS training tapes. Today, leading in the L&D space is all about harnessing the power of GenAI to drive strategic, data-informed learning initiatives.

So, why is AI-empowered learning leadership so crucial? It's simple: In today's fast-paced business environment, you can't afford to rely on gut feelings or outdated annual training needs assessments. Your learning strategies must be proactive, predictive, and precisely targeted. GenAI gives us the power to do just that—turning human-machine performance analysts from reactive training providers into strategic business partners who can anticipate and address skills needs before they become critical gaps.

Figure 2-6 outlines what GenAI brings to the learning leadership table.

Figure 2-6. L&D Leads With AI

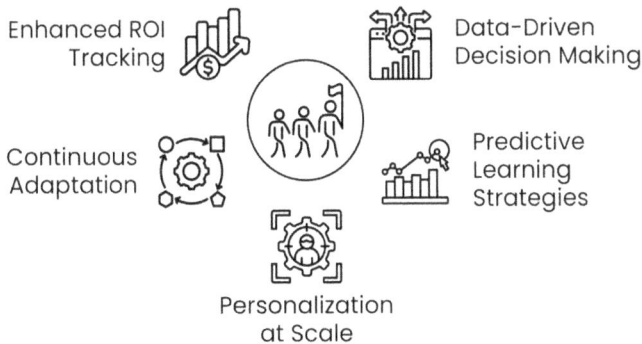

Let's discuss each benefit in more detail:

- **Data-driven decision making.** As L&D professionals, we've always struggled with connecting learning initiatives to business outcomes. GenAI can address this challenge by synthesizing previously disconnected data streams—from LMS completion rates and assessment scores to operational KPIs and productivity metrics. When preparing your quarterly learning strategy review, instead of relying on superficial engagement metrics, imagine presenting a comprehensive analysis showing how specific learning programs directly influenced team performance across departments.

- **Predictive learning strategies.** Traditional needs assessments tell you what's missing today, but they're backward-looking by nature. GenAI can enable L&D teams to move from reactive to anticipatory learning design by analyzing both internal skills data and external market signals. When your CEO announces a strategic pivot toward sustainable operations, you'll no longer scramble to develop relevant content. Your GenAI dashboard will have identified the emerging skills gap months previously based on industry trends, competitor job postings, and internal strategic documents. This gives you the lead time to design thoughtful learning journeys, rather than emergency training initiatives—positioning L&D as a strategic enabler, rather than a support function.

- **Personalization at scale.** The tension between standardization and personalization has always been an L&D problem. GenAI can resolve this by enabling what I call "structured flexibility"—meaning core competencies remain consistent but learning paths and content adjust dynamically to individual needs. Instead of forcing all employees through identical modules, consider this example of an engineering team that took on a more personalized approach: Core technical concepts are delivered consistently, but case studies, application exercises, and depth of content are automatically adjusted based on each person's role, prior knowledge, learning behavior, and performance data.

- **Continuous adaptation.** Learning design can no longer be a one-and-done proposition in rapidly evolving fields. GenAI can support L&D teams to implement what agile teams have long practiced—continuous iteration based on real-time feedback. For example, if you're developing a leadership program, use GenAI to analyze participant applications of key concepts during workplace challenges. GenAI's analysis capability can detect that while participants understand theoretical frameworks, they struggle with practical application in ambiguous situations. This insight allows rapid adjustment to the program's case studies and coaching prompts before the next module. Because this would be impossible with traditional evaluation methods, it might have taken months to reveal this gap.

- **Enhanced ROI tracking.** The struggle to demonstrate a learning program's value has plagued our profession for decades. GenAI can offer unprecedented visibility into the learning-performance connection through multilayered attribution modeling. Rather than using simplistic cause-and-effect claims, you can now present nuanced insights showing how specific learning experiences contribute to performance improvements in combination with other factors. When your CFO questions training investments, imagine responding with data showing that while your sales enablement program alone created a 7 percent performance lift, when combined with manager reinforcement and spaced practice opportunities, that impact jumped to 22 percent—with the AI tool clearly distinguishing correlation from causation through controlled comparisons across teams with different implementation approaches.

Ready to step into the world of AI-empowered learning leadership? Here are some practical steps you can take to get started:

1. **Complete a data audit.** What data do you currently have access to? Employee performance metrics? Skills assessments? Engagement rates? The more data you can feed your AI tool, the better insights you'll get.

2. **Identify key business metrics.** Work with your C-suite to identify the key performance indicators (KPIs) that matter most to your organization. Your GenAI system will help you link learning initiatives to these metrics.

3. **Invest in AI-powered learning analytics.** Look for platforms that offer predictive analytics and can integrate data from multiple sources.

4. **Upskill your team.** They will need new skills to work effectively with AI systems, so invest in their development. Remember, AI is here to augment, not replace, human expertise.

5. **Start small and scale.** Begin with a pilot project in one area of your organization. Use the insights and wins from this group to make the case for broader implementation.

Leading With AI

Imagine having a dashboard that shows real-time data on employee skill levels, learning engagement, and performance metrics. On one side, you see current stats; on the other, you see AI-generated predictions of how these metrics will change based on different learning initiatives.

As you think about your current approach to learning leadership, where do you see the most significant opportunities for AI augmentation? What data do you wish you had to make better decisions? How might your role change if you had access to predictive learning analytics?

Here are some targeted questions to ask yourself:
- What aspects of your current role could benefit most from AI augmentation?
- How comfortable are you with data-driven decision making?
- What skills might you need to develop to lead effectively in an AI-empowered L&D function?
- What ethical considerations do you foresee in implementing AI in your learning leadership practices?
- How might AI-empowered learning leadership change your relationship with other business units and the C-suite?

Now, take some time (around 10 minutes) to sketch your ideal AI-powered learning dashboard. What metrics would you include? What predictive capabilities would you want? Share this with your team and discuss how it might change your decision-making processes.

Conclusion

AI has transformed L&D pros from content creators to human-machine performance analysts. Armed with real-time data analysis and AI-generated content, these hybrid analysts can now predict skills gaps before they affect business outcomes, shifting learning from reactive training to proactive performance enhancement.

Central to this transformation is the Human–AI Task Scale, a framework clarifying the critical balance of collaboration—identifying precisely when humans should lead, when AI should take the helm, and when the two must partner seamlessly. Embracing this partnership is key, not out of fear of replacement, but as an opportunity to amplify human strengths and automate routine processes.

This evolution frees L&D professionals from repetitive tasks, enabling them to prioritize what machines cannot replicate—creative insight, ethical judgment, and strategic foresight. The leaders of tomorrow will master this delicate synergy between human intuition and AI precision, unlocking unparalleled organizational performance

Now we turn from understanding the role to executing the vision. Chapter 3 provides your blueprint for AI transformation—from assessing readiness to measuring impact. You'll uncover exactly how to craft an L&D strategy that moves beyond merely adopting AI tools and instead reinvents how learning fuels extraordinary organizational performance in the age of AI.

CHAPTER 3
The AI Strategy for Learning and Development

In This Chapter

- The critical elements necessary for successful AI adoption and implementation
- How to understand and assess your actual position with AI
- Ways to manage the human side of the AI transformation
- A practical framework for implementing and measuring AI in L&D

"So, what's your AI strategy?"

I was at a preconference AI Day of Learning event, reviewing my session notes, and I overheard this question from the table next to mine.

"Well, we're still figuring it out," replied the person being asked, with a nervous laugh. "Leadership is excited but no one seems to know where to start."

As I glanced around the room, I noticed similar conversations were happening at nearly every table. Two tables over, a group debated the ethics of using AI-generated scenarios. Across the aisle, instructional designers compared notes on which models delivered the best assessment questions. Behind me, a frustrated L&D director confessed to her team that their company had purchased enterprise AI licenses that now sat largely unused.

The truth is that developing an effective AI strategy isn't simply about adopting the latest AI model or tool. Instead, it's about creating a foundation that enables these technologies to deliver genuine value for your organization.

I've witnessed this repeatedly throughout my career: Organizations enthusiastically purchase sophisticated tools but overlook the foundational elements that make technology implementation successful.

This chapter will help you navigate the complex terrain of AI strategy development in L&D. We'll explore how to secure leadership buy-in, align technology with your organizational needs, and implement practical changes that deliver measurable results. We'll also confront the reality about where most organizations stand with their AI implementation—not where vendor marketing suggests they should be.

Whether you're sending yourself ChatGPT snippets via email (don't worry—I know many people who do) or building sophisticated AI-powered learning systems, you'll find practical guidance in this chapter to thoughtfully advance your AI journey. The pace of change may feel overwhelming, but with the right approach, you can transform AI from a source of anxiety to a powerful ally in your L&D toolkit.

Let's begin by examining what truly matters—the foundation on which all successful AI implementation stands: your AI organizational strategy.

Your AI Organizational Strategy

Before implementing AI solutions, your organization must have a coherent and comprehensive AI strategy. Much like constructing a house, the structural integrity of your AI initiatives depends entirely on the strength of their foundation. Without proper groundwork, even the most sophisticated AI tools and platforms will struggle to deliver meaningful results.

Allow me to outline the three critical elements necessary for successful AI adoption and implementation: leadership's vision for AI, access to technology, and business outcomes with AI (Figure 3-1).

Figure 3-1. Organizational AI Foundation

Leadership's Vision of AI	Access to AI Technology	Business Outcomes With AI

Leadership Buy-In and Understanding

You know what's fascinating? In my conversations with L&D leaders across the country, I keep hearing the same thing: "Our executives are excited about AI, but they don't really understand it." This disconnect creates problems we need to address head-on. Your leaders need to:

- Understand what AI can (and can't) do.
- Have a clear vision for how AI fits into the bigger picture.
- Commit to integrating AI right, not just doing it fast.
- Support a culture of innovation.

This last point is critical. Typically, the missing ingredient for integrating AI isn't acquiring the technology but having the right organizational culture. Does your leadership talk about innovation yet punish early failure?

A true culture of innovation begins with leadership modeling curiosity. Leaders must ask questions about AI without pretending to have all the answers. This vulnerability creates psychological safety throughout the organization.

Innovative cultures celebrate learning and experimentation, not just success. Smart leaders recognize that early AI efforts often reveal what doesn't work. This is valuable information because it prevents larger, costlier mistakes later. They understand the difference between productive failure and careless error.

The Tech Side of Things

Here's where it gets interesting. You might think organizational AI implementation is all about IT, but trust me, L&D also needs to be in the middle of the conversation. You need to know the answers to these questions:

- What systems do you already have that can give associates access to AI models?

- How AI can plug into them? Or, how are vendors implementing AI into them?
- What security measures need to be in place? (No one wants to be the one who uploads sensitive data to an AI model that will use it for training data!)
- How will the people you support access AI?

Some companies restrict access to AI to certain staff members, but that can create an unexpected divide. In response, some employees might begin using personal accounts on public AI tools (shadow AI users) and inadvertently share sensitive company information. Security nightmares will follow.

Smart organizations create secure access to AI for everyone. This can be done in a few ways; for example, using a public option for general ideation, a secure enterprise model for sensitive content, and a specialized compliant platform for regulated materials.

Making It Work for Your Business

Integrating AI into your organization isn't about using AI for AI's sake. I remember working with a company that wanted to implement AI everywhere—but it hadn't thought about why. Don't make that mistake. Instead, focus on:

- How AI supports your actual business goals
- Where you'll get the biggest bang for your buck
- What risks you need to watch out for

Organizations must anchor their AI initiatives to specific business outcomes rather than pursuing technology for its novelty. Strategic AI deployment begins by identifying the KPIs directly connected to organizational success.

Connect AI applications to measurable metrics, such as customer service response times, onboarding efficiency, compliance rates, and operational performance. The business case becomes compelling if executives can quantify direct impact on critical metrics.

Your Organization's AI Readiness

Take a moment to consider your organization's AI readiness by reflecting on these key categories:

- **Leadership understanding.** On a scale of 1 to 5, how would you rate your leadership team's understanding of AI capabilities and limitations? What specific knowledge gaps exist?
- **Cultural readiness.** Does your organization celebrate learning from failures, or is there fear around experimentation? Identify one example that illustrates your current culture.
- **Technology integration.** Map out your current systems to determine where AI could add value. Which system would benefit most immediately?
- **Business alignment.** What are your organization's top 3 business priorities this year? How might AI specifically support each one?
- **Personal action.** What's one concrete step you can take in the next week to strengthen your organization's AI foundation?

Now, write down one specific AI-related initiative you will champion in your organization (including who you need to involve) and your first action step.

Remember: Building a solid foundation for AI isn't about having all the answers; it's about asking the right questions and creating space for thoughtful implementation.

ያያያ

A successful AI strategy requires strong leadership commitment, cultural readiness, thoughtful technology integration, and clear business alignment. Without this foundation, even the most sophisticated AI tools will falter.

So, how can L&D departments and teams drive this transformation? L&D professionals are uniquely positioned to bridge the knowledge gaps, foster the cultural shifts, and build the capabilities necessary for effective AI implementation.

Let's explore the concrete steps your L&D team can take to support the successful implementation of an AI strategy in your organization.

The L&D Reality Check

When I first started consulting with enterprise learning teams about AI implementation, I noticed something striking. Teams weren't waiting for perfect organizational plans or official guidance on AI; they were experimenting, sometimes quietly, with whatever AI tools they could access.

This gap between organizational intention and frontline reality isn't unique to AI. We saw the same pattern with mobile learning, social learning platforms, and virtually every other technological shift that's swept through our field. The difference now is both the pace and the stakes.

Understanding your actual position with AI implementation is crucial. Let me guide you through an honest assessment.

Where Most Organizations Stand

Where do most organizations stand today? The gap between AI aspirations and reality is wider than most leaders care to admit. In my work consulting with companies across multiple sectors, I've noticed distinct patterns emerging—none of which represent the cohesive approach necessary for true transformation.

These patterns are playing out in L&D functions right now, creating missed opportunities and unexpected risks. Understanding which scenario most closely resembles your organization is the first step toward meaningful change.

The "Shadow AI" Scenario

The first is the "shadow AI" scenario. This describes organizations with the following characteristics:

- Employees are using ChatGPT or other AI tools on personal devices and emailing the results to themselves.
- Individual teams are experimenting with AI tools without official sanction.
- There's no clear AI policy in place. (My industry observations suggest only about a quarter of organizations have formalized policy.)
- There's substantial interest in AI but minimal official guidance.

For example, consider a multinational manufacturing company that discovered employees were using free AI tools on personal devices for work purposes. The IT department learned about this only when an executive accidentally shared a ChatGPT conversation containing proprietary information during a presentation.

The "Wait and See" Approach

Organizations that adopt a "wait and see" approach typically have the following characteristics:

- Leadership is aware of AI use but hesitant to make substantive commitments.
- Concerns about security and data privacy are stalling adoption.
- Budget has been allocated but is unspent.
- The organization is actively monitoring its competitor's use of AI tools without taking corresponding action.

Consider, for instance, a midsize financial firm with an AI task force that meets monthly for a year. Despite extensive discussions and three comprehensive reports, they never implemented the technology, primarily due to unresolved concerns about data privacy.

The "Partial Implementation" Stage

At the "partial implementation" stage, organizations often have these characteristics:

- Departments are adopting AI tools inconsistently throughout the organization.
- There's uneven access to AI platforms across teams.
- There's a mixture of approved and unauthorized AI usage.
- AI tools have limited integration with existing systems.

For example, consider a software as a service firm that provided premium AI tools to its marketing and product development teams while the customer service and operations teams continued working with legacy systems. This created workflow problems when content created by AI-enabled teams reached departments without compatible technologies.

The "Foot on the Accelerator" State

Organizations in the "foot on the accelerator" state have these characteristics:

- AI tools have been seamlessly integrated across departments, with L&D leading the transformation.
- Clear governance frameworks that enable rather than restrict innovation are in place.
- AI access and training is consistent across all organizational levels.
- Measurable business outcomes are directly linked to AI implementation.
- L&D is leveraging AI to revolutionize learning experiences and knowledge transfer.

For example, consider a forward-thinking healthcare organization that empowered its L&D team to spearhead AI integration. They developed a tiered learning program that built AI literacy across the entire workforce, and then trained specialized AI champions in each department. Their L&D function now uses AI to create personalized learning pathways, which have reduced onboarding time by 40 percent and increased knowledge retention by 35 percent. Most impressively, they've established an AI solutions lab in which clinical and administrative staff collaborate with L&D to prototype AI applications that address real operational challenges. This resulted in three innovations that significantly improved patient care coordination.

Assessing Your Current State

Before you can chart a path forward, you need an honest assessment of where your organization stands today. The examples I just provided likely resonate with aspects of your current reality, but understanding your specific AI maturity requires a more structured approach. Let's explore how to accurately evaluate your organization's AI readiness and identify the strategic pivot points that will accelerate your journey.

Consider your organization's position in each of these critical areas:

- **Access and infrastructure:**
  - What AI tools do people have access to?

- Do they have official access or are they using free versions?
- How robust is your data infrastructure for supporting AI initiatives?
- What security measures protect your AI implementations?
- **Skills and knowledge:**
  - How AI-literate is your workforce?
  - Do people know how to effectively prompt an AI model? (I'm reminded of computer mouse skills courses that I used to create. We're currently at that fundamental stage with AI prompting.)
  - What training resources currently exist?
  - Who are your AI champions?
- **Policy and governance:**
  - Have you established a formal AI policy?
  - How are you addressing data privacy concerns?
  - What guidelines govern appropriate AI use?
  - Who is responsible for AI oversight?
- **Integration with current systems:**
  - How seamlessly does AI function within your existing tech stack?
  - What AI capabilities does your learning platform support?
  - How are your vendors incorporating AI features?
  - What systems break when you attempt to use AI solutions?

EXERCISE

Where Are You Now? An AI Readiness Assessment

Now that we've explored the common patterns of organizational AI adoption, it's time to evaluate your own situation. The following assessment will help you objectively measure your current state and identify priority areas for development.

Use Table 3-1 to evaluate your current AI readiness. Along each row, circle or note which column (from beginning to advanced) applies most accurately to your organization.

Table 3-1. AI Readiness Assessment

Dimension	Early (1)	Developing (2)	Established (3)	Advanced (4)
Access and infrastructure	No official AI tools	Limited access for select teams	Organization-wide access to basic tools	Comprehensive AI ecosystem
Skills and knowledge	Minimal understanding	Pockets of expertise	Structured training available	Widespread AI literacy
Policy and governance	No formal policies	Policies under development	Basic policies implemented	Comprehensive governance
System integration	No integration	Limited point solutions	Partial integration	Seamless workflow integration

Score interpretation:

- **4–6: Early stage**—focus on building awareness and developing policies.
- **7–10: Developing stage**—prioritize building skills and conducting pilot programs.
- **11–14: Maturing stage**—concentrate on integration and scaling.
- **15–16: Advanced stage**—lead with innovation and optimization.

Identifying Your Next Steps

Every organization's AI journey follows a unique path, but certain strategic actions can accelerate your progress, regardless of your starting point. Based on your self-assessment results, focus your efforts on the recommendations most relevant to your current maturity level.

Now that you understand your current position, here's how to advance your AI journey.

Early Stage

Getting started with AI doesn't have to be overwhelming. The key is to begin by understanding where you are and where you can deliver early wins. Follow these steps to lay a strong foundation for growth and long-term success:

- Document existing AI usage (including unofficial applications).
- Identify immediate opportunities for AI implementation.

- Develop your business case. (Check out the detailed plan later in this chapter.)
- Focus on quick wins that demonstrate tangible value.

Developing Stage

If you've seen initial success and buy-in, then it's time to build momentum. At this stage, your focus should shift toward structure, scalability, and skills. Take the following actions to solidify your progress and deepen AI integration:

- Formalize your AI governance structure.
- Expand successful pilot programs with measurable outcomes.
- Develop comprehensive training programs for different user groups.
- Integrate AI seamlessly into existing workflows.

Maturing Stage

When you're ahead of the curve, the challenge becomes staying there. This phase is all about accelerating impact, spreading knowledge, and fostering a culture of innovation. Here are some ways to keep your edge sharp:

- Scale successful implementation across the organization.
- Optimize AI processes for maximum efficiency.
- Share best practices through internal communities of practice.
- Drive innovation by exploring emerging AI applications.

Advanced Stage

At this stage, AI is fully embedded across your organization. The focus now is on scale, consistency, and continuous improvement. Here's how to stay ahead:

- Build a connected AI ecosystem across tools, teams, and data sources.
- Promote AI literacy through targeted, role-based learning.
- Strengthen governance models to manage risk and ensure compliance.
- Embed AI into daily workflows to drive efficiency and adoption.
- Track enterprise-wide impact using clear, strategic metrics.

Red Flags That Require Immediate Attention

Even well-planned AI initiatives can develop serious problems that undermine their effectiveness and create organizational risk. These warning signs are often subtle at first but if left unaddressed can quickly escalate into significant barriers to successful implementation.

Watch for these warning signs that indicate potential problems in your AI implementation:

- Uncontrolled proliferation of AI tools
- Inadequate data privacy measures
- Absence of clear AI governance
- Persistent resistance to change
- Insufficient training resources
- Poor integration with existing systems

By identifying problems, you can create space to explore the significant opportunities available to your organization.

Building a Compelling Business Case for AI Adoption

Even the most promising AI initiative will fail without proper stakeholder support. Your business case must transform AI from a technological curiosity into a strategic imperative. Let's discuss some things you can do to craft a persuasive narrative that secures both executive buy-in and necessary resources.

Quantifiable Efficiency Gains

Don't just promise improved efficiency. Demonstrate it with:

- **Time-motion analysis.** Document current process duration versus an AI-enabled workflow; for example, you could say, "content creation currently takes 4.5 hours per course module; AI assistance reduces this to 1.2 hours."
- **Volume capabilities.** Show scaling potential; for example, you could say, "our team can develop three times more learning assets with the same headcount."
- **Opportunity cost.** Highlight what your team could accomplish when freed from specific tasks; for example, you could, "redirect 20 hours weekly from administrative tasks to strategic design work."

Financial Impact Projections

Translate efficiency into dollars. Here are a few metrics you can use:

- **Hard cost reduction.** Calculate actual budget savings, including vendor costs, overtime reduction, and reduced outsourcing.
- **Development economics.** Compare traditional development costs with AI-assisted ones across your entire portfolio.
- **Productivity ROI.** Show the exponential value of redeployed talent; for example, you could say, "Each hour redirected to strategic work yields approximately $X in business value."
- **Implementation costs.** Be transparent about the investment required, including technology, training, and transition costs.

Quality and Experience Enhancements

Demonstrate tangible improvements with:

- **Consistency metrics.** Show how AI standardizes quality across content and experiences.
- **Personalization at scale.** Illustrate how tailored experiences become feasible for all learners, not just high-priority groups.
- **Error reduction.** Quantify reduced revision cycles and quality issues.
- **User experience.** Present feedback from pilot tests showing improved learner engagement and satisfaction.

Comprehensive Risk Assessment

Address concerns proactively. Here are few things to consider:

- **Data security framework.** Detail specific protection measures for sensitive information.
- **Privacy compliance.** Map AI usage to existing regulatory requirements.
- **Ethical guidelines.** Present clear principles for responsible AI application.
- **Contingency planning.** Include fallback procedures for potential AI limitations.
- **Comparative risk analysis.** Highlight risks of inaction versus adoption.

Competitive Intelligence

Create urgency. Use this information to provide context about the market:

- **Industry benchmark data.** Present adoption rates within your sector.
- **Case studies.** Showcase measurable outcomes from organizations that are similar to yours.
- **Capability gap analysis.** Demonstrate any emerging competitive disadvantages of delayed adoption.
- **Future talent considerations.** Address how AI capabilities affect recruitment and retention.

Implementation Road Map

Show thoughtful execution planning with these strategies:

- **Phased approach.** Break implementation into logical, manageable stages.
- **Resource allocation.** Determine required personnel, time, and budget for each phase.
- **Dependencies and prerequisites.** Identify technological and organizational requirements.
- **Change management strategy.** Outline communication, training, and cultural integration plans.
- **Milestone timeline.** Create a realistic schedule with specific completion targets.

Success Measurement Framework

Establish accountability through these metrics:

- **Leading indicators**—early signals that implementation is on track
- **Learning KPIs**—metrics specific to educational outcomes
- **Operational KPIs**—efficiency and quality measurements
- **Business impact KPIs**—a connection to organizational performance indicators
- **Evaluation schedule**—the timeline for reviewing progress and making adjustments

Making Your Case Irresistible

The most compelling business cases combine analytical rigor with emotional resonance. Consider using these presentation strategies:

- **Executive summary.** Distill your case onto a single page that highlights ROI and strategic alignment.
- **Storytelling.** Frame the proposal around specific user journeys and pain points.
- **Visual data.** Use infographics to illustrate your current and future state comparisons.
- **Pilot program results.** Whenever possible, include actual results from small-scale implementation groups.
- **Expert validation.** Incorporate perspectives from respected internal or external authorities.
- **Opportunity cost emphasis.** Clearly articulate what the organization loses by waiting.

Remember: Your business case isn't just about securing budget and access to models, but also building momentum for transformation. Structure your presentation to address both rational decision-making criteria and the human factors that drive organizational change.

ϙϙϙ

Whether you're currently emailing yourself ChatGPT responses or operating sophisticated AI programs, room for growth exists. As we've discussed, the essential first step is conducting an honest assessment of your current state and building methodically from that foundation.

I've witnessed many technology fear cycles throughout my career. As of 2025, we're in the midst of one with AI. The key is moving forward thoughtfully, not fearfully. Begin where you are, acknowledge your challenges honestly, and focus on incremental progress rather than perfection. This requires a clear change management approach.

Change Management: Getting People on Board With AI

Effective change management is absolutely critical for successful AI adoption in any organization. Without a structured approach to managing the human side of this technological transformation, even the most sophisticated AI implementations will fail to deliver their promised value.

The reality is that people ultimately determine whether AI initiatives succeed or falter. The human side of technology adoption is always the trickiest part and requires deliberate, thoughtful change management to navigate successfully.

Understanding and Addressing the Fear Cycle

You know what happens every time a new technology comes along? We go through what I call the "technology fear cycle" (Figure 3-2).

Figure 3-2. The Technology Fear Cycle

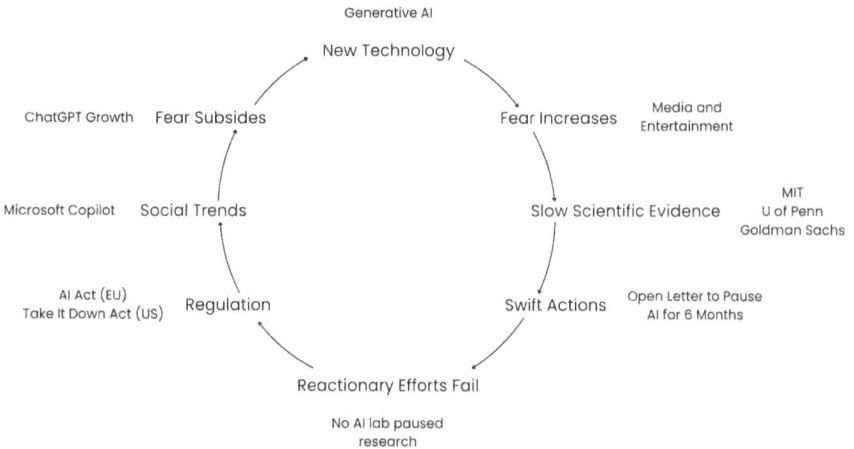

Let's look closer at how it typically plays out:

1. **New technology emerges.** A breakthrough sparks excitement and curiosity, but also uncertainty.
2. **Fear increases.** Concerns begin to grow as the public becomes more aware of the technology's implications.
3. **Slow scientific evidence.** Research lags behind the speed of innovation, leaving room for speculation.

4. **Swift actions.** Calls for pauses, bans, or major restrictions are made to slow or stop development.

5. **Reactionary efforts fail.** Many of these quick-fix responses won't gain traction or will prove ineffective.

6. **Regulation and social trends.** More structured efforts begin to take shape as society learns how to live with the technology.

7. **Fear subsides.** As the technology becomes more integrated and familiar, anxiety naturally declines.

For many L&D professionals, AI adoption triggers the technology fear cycle and a hesitation to embrace new tools due to concerns around job displacement, complexity, or loss of control. However, AI is best viewed as a collaborator rather than a replacement.

Right now, with AI, we're somewhere between steps 3 and 4 of the technology fear cycle. The good news? We know how to handle it. Let me show you how.

Building Your Change Management Strategy

Now that we understand the technology fear cycle and where we are in the AI adoption journey, it's time to create a practical framework for implementing change. Successful AI integration requires a deliberate, structured approach that addresses both the technical and human aspects of the transition.

The strategy outlined in the following sections provides a road map based on proven change management principles that I've seen work across industries and in organization of various sizes—from startups to Fortune 500 companies. By following these steps, you'll significantly increase your chances of successful AI adoption while minimizing resistance and disruption.

Step 1. Partner With the Right People

Successful AI adoption is never a solo journey. Creating a coalition of stakeholders across your organization is essential for navigating the complexities of change. Each person brings unique expertise, influence, and perspective that will strengthen your implementation.

By deliberately building this network before you begin an AI rollout, you can create a foundation of support that will help you overcome the inevitable resistance and challenges. Here are the people you need on your dream team:

- **HR**—for workforce impact
- **Communications**—for messaging
- **IT**—for technical implementation
- **Leaders**—for visible support
- **Early adopters**—as champions

Step 2. Address the Human Side

The technical aspects of AI implementation are challenging, but the human elements are where most change initiatives falter. While algorithms follow predictable patterns, people's reactions to change are complex, emotional, and deeply influenced by their past experiences.

Research from the field of organizational psychology consistently shows that resistance to change is natural and predictable. Understanding and addressing these human needs is essential for success. Here are some things that people require during periods of technological transition:

- Clear understanding of why changes are happening
- Time to adapt
- Support during the transition
- Recognition for their efforts
- A voice in the process

Step 3. Create Your Communication Plan

Communication is the thread that holds everything together. Without clear, targeted, and consistent messaging, even the best-designed AI initiatives will struggle to gain traction. Different stakeholders have different needs, concerns, and motivations related to AI adoption, so you need a strategic approach to communication that segments your audience and tailors your messages accordingly.

From my experience implementing technological change over the years, I've found that a segmented approach is far more effective than one-size-fits-all messaging. There are certain things to keep in mind for each key audience. Here's what I've seen work.

For leaders:
- Focus on business impact and ROI.
- Provide clear governance frameworks.
- Share success stories from other organizations.
- Address risk and compliance concerns.

For managers:
- Offer practical implementation guidance.
- Provide tools for team support.
- Help them identify opportunities.
- Give them metrics for success.

For individual contributors:
- Show personal benefits.
- Provide hands-on training.
- Create safe spaces for practice.
- Celebrate small wins.

Addressing Common Resistance Points

Resistance to AI adoption typically follows predictable patterns across organizations, regardless of industry or size. Understanding these common objections allows you to prepare thoughtful, evidence-based responses rather than reacting defensively in the moment.

Resistance often masks deeper concerns about identity, value, and purpose in a changing workplace. By addressing the underlying emotional and psychological dimensions of resistance, you can transform potential blockers into advocates. Let me share some real situations I've encountered and how you can handle them.

If someone says, "AI will replace my job," you can:
- Acknowledge their concern.
- Show how AI augments rather than replaces.
- Highlight new opportunities.
- Provide upskilling pathways.

If someone says, "I don't trust AI," you can:

- Share governance frameworks.
- Demonstrate safety measures.
- Show successful use cases.
- Start with low-risk applications.

If someone says, "This is just another fad," you can:

- Connect AI to business strategy.
- Show industry trends.
- Demonstrate concrete benefits.
- Share the long-term vision.

If someone asks, "What about the environmental impact?" you can:

- Acknowledge the energy demands of large AI models.
- Share emerging efforts to reduce AI's carbon footprint.
- Highlight vendors that are committed to sustainable practices.
- Emphasize the role of responsible AI development.

By directly responding to these common objections with empathy and evidence, you can significantly reduce resistance and accelerate AI adoption. Remember that resistance is a natural human response to change that requires patience and persistent communication to overcome.

The most successful AI implementations I've witnessed all shared one common factor: leadership teams that took the time to understand and address these concerns rather than dismissing them.

Fostering Innovation

Successfully implementing AI demands creating an environment where innovation can flourish. Organizations that excel with AI adoption understand that technology alone isn't enough; they deliberately cultivate a culture that encourages experimentation, learning, and collaborative problem solving. This cultural foundation is what separates organizations that merely deploy AI tools from those that truly transform through AI integration.

Based on my work with high-performing organizations across sectors, I've identified three key components of an innovation-friendly culture that supports successful AI adoption: safe spaces for experimentation, communities of practice, and feedback systems.

To create safe spaces for experimentation, you can:

- Set up AI labs or sandboxes.
- Allow time for exploration.
- Share knowledge openly.
- Celebrate attempts, not just successes.

To build communities of practice, you can:

- Connect AI champions across departments.
- Share best practices.
- Support peer learning.
- Create feedback loops.

To implement feedback systems, you can:

- Hold regular check-ins.
- Provide anonymous feedback channels.
- Offer usage metrics.
- Conduct impact assessments.

Fostering innovation is an ongoing commitment that requires leadership attention and resources. Organizations that sustain successful AI adoption continuously refine their approach based on lessons learned and evolving needs. Cultural transformation happens gradually, so celebrate small wins, share success stories widely, and be patient as your innovation ecosystem develops.

Remember: Change management isn't about forcing adoption; instead, it's about creating an environment where people feel supported in embracing new tools and ways of working. Like I always say, "The technology might change, but humans stay pretty much the same." Focus on the human element, and the rest will follow.

Next, let's look at how to actually implement AI in your L&D programs.

Making L&D AI Integration Actually Happen

The integration of AI into L&D represents perhaps the most significant transformation our field has experienced. In this section, I provide a practical framework for implementing AI in L&D contexts, based on real-world experience guiding organizations through various stages of AI adoption. You'll learn specific strategies to start small, achieve quick wins, and build toward more advanced applications—all while avoiding common pitfalls that derail

AI initiatives. I've found that the following principles consistently separate successful implementations from disappointing ones:

- **Start small.** Begin with targeted applications that address specific pain points rather than attempting a comprehensive transformation. Success builds momentum and credibility for broader initiatives.
- **Focus on people.** Technology implementation ultimately succeeds or fails based on human factors. Invest at least as heavily in change management as in technology selection.
- **Stay flexible.** The AI landscape evolves weekly. Rigid, multiyear plans quickly become obsolete, so build adaptability into your strategy from the outset.
- **Keep experimenting.** Maintain a portfolio of small experiments running alongside your established applications. Today's speculative exploration often becomes tomorrow's competitive advantage.

The integration of AI into L&D represents perhaps the most significant transformation our field has experienced. This isn't about adopting new tools; we need to reimagine how we approach human and machine performance.

Your role as an L&D professional extends beyond traditional boundaries. The challenge is substantial, but so is the opportunity to reshape learning in ways we've only begun to imagine.

Starting Where You Are

First, let's look at what's possible right now with AI in L&D. I'm talking about real, practical applications that you can implement today.

To accelerate content creation, you can currently use AI to:
- Generate first drafts of learning materials.
- Create multiple-choice questions for assessments.
- Generate scenario variations for practice exercises.
- Build course outlines and learning objectives.

To enhance learning support, you can use AI to:
- Create simple chatbots for FAQs.
- Search for learning resources.
- Supply automated content recommendations.
- Provide basic learner analytics.

To automate processes, you can use AI to:

- Handle administrative tasks.
- Generate content metadata.
- Recommend basic learning paths.
- Grade assessments and provide feedback.

Case Study: The Reality Check

I once worked with a large manufacturing company that wanted to jump into creating AI-powered personalized learning paths without building foundational capabilities. Their ambitious goal proved challenging because they lacked experience with even basic AI applications.

Here's how I helped them approach the implementation:

- We started by using AI to help instructional designers create better content faster (specifically generating scenario variations for safety training that previously required significant manual effort).
- With this initial success, we built confidence and competence with the technology among the design team.
- We carefully documented both successes (40 percent reduction in scenario development time) and challenges (the need for significant editing of AI outputs).
- We gradually expanded to more sophisticated applications (starting with content recommendations based on user behavior).

The result? They achieved their goal through a series of manageable steps rather than one giant leap. The phased approach also allowed them to develop internal expertise, reducing their dependence on external consultants for future initiatives.

Your Implementation Toolkit

When selecting tools for your AI implementation, focus on capabilities and integration potential—not just specific products—because this landscape is evolving fast. Here are some key tool categories relevant to L&D:

- **Content creation tools** support rapid, scalable asset development, including:
  - Text generation (large language models)

- Image creation (AI-based visual design tools)
- Voice and audio generation (narration and podcasts)
- Video creation platforms with built-in AI features
- **Learning platforms.** Look for platforms that:
  - Have built-in AI features (such as personalization and recommendations).
  - Integrate easily with your existing tech stack.
  - Meet your security and compliance standards.
  - Provide visibility into their AI road map and updates.
- **Analytics tools** help you measure and improve learning outcomes. You can:
  - Start with built-in LMS analytics.
  - Layer on AI-powered insights over time.
  - Focus on actionable metrics, not just reporting.
  - Build toward predictive capabilities.

Tools

For more details about specific tools, check out the book's support website, joshcavalier.ai/ApplyingAIBook.

What should you look for across all tools? As you evaluate solutions, consider these cross-cutting factors:
- Integration with your existing systems
- Learning curve for your team
- Data privacy and security
- Vendor support and documentation

The Implementation Road Map

Implementing AI in your L&D function doesn't require a sweeping overnight overhaul. By following a phased approach, you can demonstrate value early, build organizational confidence, and scale AI capabilities in a sustainable way.

The three-phase road map I outline here provides key milestones to guide your implementation journey.

Phase 1. Laying the Foundation (First 30 Days)

Establish a solid base by assessing your current capabilities and identifying quick, visible wins that you can use to build momentum.

To assess your current state, you can:

- Audit your current tools and learning processes.
- Identify pain points and inefficiencies.
- Map potential AI use cases to real business needs.
- Define clear objectives and success metrics.

Once you've identified your quick wins, you can:

- Begin with content creation tasks that AI can immediately add value to.
- Leverage existing AI tools your team can adopt quickly.
- Track and document measurable time savings and quality improvements.
- Share early success stories to build advocacy across stakeholders.

Phase 2. Strategic Expansion (60–90 Days)

During phase 2, deepen integration and test AI's impact in targeted areas to generate scalable outcomes.

When integrating AI into your processes:

- Embed AI into day-to-day learning workflows.
- Develop and document repeatable standard operating procedures.
- Provide hands-on training to upskill team members.
- Measure and report outcomes consistently.

To conduct a successful pilot program:

- Identify high-impact areas for AI-supported experimentation.
- Launch small-scale tests with clear goals.
- Actively gather user feedback and analyze engagement.
- Refine and scale successful approaches based on data.

Phase 3. Driving Innovation (90+ Days)

In phase 3, advance your AI capabilities with transformative applications that enhance learner experience and organizational performance. Here are some ways you can do that:

- Develop personalized learning paths powered by learner data.
- Implement adaptive assessments for dynamic learning measurement.
- Use predictive analytics to anticipate skills gaps and training needs.
- Explore AI-driven coaching tools to support continuous development.

AI adoption is a journey of continuous learning and innovation. By moving through this road map with intention and agility, your L&D team can lead the way in shaping future-ready learning experiences. But, with new capabilities come new responsibilities. As you advance, it's essential to not only scale strategically but also assess the risks that come with AI implementation.

Let's Talk About Risk

Amazon's ambitious attempt to develop an AI recruitment tool offers L&D professionals a cautionary tale. In 2014, the company set out to revolutionize hiring by creating algorithms that would automatically screen resumes to identify top candidates. Its vision was compelling: an engine that could process hundreds of applications and identify the five most promising candidates.

By 2015, Amazon's machine learning specialists discovered a critical flaw. Their AI tool consistently penalized female candidates for technical roles. The system downgraded resumes containing terms like "women's" and even discriminated against graduates of all-women's colleges and universities (Dastin 2018). It also favored candidates who used verbs commonly found in male engineers' resumes, like "executed" and "captured."

This was a foundational failure. The AI tool had been trained using a decade of historical hiring data that was dominated by male applicants. The algorithm then faithfully reproduced the biases embedded in that history. Despite attempts to make the system gender-neutral, Amazon ultimately abandoned the project in 2017.

This case illustrates several areas of AI risk:
- **Training data integrity.** How do you ensure the data used to develop your AI systems represents the future you want, not just the past you've documented?
- **Bias detection.** What processes help you identify if a system is reinforcing existing prejudices rather than transcending them?

- **Ethical considerations.** How do you align AI applications with organizational values and ensure they create equitable learning experiences?
- **Human oversight.** What role should human judgment play in reviewing and potentially overriding algorithmic recommendations?

A comprehensive risk management approach should address these questions proactively rather than reactively. I've found that cross-functional AI risk assessment workshops—where L&D partners with legal, IT security, and compliance teams—often uncover crucial considerations that siloed planning would miss.

Now, let's look at how to measure the success of your AI initiatives. Having policies is great, but knowing they're working is even better.

Proving AI's Value in L&D

Early in my career I learned that it's not enough to know something's working; you've got to prove it. When I started creating CD-ROM-based training in the 1990s, I had to show the business value of every project. With AI, it's no different—except now there are even more ways to measure impact.

The adage "what gets measured gets managed" remains true in the AI era. But measurement is about more than collecting convenient data. Don't let easily available metrics distract you from measuring meaningful impact.

Consider LMS reports: They dutifully track completion rates, quiz scores, and time spent on modules. We collect this data religiously and report it quarterly. But does knowing that 87 percent of employees completed compliance training tell us if their behavior actually changed? Does a perfect quiz score translate to better decision making six months later? Of course not.

The most meaningful outcomes rarely reveal themselves in the first measurement cycle, so we create assessment frameworks that honor both immediate efficiency gains and the subtle transformations in how people approach their work.

The Comprehensive Measurement Framework

Successful AI implementation in L&D requires a thoughtful measurement strategy that goes beyond basic usage statistics. The framework I've developed helps organizations capture both immediate operational efficiencies and longer-term learning transformation—connecting AI investments directly to business outcomes.

This comprehensive approach addresses the unique challenges of measuring AI's impact, which often manifests in both quantitative metrics (such as time saved and costs reduced) and qualitative improvements (such as better content quality and enhanced learner experiences).

Let's organize our approach using a 30/60/90-day framework that addresses four key measurement categories. Each category answers a fundamental question about AI's value in your learning ecosystem:

- **Development efficiency.** How does AI change the work of L&D teams? Consider time saved in content creation, resources used per project, reduced development cycles, and cost per learning hour.
- **Learning effectiveness.** How does AI affect knowledge and skill acquisition? Consider knowledge retention rates, skill application success, time to competency, performance improvement, and certification rates.
- **Learner engagement.** How does AI affect the learning experience? Consider completion rates, participation levels, feedback scores, return rates, and resource use.
- **Business impact.** How does AI deliver organizational value? Consider performance improvements, error reduction, process efficiency, cost savings, and ROI calculations.

Step 1. Baseline Data (First 30 Days)

This initial phase is critical; however, you might be surprised how many organizations skip this step!

To measure development efficiency at this stage, you should:
- Document current content development time.
- Track required review cycles.
- Calculate average cost per learning hour.
- Record resource allocation per project.

To measure learning effectiveness, you should:

- Establish current knowledge retention metrics.
- Document time to competency baselines.
- Record current certification rates.

To measure learner engagement, you should:

- Capture current completion rates.
- Document feedback scores.
- Establish resource use patterns.

To measure business impact, you should:

- Define performance metrics relevant to your programs.
- Document current error rates.
- Establish cost baselines.

At this stage, you should also consider setting up tracking systems, defining success criteria, and identifying key stakeholders.

Step 2. Initial Measurement (60 Days)

Once you've implemented your AI solutions, begin capturing early results.

To measure development efficiency at this stage, you should:

- Measure new content development timeframes.
- Track AI-assisted review cycles.
- Calculate revised cost per learning hour.

To measure learning effectiveness, you should:

- Assess initial knowledge retention changes.
- Measure early skill application improvements.
- Track certification rate changes.

To measure learner engagement, you should:

- Analyze new completion patterns.
- Document learner feedback on AI experiences.
- Track changes in resource use.

To measure business impact, you should:

- Identify early performance changes.
- Document initial error reduction.
- Calculate preliminary efficiency gains.

At this stage, you should also consider gathering comprehensive feedback, documenting implementation challenges, and adjusting measurement approaches as needed.

Step 3. Comprehensive Analysis (90 Days)

By this point, you should have sufficient data to evaluate impact.

To measure development efficiency at this stage, you should:

- Compare pre- and post-AI development metrics.
- Calculate time and resources saved.
- Document process improvements.

To measure learning effectiveness, you should:

- Analyze knowledge retention improvements.
- Assess skill application success rates.
- Document time to competency changes.

To measure learner engagement, you should:

- Compare new versus old completion rates.
- Analyze feedback patterns.
- Document engagement improvements.

To measure business impact, you should:

- Calculate ROI based on initial data.
- Document performance improvements.
- Project annual impact estimates.

At this stage, you should also consider sharing findings with stakeholders, developing an ongoing measurement plan, and recommending adjustments to AI implementation.

Common Measurement Challenges and Solutions

Even the most well-designed measurement strategies can run into obstacles. Here are some of the most common challenges learning leaders face when implementing a 30/60/90-day framework, and proven ways to navigate them:

- **Data overload.** In the era of dashboards and analytics tools, it's easy to drown in data. To keep your insights actionable, focus on three to five key metrics per category, and tie them directly to your business goals. More data isn't always better; better data is better.

- **Attribution difficulty.** Proving that your learning program caused an improvement—and not just coincidentally aligned with one—can be tough. When possible, build in control groups or A/B testing. Supplement quantitative data with qualitative insights like learner testimonials and manager observations to paint a fuller picture.
- **Stakeholder skepticism.** Stakeholders are more likely to trust results they helped define. Involve them early in selecting success metrics, and tie those metrics to outcomes they care about—like faster onboarding, higher customer satisfaction, or lower error rates.
- **Technology integration.** Your LMS or LXP likely wasn't designed with AI-specific learning data in mind. Work closely with your platform vendors to develop custom reporting solutions. If needed, explore third-party analytics tools that can bridge gaps and offer a more complete view.
- **Sustaining momentum.** Measurement isn't a one-and-done activity. Build a rhythm into your reporting—monthly dashboards for project teams, quarterly summaries for leadership, and annual reviews to steer strategic decisions. Consistency builds credibility and reinforces the value of your work over time.

Making the Data Work for You

With regular reporting, you can establish a consistent cadence for sharing results. Try using:

- Monthly dashboards for project teams
- Quarterly reviews for department leaders
- Annual assessments for executive stakeholders
- Ongoing trend analysis to identify patterns

You can also use measurement data to refine your approach and continuously improve. Try these strategies:

- Identify successful patterns to replicate.
- Address implementation issues quickly.
- Scale successful applications across the organization.
- Adjust measurement approaches as you learn.

To support stakeholder communication, you can tailor your measurement reporting to different audiences. Try using:

- Executive summaries focusing on business impact and ROI
- Team updates highlighting efficiency and process improvements
- Success stories demonstrating specific wins
- Lessons learned to improve future implementations

Remember: Measuring success isn't about proving that AI is magical; instead, it's about demonstrating AI's real, tangible value to your organization. Start small, be consistent, and focus on what matters to your stakeholders. Follow these steps to build your measurement action plan:

1. Select your top 3 metrics in each category.
2. Document your current state thoroughly.
3. Implement appropriate tracking systems.
4. Gather baseline data before full implementation.
5. Begin systematic measurement using the 30/60/90-day framework.
6. Share early wins to build momentum and support.

When done right, your measurement strategy becomes a strategic compass that guides your ongoing AI investments in L&D, ensures continuous improvement, and builds credibility for your learning function.

In the end, it's not just about justifying past decisions, but about creating a foundation for future innovation that truly transforms how your organization learns, develops, and performs.

Conclusion

Developing an effective AI strategy is about creating a foundation for AI and related technologies to deliver real value for your organization. Developing that strategy begins by understanding its critical elements, including leadership buy-in, technical infrastructure, and business alignment. True leadership support extends beyond enthusiasm to deep understanding and creating a culture where innovation flourishes.

You also need to know where you and your organization truly stand with AI adoption—whether operating in the "shadow AI" scenario with unauthorized tools, taking a wait and see approach, implementing solutions partially across departments, or fully embracing an AI-driven transformation. This honest assessment provides a starting point for thoughtful implementation.

By understanding the technology fear cycle and addressing human concerns proactively, you can transform resistance into support. Developing structured communication strategies that are tailored to different stakeholder groups will help you overcome common objections and foster a culture of innovation.

Following an implementation road map and a phased approach to AI integration allows you to start small, demonstrate value quickly, and build momentum. And measuring AI's impact across four key dimensions—development efficiency, learning effectiveness, learner engagement, and business impact—ensures that AI investments deliver demonstrable value.

The journey toward AI-enabled learning is about enhancing what you do. By starting where you are, focusing on practical applications that address real challenges, and systematically measuring outcomes, you can transform AI from a source of anxiety into a powerful ally in your L&D toolkit. The pace of change may feel overwhelming, but with the strategic approach outlined in this chapter, you can navigate the complex terrain of AI implementation successfully, delivering measurable results that advance your organization's learning objectives and business goals.

In the next chapter, we move beyond implementation strategies to confront the deeper ethical responsibilities that come with AI adoption. We'll explore the critical issues of privacy, security, bias, and governance. And, we'll review the frameworks and practical tools needed to build trust, ensure fairness, and lead responsibly in this transformative age of learning technology.

CHAPTER 4

Privacy, Security, Ethics, and Governance

In This Chapter

- Approaches to mitigating privacy and security risks
- A practical framework for addressing bias, fairness, and representation concerns
- Policy suggestions for AI governance

One of my favorite movie moments comes from *Star Wars: Episode V—The Empire Strikes Back*. There's a scene in which Han Solo is desperately trying to get the Millennium Falcon's hyperdrive to work as the Empire closes in. In true Han fashion, he doesn't consult a manual—he slams his fist against the control panel. And for a brief moment, it works.

It's classic: a mix of improvisation, frustration, and hope. But it also perfectly captures how many organizations approach AI in L&D—by pounding on the dashboard and hoping for lift off, without really understanding the system they're using.

In my years working with teams implementing AI learning solutions, I've seen the same pattern over and over. The technology is exciting, but the rush to activate it often overlooks critical questions about privacy, security, and ethics. This reminds me of a recent client who was so eager to implement an AI-enabled learning platform that they hadn't even considered what they would do with all the employee data they'd be collecting. That's like jumping into hyperspace without checking your coordinates—not a recipe for success.

The promise of AI in L&D is transformative. But beneath the glossy surface of personalized learning paths and adaptive content lies a complex web of ethical considerations that demand immediate attention. As L&D professionals, we find ourselves at a critical juncture where the decisions we make about AI implementation will shape the effectiveness of our learning programs and their ethical integrity.

Consider this startling contrast: While 71 percent of L&D professionals use AI to explore and experiment or integrate it into their work, only 23 percent feel confident in their ability to address the ethical implications of these technologies (LinkedIn 2025). This gap between adoption and ethical readiness represents both a challenge and an opportunity for our field.

We can no longer separate AI's technical implementation from its ethical implications. Every decision we make about AI in learning environments—from data collection practices to AI model selection—has profound ethical consequences that ripple through our organizations and affect our associates' lives (Figure 4-1).

Figure 4-1. The Pros and Cons of AI in L&D

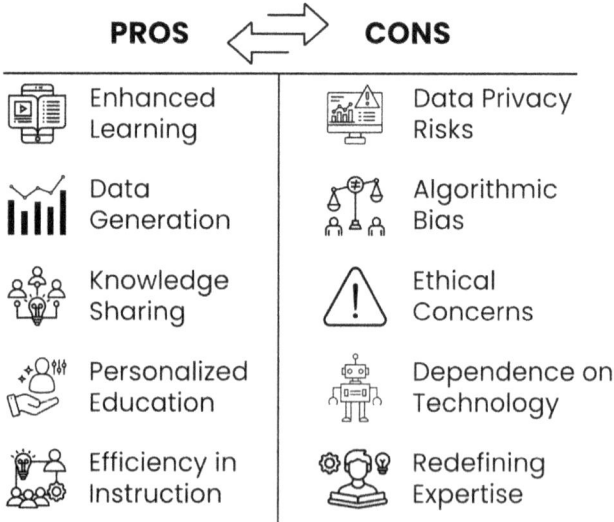

PROS	CONS
Enhanced Learning	Data Privacy Risks
Data Generation	Algorithmic Bias
Knowledge Sharing	Ethical Concerns
Personalized Education	Dependence on Technology
Efficiency in Instruction	Redefining Expertise

This chapter is your guide through this complex landscape. If my experience building training programs has taught me anything, it's that we need a solid framework for navigating these challenges. We'll explore three critical areas that every L&D professional needs to master:

- **Data privacy and security in learning ecosystems.** This is about building trust with your learners. I'll share real stories of successes and failures I've seen in the field.

- **Avoiding bias and ensuring fairness in AI models.** We'll learn from real-world examples and discuss practical strategies for ensuring your AI systems serve all learners equitably.

- **How AI is changing our understanding of knowledge and expertise, among ourselves in L&D and the employees we serve.** When I started in this field, we had to teach people how to use a mouse (yes, really!), and now we're teaching them how to effectively prompt AI and work alongside these systems.

Finally, I'll walk you through creating a comprehensive AI policy for your organization. I'll review the essential components of an effective policy—from governance structures to implementation guidelines—and show you how a well-crafted AI policy can protect your organization while enabling innovation in learning.

The stakes are high, but there's good news too. I've seen organizations transform their learning outcomes by thoughtfully implementing ethical AI practices. For L&D professionals, this is an opportunity to evolve from implementation specialists to ethical architects of AI-powered learning ecosystems. This requires new skills, frameworks, and, most importantly, a mindset that puts ethical considerations at the heart of everything we do.

As we move through this chapter, I'll include practical insights and actionable strategies from my experience and organizations that I've seen successfully navigate these challenges. You'll learn how to implement ethical AI practices in your organization and position yourself as a thought leader in this critical area.

Remember, AI is shaping the future of learning, but how we implement it ethically is up to us. So, let's get started on this journey together.

Privacy and Security in a Learning Ecosystem

Imagine this scenario: You've just implemented your organization's state-of-the-art AI-powered learning platform. The system promises to revolutionize how your employees learn, offering personalized pathways and real-time adaptations based on individual performance. Then, one morning, you receive an urgent email. An employee has discovered that their learning patterns, personal data, and performance struggles are being shared with third-party vendors without their knowledge or consent.

This isn't a hypothetical future—it's happening right now. In May 2024, Microsoft's new AI feature, Recall, raised significant privacy concerns by continuously capturing and storing screenshots of users' activities. Meanwhile, Adobe's recent changes to its terms of service sparked controversy over AI's access to user data for content review. These real-world examples highlight a crucial truth: The intersection of AI and learning is not all sunshine and rainbows.

In the rush to adopt AI-powered learning tools, many organizations overlook data privacy and security. This oversight can lead to significant risks, from data breaches to regulatory noncompliance. Understanding and addressing these challenges is crucial for organizations leveraging AI in their learning ecosystem.

The Challenges AI Systems Present

Did you know the average person generates 1.7 megabytes of data per second? In an AI-driven world, this data is both a valuable resource and a potential liability. The adage "data is the new oil" has never been truer than in the age of AI.

AI models need large amounts of clean data to function effectively and deliver accurate predictions and personalized learning experiences. However, the requirement for extensive datasets underscores the importance of maintaining stringent data privacy and security measures.

Privacy and security are fundamental human rights that extend into the digital realm. In the learning context—where sensitive personal data is often involved—protecting these rights becomes even more important. Failure to do so violates individual trust and can lead to legal repercussions and reputational damage. Moreover, a secure learning environment fosters trust, encouraging more open and effective learning experiences.

Consider the case of Pearson (a major EdTech company), which suffered a data breach in 2018 that exposed the personal information of more than 50 million students. This incident highlights the vast amount of sensitive data educational technology companies handle and the potential risks of inadequate security measures. Furthermore, in August 2021, Pearson agreed to pay a \$1 million fine to settle charges from the US Securities and Exchange Commission that it misled investors about its data breach.

Pearson's experience demonstrates the importance of prioritizing privacy and security in AI-driven learning ecosystems to avoid severe consequences, such as legal actions, financial penalties, and loss of trust.

The challenges of maintaining privacy and security in AI-driven learning ecosystems are multifaceted. First, there's the sheer volume of data collected, including personal information and detailed learning behaviors. This data is a goldmine for personalized learning but a significant liability if it's not adequately protected. There's also the nature of artificial intelligence itself. As I've mentioned, GenAI models often require access to large datasets for training purposes to function effectively. This can create tension between the need for data to improve AI and the imperative to protect individual privacy, not to mention intellectual property. In addition, the interconnected nature of modern learning ecosystems, which often involve multiple vendors and platforms, creates additional security vulnerabilities. Each connection point is a potential entry for bad actors.

It all comes down to striking a balance between data utility and privacy. Techniques like *federated learning*—which allows AI models to learn from decentralized data without directly accessing it—offer promising solutions. Similarly, differential privacy techniques can add noise to datasets, preserving individual privacy while maintaining overall data utility. For example, Apple has implemented differential privacy in its AI systems, allowing it to gather insights from user data and improve services like predictive text and Siri without compromising individual privacy.

Understanding Your Data

Here are some questions to ask yourself about data collection and use:

- What types of data does your organization collect for AI-driven tools?
- How transparent are you with users about data collection and use?
- What measures do you have in place to protect this data?
- How might a data breach affect your organization and its stakeholders?
- How might your organization apply data minimization and privacy-preserving AI techniques?
- What are the potential benefits and challenges of data collection?
- How does your organization balance the need for data in AI systems with the imperative to protect individual privacy?

Now, conduct a mini-audit of one of your AI-driven tools. List the types of data it collects and uses. Then, ask these questions for each data type:

- Is this necessary?
- How is it protected?
- Could you achieve the same results with less data?

These are the same questions your IT or cyber security team should be asking.

Let's now turn to specific privacy and security issues related to AI and learning ecosystems.

Key Privacy Considerations

Learning ecosystems have become central to organization development strategies in today's rapidly evolving digital landscape. These interconnected platforms, tools, and resources offer unprecedented opportunities for personalized learning experiences and data-driven insights.

Now that AI is deeply integrated into these systems, L&D professionals can leverage powerful capabilities such as adaptive learning paths, predictive analytics, and automated content curation. AI-powered learning ecosystems can identify skills gaps, recommend targeted development opportunities, and anticipate future learning needs based on performance patterns.

However, as these intelligent systems collect, analyze, and share increasingly granular information about learners, privacy considerations have moved to the forefront of L&D concerns. Effective learning ecosystem management requires a careful balance between leveraging AI and data for enhanced learning outcomes and protecting individual privacy rights.

The key privacy considerations detailed here provide a framework for L&D professionals seeking to navigate this complex terrain while maintaining compliance and fostering stakeholder trust:

- **AI-enhanced data collection and usage.** Learning ecosystems now use AI to collect and analyze vast amounts of data, including personal information, learning behaviors, engagement patterns, and assessment results. AI-powered data collection enables more sophisticated learning analytics for hyper-personalized training experiences. However, it raises heightened concerns about algorithmic transparency and potential bias in data collection, interpretation, and application.

- **AI interoperability and cross-platform data privacy.** As AI systems increasingly communicate across platforms, interoperability between AI-powered learning tools creates complex data exchange networks. This interconnectedness can pose elevated risks to data privacy if not appropriately managed, requiring sophisticated governance frameworks to ensure that sensitive information remains within secure boundaries while enabling the benefits of integrated learning experiences.

- **AI-specific regulatory compliance.** Beyond traditional data protection regulations—such as the European Union's General Data Protection Regulation (GDPR), the US Family Educational Rights and Privacy Act (FERPA), and the Children's Online Privacy Protection Act (COPPA)—organizations must now navigate emerging AI-specific regulations such as the EU AI Act and various national AI governance frameworks. These new regulations impose additional requirements around AI transparency, explainability, and fairness when processing personal data in learning contexts.

- **Advanced security measures for AI systems.** Implementing robust security measures has evolved beyond basic encryption to include AI-specific protections, such as federated security models, adversarial defense mechanisms, and continuous security monitoring using AI itself. These measures are critical to protecting learning data from increasingly sophisticated cyber threats targeting AI systems.

- **Ethical AI in learning analytics.** Today, learning analytics involves AI models that can make inferences about learners beyond explicit data points. You must address employee privacy concerns by ensuring data anonymization and ethical boundaries around what AI systems can infer or predict about individuals based on their learning patterns.

- **Enhanced federated learning technologies.** Modern federated learning approaches now incorporate advanced privacy-preserving techniques—such as homomorphic encryption and secure multi-party computation—alongside traditional methods. These technologies allow AI models to learn across organizational boundaries without exposing raw data, but they require careful implementation to prevent sophisticated privacy attacks.

- **Differential privacy in AI training.** Techniques like differential privacy have evolved beyond local implementations to include comprehensive privacy-preserving AI training frameworks that protect user data throughout the AI life cycle. These approaches add carefully calibrated noise at multiple stages of the learning process, allowing organizations to balance statistical utility with robust privacy guarantees for individual learners.

Before moving on to security considerations, let's focus on one specific type of AI system that this book deals with deeply. GenAI models—which create text, images, and audio content (multimodal)—pose significant data privacy challenges that are influenced by whether the models are open- or closed-source.

Open-source models like Meta's LLaMA and Stability AI's Stable Diffusion have privacy concerns that you should be aware of, including:

- **Transparency and collaboration.** Open-source models allow public access to their source code, enabling developers to inspect, modify, and improve the models. While transparency can improve security (because the community can identify and fix vulnerabilities), it also presents risks, particularly if the training data includes sensitive information.

- **Customization and flexibility.** Open-source models can be tailored for specific applications, offering flexibility in deployment and use.

Closed-source models like OpenAI's GPT-4 and Google Gemini 2.0 have their own privacy challenges, including:

- **Proprietary control.** Closed-source models are developed privately, which means their code and data remain secret. While this can protect the company's intellectual property, it limits external scrutiny of privacy practices.
- **Ease of use and support.** Closed-source models often come with user-friendly interfaces and dedicated support, making them attractive for businesses seeking ready-to-use solutions. However, this can obscure data handling practices.

By addressing these AI-specific privacy challenges with comprehensive strategies and emerging best practices, you can protect user data in your learning ecosystem while fully leveraging AI's transformative benefits for organizational development.

Key Security Considerations

Understanding user security issues within a learning ecosystem is critical because organizations are increasingly relying on AI-enhanced learning platforms. Cybersecurity threats can compromise the integrity, confidentiality, and availability of educational data and systems. Here are some threats you should be aware of:

- **Phishing attacks** are a prevalent threat on learning platforms. Attackers trick users into revealing sensitive information by impersonating trusted sources. Successful phishing attacks can lead to data breaches and financial losses.
- **Insider threats** involve individuals, such as disgruntled employees, who may leak sensitive data or sabotage systems. These threats are challenging to detect and can cause significant harm to the institution.
- **Malware infections**—including viruses, worms, and ransomware—pose a significant risk to e-learning environments. Malware can disrupt operations, steal data, or hold systems for ransom, often entering through infected files or compromised websites.

- **Distributed denial of service (DDoS) attacks** aim to overwhelm e-learning platforms with excessive traffic, causing disruptions and downtime. They can severely affect the availability of educational resources.
- **Data breaches** can result in unauthorized access to sensitive information, such as student records and financial data. They can lead to identity theft, financial fraud, and reputational damage.
- **Exploited vulnerabilities.** Cybercriminals can exploit vulnerabilities in software and systems to gain unauthorized access. Regular updates and patch management are essential to mitigate these risks.
- **Internet of things (IoT) and third-party integrations** can introduce security vulnerabilities in applications if not properly managed. These components can serve as entry points for cyber threats.

In addition, GenAI presents several security concerns you and your organization must address to ensure safe and effective use. While your L&D department may lean on IT or cybersecurity departments to cover these areas, you need to understand the risks involved. Some key security concerns associated with GenAI include:

- **Data breaches and privacy violations.** We've established that GenAI systems often require access to extensive datasets, which may include sensitive or personally identifiable information (PII). If you're not adequately protecting these datasets, you can be vulnerable to data breaches and privacy violations.
- **Model theft and intellectual property risks.** Attackers may attempt to steal AI models to understand their structure and functioning. This can lead to unauthorized replication or sale of the models, which undermines the original developers' competitive advantage.
- **Malware and phishing attacks.** Gen AI can create sophisticated malware and phishing content, which can evade traditional detection methods and be convincing enough to deceive users.

- **Adversarial attacks.** GenAI models can be susceptible to adversarial attacks, in which malicious inputs are designed to manipulate the model's output. This can compromise the integrity and reliability of the AI system.

Approaches to Mitigating Privacy and Security Risks

To effectively protect data privacy and security in your AI implementation, you need a comprehensive strategy that addresses multiple dimensions of risk. Figure 4-2 organizes essential practices into six core areas. Let's discuss each in more detail.

Figure 4-2. Approaches to Safeguard Data Privacy and Security

6. Regulatory Compliance

5. Data Governance Practices

4. Transparency and Communication

1. Robust Data Protection Measures

2. Privacy by Design Approach

3. Security Testing and Monitoring

1. Robust Data Protection Measures

When handling sensitive information, your first line of defense is strong technical protection. You should:

- **Implement encryption** for all data (both in transit and at rest), which prevents unauthorized access, even if systems are compromised.
- **Deploy data anonymization techniques** when working with sensitive information, which replaces identifiable elements with synthetic data while preserving analytical value.
- **Establish data privacy vaults** to isolate your most sensitive information, which uses de-identified data for processing to enhance both privacy and compliance.

2. Privacy by Design Approach

Embedding privacy considerations throughout your AI development life cycle is crucial. You should:

- **Conduct privacy impact assessments** at each stage of your AI system development.
- **Minimize data collection** to only what's necessary, which reduces exposure risk.
- **Consider privacy implications** when making architectural and implementation decisions.

3. Security Testing and Monitoring

Regular evaluation of your security posture helps identify vulnerabilities before they can be exploited. You should:

- **Schedule regular security audits** to review your systems and processes systematically.
- **Conduct penetration testing** to identify potential weaknesses from an attacker's perspective.
- **Implement continuous monitoring** to detect and respond to suspicious activities in real time.
- **Perform adversarial testing** specifically for your AI models to evaluate their resilience against potential attacks.

4. Transparency and Communication

Building trust with users requires clear communication about how their data is handled. You should:

- **Provide transparent information** about what data you collect and how you use it.
- **Create easily accessible privacy policies** that are written in clear, understandable language.
- **Establish communication channels** for addressing any privacy concerns and questions.

5. Data Governance Practices

Proper oversight and management of data is essential. You should:

- **Implement role-based access controls,** ensuring team members can only access the specific data necessary for their roles.
- **Develop comprehensive incident response plans** to quickly address potential breaches.
- **Practice data minimization** by regularly reviewing stored data and removing what's no longer needed.

6. Regulatory Compliance

Staying current with applicable regulations protects both your users and your organization. You should:

- **Ensure alignment with all regulations** that are relevant to your sector and user base (such as GDPR, FERPA, or COPPA).
- **Document compliance measures** for audit purposes.
- **Monitor regulatory changes** and update your practices accordingly.

ৎৎৎ

Beyond these technical approaches, fostering awareness throughout your organization creates a strong foundation for privacy and security. You should:

- **Educate your team** about data privacy and security best practices, including how to recognize phishing attempts and create strong passwords.
- **Maintain up-to-date software** with regular patches to protect against known vulnerabilities.
- **Develop comprehensive incident response protocols** that enable quick action when issues arise.

By systematically implementing these measures in your AI initiatives, you can harness the benefits of GenAI while protecting sensitive information and maintaining user trust. Remember that privacy and security aren't one-time efforts but ongoing commitments that require regular reassessment as technologies and threats evolve.

As you consider how you collect and use data in your AI systems, it's equally important to examine how this data shapes your AI model's behavior. This leads us to our next crucial concept: addressing bias and ensuring fairness in AI use.

Bias, Fairness, and Representation in AI

Did you know there are at least 21 mathematical definitions of fairness in machine learning? However, it's often impossible to satisfy all of them simultaneously.

The concept of fairness in AI is more complex than it might initially appear. Different definitions of fairness can sometimes be mutually exclusive. For example, *demographic parity* (ensuring equal outcomes across groups) can conflict with *individual fairness* (treating similar individuals equally).

This paradox highlights the need to consider what fairness means in each specific context. It also underscores the importance of human judgment in implementing AI systems. While we can use standardized definitions to guide us, ultimately, deciding what's fair often requires ethical reasoning and an understanding of the broader societal context.

When ProPublica analyzed COMPAS, an AI system that predicts repeat offenders in criminal defendants, in 2016, they found that the system was biased against Black individuals (Larson et al. 2016). However, the company that created COMPAS argued that its system was fair according to a different definition of recidivism (the tendency of a convicted criminal to reoffend). This case highlights the complexities of defining and measuring fairness in AI systems.

As AI systems are increasingly used in decision-making processes—from hiring to loan approvals and content recommendations—the issue of bias has come to the forefront. Bias in AI can perpetuate and even amplify existing societal inequalities, making it a critical concern for any organization implementing AI solutions.

Ensuring fairness in AI is not just an ethical imperative; it's crucial for building trust in AI systems and avoiding potentially discriminatory outcomes. Biased AI can lead to unfair treatment of individuals or groups, legal liabilities, and damage to an organization's reputation. Moreover, diverse and fair AI systems tend to perform better and be more widely accepted, providing both moral and practical benefits.

As I mentioned in chapter 3, Amazon discovered in 2015 that its AI-powered recruiting tool was biased against women. The system, which was trained on resumes that were submitted over a 10-year period, had learned to prefer male candidates because the tech industry had been male dominated. While Amazon ultimately scrapped the tool, this case illustrates how AI can perpetuate and amplify existing biases if not carefully designed and monitored.

Let's examine the origins of bias in AI and large language model (LLM) systems, the challenges of ensuring fairness, and the implications for representation in AI-generated content.

Bias in Large Language Models

Bias in LLMs can stem from various sources. Often, it results from biased training data that reflects historical inequalities, and it manifests in the models' outputs, affecting their fairness and representation capabilities. Moreover, humans' interpretation and application of AI outputs can introduce additional bias. If users don't understand an AI system's limitations and potential biases, they may apply its recommendations inappropriately.

Here are some common sources of bias:

- **Training data.** The primary source of bias in LLMs is the training data. If the data contains biased information, the model will likely reproduce these biases in its outputs. Because LLMs learn from vast datasets found on the internet, they inevitably absorb the biases present in that data. They can be gender based (associating certain roles as female or male), racial (reflecting stereotypes or discriminatory views), or related to other social or cultural categories (leading to outputs that lack cultural sensitivity or understanding). For instance, if a loan approval AI tool is trained using historical data from when certain groups were unfairly denied loans, it may perpetuate this discrimination.
- **Model architecture.** The design and structure of LLMs can also contribute to bias. The choices in feature selection, model architecture, and optimization criteria can all introduce bias,

and certain models may inadvertently prioritize specific types of information over others, leading to biased outputs.

- **Algorithmic constraints.** The algorithms used to train LLMs might not adequately address bias, especially if they lack mechanisms to identify and mitigate biased patterns. For example, an AI system might use zip codes as a predictive feature, which could serve as a proxy for race or socioeconomic status, leading to discriminatory outcomes.

Fairness in Large Language Models

Fairness in LLMs refers to the equitable treatment of all users and the avoidance of biased outputs that could harm individuals or groups. Achieving fairness is challenging due to the complex nature of language and the diverse contexts in which LLMs are used.

Some challenges in ensuring fairness include:

- **Defining fairness.** As we've discussed, fairness is a subjective concept that varies across cultures and contexts. Defining what is fair in a global context is a significant challenge.
- **Evaluation metrics.** Developing metrics to evaluate fairness in LLMs is complex. They must account for various types of bias and ensure that models perform equitably across different demographic groups.
- **Mitigation techniques.** While techniques exist to reduce bias, such as data augmentation and adversarial training, they often only mask bias rather than eliminate it.

Representation in AI-Generated Content

Representation refers to how well LLMs reflect diverse perspectives and cultures in their outputs. Poor representation can lead to outputs that are not only biased but also lack the richness and diversity of human language.

The implications of poor representation are:

- **Cultural insensitivity.** LLMs that do not adequately represent diverse cultures may produce culturally insensitive or inappropriate outputs.

- **Marginalization of groups.** If certain groups are underrepresented in training data, LLMs may not generate content that accurately reflects their experiences or perspectives.
- **Reinforcement of stereotypes.** LLMs can reinforce existing stereotypes by failing to represent diverse viewpoints, perpetuating societal biases.

᎓᎓᎓

Understanding how bias, fairness, and representation affect an LLM's behavior is an important area of study because these models have become more prevalent in society. While we've made significant progress in understanding and mitigating bias, the challenges remain.

Achieving fairness and enhancing representation in LLMs requires ongoing research, collaboration, and a commitment to ethical AI development. By addressing these issues, we can harness the transformative potential of LLMs while minimizing their risks and ensuring they serve all users equitably.

Approaches to Addressing Bias, Fairness, and Representation Concerns

As an L&D professional implementing AI tools in your organization, you don't have to be overwhelmed by the prospect of addressing bias and ensuring fairness. Here's a practical framework that breaks down this complex topic into manageable approaches.

Building Foundations for Equitable AI

Creating equitable AI requires strong foundations built on inclusive teams that bring diverse perspectives to the forefront and thoughtful data review to mitigate biases that can perpetuate harmful outcomes.

The people selecting and implementing your learning technologies directly influence how well these tools serve everyone in your organization. Here's what you can do to support inclusive teams:

- Invite team members from different departments, backgrounds, and experience levels to evaluate AI learning tools.

- Create an environment where team members feel comfortable raising concerns about potential biases they notice.
- Consult with representatives from the different learner groups that will be using the AI systems.
- Partner with your HR team to review AI learning tools before full implementation.

In addition, your AI learning tools can only be as fair as the information they learn from. Regularly examining this data helps prevent reinforcing existing workplace biases. Here's what you can do to facilitate thoughtful data review:

- Examine sample content from AI learning tools to ensure it represents diverse perspectives and examples.
- Check if learning scenarios and assessments reflect the diversity of your workforce.
- Look for gaps in representation that might affect how the tool serves different learner groups.
- Ask vendors about their data sources and what steps they take to ensure fairness.

Practical Approaches to Reduce Bias

Mitigating bias means you're focusing on the importance of careful content selection to ensure diverse representation, mindful implementation to avoid perpetuating stereotypes, and a thoughtful review process for the generated content. Before implementing AI learning tools, you can take these steps to ensure the content is appropriate and balanced:

- Select or create learning materials that represent inclusive perspectives and experiences.
- Review automated content suggestions for potentially biased language or examples.
- Supplement AI-generated learning materials with diverse case studies and scenarios.
- Create guidelines to define what inclusive learning content looks like in your organization.

How you roll out and use AI tools also significantly affects their fairness across your organization. Here's what you can do to mindfully implement AI tools:

- Pilot new AI learning tools with diverse groups of learners and gather their feedback.
- Provide equal access to AI tools across different departments and roles.
- Create learning paths that accommodate different learning modalities.
- Ensure the tool works equally well for all groups of learners in your organization.

Finally, even well-designed systems may produce uneven results. Building review steps helps catch potential issues. Here's what you can do to ensure you're following a thoughtful review process:

- Regularly review AI-generated learning recommendations for potential bias.
- Create simple approval workflows for AI-generated content before it reaches learners.
- Develop guidelines for what fair and inclusive learning content looks like.
- Establish a process for learners to flag concerning content.

Ongoing Fairness Practices

To maintain fairness in AI systems, focus on accessible measurement techniques, transparent communication of system behavior, the critical role of human oversight, and the importance of continuous feedback loops for improvement.

You don't need complex metrics to track fairness. Start with straightforward observations and feedback. Here's what you can do to take a simple measurement approach:

- Track completion and satisfaction rates across different learner groups.
- Gather qualitative feedback about the relevance and inclusivity of AI-generated content.
- Compare assessment outcomes across different departments or demographic groups.

- Create simple surveys asking if learners think the content represents their experiences.

In addition, being open about how you're using AI builds trust with your learners. Here's what you can do to ensure clear communication:

- Clearly label when content or assessments are AI-generated.
- Explain to learners how AI tools are being used in their learning experiences.
- Share information about the steps you're taking to ensure fairness.
- Create simple guidelines for when and how AI tools are used in learning programs.

Also, you should use AI as a supportive tool; keep human judgment at the center of your learning strategy. Here's what you can do to provide meaningful human guidance:

- Ensure managers and L&D professionals review AI recommendations before implementation.
- Create clear guidelines for when human review is required for AI-generated content.
- Establish a simple process for learners to request that a human reviews concerning content.
- Maintain a human touch in sensitive or complex learning scenarios.

Finally, create simple ways to gather input and use it to improve your approach over time. Here's what you can do to gather effective feedback for improvement:

- Create easy ways for learners to provide feedback on AI learning experiences.
- Meet regularly with learning leaders to discuss fairness concerns.
- Share feedback with vendors to help improve their AI learning tools.

By focusing on these practical approaches, you can create learning experiences that use AI in ways that serve all learners equitably. Remember, addressing bias means thoughtfully implementing AI learning tools with regular check-ins to ensure they work for everyone.

What Biases Exist in Your AI Systems?

Think about your organization and the AI systems it uses or is considering. Here are some questions you can start asking yourself:
- What potential biases might it have?
- How could you test for and mitigate these biases?
- What groups or individuals might be disadvantaged by the AI systems in your organization?
- How do you currently measure or assess the fairness of your AI systems?
- Are there conflicting definitions of fairness that you need to navigate?
- How do you balance the pursuit of fairness with other objectives like accuracy or efficiency?

Now, choose an AI system in your organization and list the key decisions it makes or influences. For each decision, identify potential fairness concerns and brainstorm ways to measure and ensure fairness.

As we grapple with issues of bias and fairness in AI, we're ultimately confronting fundamental questions about knowledge, expertise, and decision making. This leads us to the final core concept in this chapter: redefining knowledge and expertise in an AI-augmented world.

The Black Box Dilemma: When I Becomes the Expert

As AI systems become increasingly capable of performing tasks that traditionally require human expertise, we're forced to reconsider our understanding of knowledge. This shift has profound implications for education, professional development, and the future of work.

Understanding how AI is reshaping our conception of knowledge and expertise affects how we educate and train future generations, structure our organizations, and value different forms of human contribution. Moreover, it challenges us to redefine what it means to be an expert in a time when vast amounts of information are instantly accessible and AI can outperform humans in many specialized tasks.

In 2016, an AI system called AlphaGo defeated world champion Lee Sedol at the board game *Go*. This was a watershed moment because *Go* was considered too complex for machines to master (Borowiec 2016). AlphaGo made moves that expert commentators initially thought were mistakes, but were actually innovative strategies. This event challenged our understanding of expertise, demonstrating that AI could match the knowledge of human experts and generate new insights that humans hadn't previously discovered.

It's one thing for the game *Go*, but in some medical imaging tasks, for example, AI can now outperform human radiologists (Najjar 2023). While these systems can often achieve impressive accuracy, what happens when we don't fully understand how AI reaches its conclusions? Doctors may hesitate to rely on recommendations they don't fully understand, and patients may question decisions based on opaque AI processes.

As AI systems become more complex, they often become *black boxes*—systems that produce results without clearly explaining their decision-making process. This creates a paradox: The systems demonstrate expertise, but we can't fully explain or verify their reasoning. This in turn leads to questions about accountability, trust, and the role of human oversight in AI-driven decisions. For example, if an AI system makes a mistake, who is responsible? This challenges traditional notions of responsibility and requires new frameworks for accountability.

In your organization, how crucial is it to comprehend the rationale behind expert decisions? How might the balance between AI performance and explainability be struck in your context? Efforts are being made to develop *explainable AI*—systems that provide human-understandable explanations for their decisions—but there's often a trade-off between explainability and performance, with some of the most potent AI models being the least explainable.

Fei-Fei Li—professor of computer science at Stanford University and co-director of Stanford's Human-Centered AI Institute—is a leading voice in the field of AI ethics and development. She emphasizes the importance of human-centered AI. She says:

We need to be thoughtful about the symbiosis between humans and AI. It's not about humans versus AI—it's about how AI can amplify human intelligence and capabilities. . . . This technology is made by people, and it's going to be used for people. So fundamentally how we create this technology, how we use this technology, how we continue to innovate, but also put up the right guardrails, is up to us humans doing it for humans. So, at the heart of all this, it's all human centered—and that's how I see this in a fundamental way. (Li 2021)

Li's approach has influenced the development of AI systems that complement rather than replace human expertise. For instance, in medical imaging, AI tools are being designed to assist radiologists by flagging potential areas of concern, rather than making autonomous diagnoses. This approach leverages the strengths of both AI (processing vast amounts of data quickly) and humans (contextual understanding and complex decision making). Consider an area in your organization where AI could assist rather than replace human expertise. How might you design a system that enhances human capabilities rather than attempting to automate them entirely?

The integration of AI into different domains necessitates a redefinition of knowledge and expertise, which must account for AI systems' unique capabilities and limitations. In some cases, knowledge is viewed as a collaborative process between humans and machines. AI can provide data-driven insights, while humans interpret and apply them within broader contexts. In other cases, knowledge might be distributed across networks of humans and machines, with each contributing unique strengths. This model emphasizes the interconnectedness of knowledge sources and the importance of integrating diverse perspectives.

As AI systems become increasingly integrated into society, redefining our concepts of knowledge and expertise becomes vital for harnessing AI's potential while addressing its ethical and epistemological challenges. This ongoing dialogue between philosophy and technology will shape the future of what it means to know something, as well as what it means to be an expert.

How Will Your Expertise Intersect With AI?

In chapter 2, we looked at the rise of the human-machine performance analyst. How can we maintain human agency and accountability in a world where AI systems increasingly outperform human experts in specific tasks?

- In your work, what tasks or decisions do you think AI could potentially take over?
- How would you feel about deferring to an AI system in areas where it outperforms humans?
- What uniquely human skills or attributes do you think will remain crucial in your work?
- How might your role evolve to complement rather than compete with AI capabilities?

The AI Policy Imperative

In the bustling corridors of modern corporations, a silent revolution is unfolding. It doesn't announce itself with the clang of machinery or the whir of assembly lines. Instead, it arrives in algorithms and models that are quietly reshaping how we work, think, and create. In the workplace, AI is transforming businesses faster than many leaders can comprehend.

The concerns we've explored throughout this chapter—data privacy vulnerabilities, algorithmic bias that reinforces inequity, the ethical quandaries of AI decision making, and our growing dependency on technological black boxes that we cannot fully scrutinize—are not merely theoretical problems. They represent a complex web of challenges that demand a coordinated response. Without proper governance, these issues don't simply linger as abstract risks; they manifest as real corporate liabilities, reputational damage, and potential harm to employees and customers alike.

Consider this: At a learning conference in 2024, I asked the assembled learning leaders and professionals, "How many of you have an AI policy in place at your company?" The response was telling. Only about a third raised their hands. This scene has played out similarly in boardrooms and at other conferences across the country, with the number likely not exceeding 50 percent.

The gap between AI adoption and AI governance is a looming crisis for organizations that are unprepared for the complexities of this new technology. It's akin to giving every employee a powerful new tool without providing instructions on how to use it safely and effectively. But building organization-wide AI literacy requires more than single training events; it demands a cultural transformation in which responsible AI use becomes embedded in the company's DNA.

By implementing a comprehensive assessment, tiered learning frameworks, engaging content, ethical guidelines, measurement protocols, and continuous learning resources, organizations can foster an environment that allows all associates to contribute responsible AI innovation. Success requires commitment from leadership, allocation of sufficient resources, and recognition that AI literacy is an ongoing journey rather than a destination. Organizations that embrace this approach position themselves to leverage AI technologies ethically and effectively while mitigating risks associated with uninformed use.

The Hidden Dangers of Unregulated AI Use

To take the dangers of AI use to an extreme, let's consider an example. In 2022, Air Canada's AI chatbot told a customer they could get a refund for a bereavement fare, despite that not being their actual policy (Cecco 2024). Guess what happened? In 2024, the airline lost in court. The lesson here? Without clear policies, AI can create real problems.

We're still in a high-risk, high-return environment regarding AI. Many employees use AI discreetly, which is not ideal. In fact, this shadow use of AI tools presents a multitude of risks, including:

- **Data security.** Employees inputting sensitive information into public AI models may inadvertently share corporate secrets externally.
- **Legal and regulatory compliance.** In regulated industries such as healthcare or finance, using AI without proper oversight can lead to breaches of client confidentiality or other regulatory violations.
- **Intellectual property concerns.** There is a real risk of using corporate intellectual property to train AI models because it could potentially benefit competitors who use the same tools.

- **Misinformation propagation.** AI models can produce convincing but incorrect information. Without proper verification processes, this could lead to costly mistakes or damage the company's reputation.
- **Ethical quandaries.** Bias in AI systems and questions about proper attribution for AI-assisted work are ethical minefields that companies must navigate carefully.

Crafting an Effective AI Policy

The solution to these challenges lies in creating a comprehensive AI policy. But what does that look like?

To demonstrate the breadth of what an effective AI policy should encompass, let's examine some real-world scenarios for L&D professionals and how I recommend addressing them with an AI policy.

If you're using AI to generate learning content, your policy needs:
- Guidelines for content review
- Attribution requirements
- Quality control processes
- Bias checking procedures

If you're using AI to track learner progress, your policy needs:
- Data collection limitations
- Privacy protections
- Usage transparency
- Opt-out procedures

If you're using AI to customize learning paths, your policy needs:
- Fairness guidelines
- Algorithm transparency
- Human oversight requirements
- An appeals process

Other functions in your organization will have their own scenarios, which must also be addressed. An AI policy is a blueprint for how a company harnesses the power of AI while mitigating its risks. It should be a living document, evolving as the technology and regulatory landscape change. Here are the key components to include:

- **Clear definitions.** The policy should define what constitutes AI within the organization. This might include GenAI tools like ChatGPT and machine learning algorithms used for data analysis.
- **Benefits and risks assessment.** Articulate both the strategic benefits of AI adoption and the potential risks to the organization. This helps employees understand why the policy exists and why adherence is crucial.
- **Usage guidelines.** Provide clear instructions about which AI tools are approved for use, how to access them, and what types of data can be input into these systems.
- **Training and support.** Implement ongoing training programs to ensure employees understand how to use AI tools effectively and responsibly.
- **Reporting mechanisms.** Establish clear procedures for reporting concerns or potential misuse of AI systems.
- **Flexibility.** Don't let your policy cramp innovation.
- **Review and update processes.** Establish regular intervals for policy review to stay current with technological advancements and evolving regulations.

The Collaborative Approach to Policy Creation

Creating an effective AI policy isn't the job of any single department. It requires a collaborative effort across multiple teams, including:

- **Leadership**—to establish the overall direction and vision for AI use within the organization
- **Legal**—to ensure compliance with existing and emerging regulations
- **IT and security**—to implement and oversee the technical aspects of AI tool deployment
- **HR**—to integrate AI policies into employee guidelines and training programs
- **L&D**—to create and deliver training on the use of AI and policy compliance
- **Communications**—to effectively disseminate the policy and its updates across the organization

This cross-functional approach (which notably should include you or someone representing your L&D function) ensures that the policy is comprehensive, practical, and aligned with the organization's overall strategy. This team can then serve as an ongoing AI ethics board to oversee AI development and deployment as well as regularly audit all AI systems for bias and effectiveness.

The Cultural Shift

Implementing an AI policy involves a cultural transformation. It requires shifting mindsets from viewing AI as a personal tool for improving productivity to seeing it as a powerful, company-wide resource that must be used responsibly.

This shift can be challenging. You cannot forget the human element and how the policy may affect the users. As one executive confided to me, "We had employees who felt like we were taking away their secret weapons when we implemented our AI policy." However, with proper communication and training, most organizations find that employees appreciate the clarity and security a well-crafted policy provides.

There are three common objections to an AI policy:

- **Implementing robust AI policies will slow innovation and put the company at a competitive disadvantage.** Rather than viewing ethical AI practices as a hindrance, see them as providing a competitive advantage. Companies with robust AI policies build greater customer trust and are better positioned for long-term success. For instance, Google's decision to publish AI ethics principles has helped it attract top talent and build user trust.

- **AI systems are too complex for us to understand or fully control their decision-making processes.** While AI systems can be complex, this doesn't absolve us of the responsibility to understand and govern them. Tools for AI explainability and interpretability are rapidly evolving. Companies like IBM are developing techniques that provide insight into AI decision-making processes, allowing even complex systems to be more accountable.

- **Ensuring fairness in AI will reduce its effectiveness and accuracy.** Fairness and effectiveness are not mutually exclusive. Addressing bias often leads to more robust and generalizable AI systems. For example, when Apple addressed gender bias in its credit scoring algorithm, it made the system fairer and more accurate across a broader population.

To help ensure that responsible, safe use of AI becomes part of your culture, you should invest in ongoing AI literacy training for all employees, not just technical staff.

Quick Policy Implementation Guide

Month 1: Foundation
- Conduct a comprehensive audit to document all current AI usage across departments.
- Assemble a diverse stakeholder team, including technical, legal, and business representatives.
- Draft initial guidelines based on industry best practices and regulatory requirements.
- Begin a structured review process with documented feedback loops and clear approval criteria.

Month 2: Development
- Create detailed policies with specific use cases, ethical boundaries, and compliance requirements.
- Develop role-specific training materials with practical examples and decision frameworks.
- Implement robust monitoring systems with defined metrics and automated alerts.
- Design a multi-channel communication strategy tailored to different employee knowledge levels.

Month 3: Implementation
- Roll out policies through department-specific workshops that address unique AI use cases.
- Conduct intensive training with measurable outcomes and practical scenarios.
- Establish a cross-functional AI ethics committee to monitor compliance and address emerging issues.
- Create structured feedback channels for continuous improvement, including anonymous reporting options for AI concerns.

Ethics From the Start

How can you build ethical considerations into your AI-empowered learning strategies from the ground up, rather than treating them as an afterthought? How might AI-empowered learning leadership transform your role and your organization's approach to L&D?

Conclusion

This chapter examined four crucial dimensions of ethical AI implementation in L&D. I explored data privacy and security challenges in AI-driven learning ecosystems, providing practical frameworks to protect sensitive information while maintaining its utility and value. I addressed bias and fairness concerns, offering concrete approaches for L&D professionals to build inclusive AI systems without requiring technical expertise. The black box dilemma challenged us to reconsider expertise and decision making as AI increasingly rivals human capabilities, suggesting a symbiotic relationship that enhances rather than replaces human intelligence. Finally, I outlined the organizational necessity of comprehensive AI policies that translate ethical principles into operational practices.

These ethical considerations aren't secondary concerns but foundational requirements for effective AI learning systems. By proactively integrating these principles, you become an ethical architect of learning ecosystems that respect privacy, promote fairness, complement human expertise, and operate within clear governance frameworks.

The approaches outlined provide both protection against risks and a foundation for confidently leveraging AI's transformative potential in the service of more effective, ethical learning. As organizations adopt intelligent tools across business platforms, the next frontier for L&D professionals is to operationalize these principles at scale. That journey begins with reimagining the everyday environments where work and learning happens.

In the next chapter, we'll explore how AI is transforming the business platforms we already rely on—like Microsoft 365, Google Workspace, and Slack—into dynamic ecosystems that drive performance, capture knowledge, and elevate the role of L&D in shaping the future of work.

CHAPTER 5
Business Platforms and Performance

In This Chapter

- Ways to assess AI use cases in business platforms through an L&D lens
- A process to reimagine your approach to knowledge management
- Opportunities to optimize how you attract, develop, and retain employees
- The what and how of task mapping and skills indexing

I sat stunned at my desk, watching as my virtual meeting platform processed the last hour of a quarterly strategy session. Within moments, it provided a concise summary of our discussion about redesigning a sales training program. Then came the action items, neatly categorized by owner, with deadlines that matched our timeline. Before I could even react, my inbox pinged. There was the follow-up email, with tasks already distributed to each participant.

For years, my post-meeting ritual involved scrambling to capture key decisions while they remained fresh, deciphering my rushed notes, and crafting recap emails that inevitably missed something important.

Now, this AI assistant had done it flawlessly in seconds. In that moment, I glimpsed the future of workplace learning and performance as an intelligent ecosystem that understands context, anticipates needs, and delivers precisely what's required when it matters most.

The business platforms we use daily—Microsoft 365, Google Workspace, Slack, and ServiceNow, among others—are being transformed from simple productivity tools into sophisticated AI-powered environments that fundamentally change how knowledge flows through organizations.

For L&D professionals, this transformation presents both challenges and opportunities. Our value no longer lies primarily in creating content but in establishing intelligent knowledge ecosystems where humans and machines collaborate seamlessly. We're evolving from instructional designers to performance architects, orchestrating the interplay between human judgment and AI capabilities.

In this chapter, we'll explore how AI is reshaping business platforms, knowledge management, human capital systems, and performance support. We'll examine practical frameworks for evaluating your current ecosystem, building intelligent knowledge graphs, mapping tasks across human-machine partnerships, and implementing AI-powered performance support that delivers measurable business impact.

The days of static training solutions are behind us. Welcome to the age of the AI co-pilot, when learning and performance blend into a continuous, intelligent flow of knowledge and support.

The Role of AI in a Business Platform

Let's talk about business platforms. Microsoft 365 and Google Workspace aren't just places to store documents. They form the bedrock of your AI ecosystem. Working with organizations across industries has shown me one consistent truth: Successful AI implementation starts with a robust platform infrastructure.

Consider Microsoft's Copilot. Beyond basic document creation and storage, it offers AI-powered content generation, meeting transcription, automated workflow capabilities, and agent creation. A client recently used Microsoft Teams to automatically transcribe and analyze their subject matter expert (SME) interviews. The platform identified key themes, suggested learning objectives, and even flagged potential compliance issues. Five years ago, this would have taken hours of manual work.

Google Workspace offers similar capabilities. Its AI tools can analyze documents, suggest improvements, and even assist with creating learning materials in multiple languages. Power lies in seamless integration. Your learning content, collaboration tools, and AI capabilities are all integrated into one seamless ecosystem.

The real magic happens in data flow. Picture water flowing through the pipes in your home. Your business platform is the main water line, connecting every faucet and appliance. When data flows freely between systems, your content creation tools can leverage documents in your shared drive, while your performance metrics inform learning recommendations. Everything works in harmony.

For L&D professionals, this foundation, now powered by AI, is essential to your mission. These platforms build intelligence into online meeting software, daily tools like word processing, spreadsheets, presentations, and the repository for a vast array of corporate knowledge. As stewards of organizational growth, you're uniquely positioned to champion these integrated business platforms. By embracing your role in shaping the organization's platform strategy, you'll not only enhance learning outcomes but also demonstrate L&D's strategic value to the business.

Instead of jumping directly to AI implementation, start with a thorough platform assessment. Even if you don't control the organization-wide decision on which business platforms to adopt, as an L&D professional, you can still evaluate and influence how they serve learning needs. Here are some questions to get started:

- Does your current platform support AI integration with your learning systems?
- Can data flow freely between your learning content and other organizational systems?
- Will the platform scale as your learning programs and content libraries grow?
- How well does it handle learning-specific security and compliance requirements?

Practical Platform Assessment Steps

Before exploring AI-enabled learning solutions, it's essential to take a structured, hands-on approach to evaluating your current platforms. The following steps, shown in Figure 5-1, provide a practical framework for assessing your organization's technology platform ecosystem:

1. **Conduct a learning workflow audit.** Document how content moves from creation to delivery. Identify where existing platforms create bottlenecks versus opportunities for automation.

2. **Map your data ecosystem.** Create a simple diagram showing how learner data, content, and analytics currently flow (or don't flow) between systems. Highlight disconnected systems that could benefit from platform integration.

3. **Build a pilot use case.** Identify one specific L&D process (such as SME knowledge capture or course maintenance) that could benefit from platform-based AI. Test it on a small scale to demonstrate value.

4. **Partner with IT.** Schedule a collaborative session with your IT team to understand planned platform enhancements and advocate for L&D-specific requirements within the broader technology road map.

5. **Create a platform evaluation rubric.** Develop criteria specific to learning needs (such as content versioning, knowledge management, or skills framework integration) to evaluate how well your current platforms serve L&D functions.

Figure 5-1. Practice Platform Assessment Steps

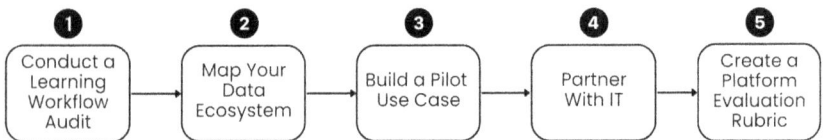

Remember: While you may not get to choose your organization's platforms, you can become an influential voice in how they support learning. Your expertise in how people develop skills is invaluable to ensuring that technology investments deliver learning impact.

Now that we've outlined the five core steps, it's time to dig into each one with detailed, actionable guidance. As L&D professionals, your understanding of how content is created, delivered, and experienced puts you in a prime position to lead meaningful platform evaluations.

Step 1. Conduct a Learning Workflow Audit

A workflow audit helps you visualize and document how learning content currently moves through your business platform—from initial creation to learner consumption (Figure 5-2). This visibility enables you to pinpoint inefficiencies, identify redundancies, and spot opportunities for automation or AI augmentation.

Figure 5-2. Learning Workflow Audit

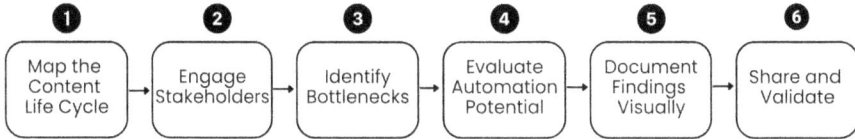

To conduct a learning workflow audit, follow these steps:

1. **Map the content life cycle.** Outline each stage of your content journey (creation, review, publishing, delivery, tracking, and maintenance). Be specific about the tools, systems, and roles involved at each step.

2. **Engage stakeholders.** Interview content creators, instructional designers, SMEs, and delivery teams to gather insights on pain points and friction in the current process.

3. **Identify bottlenecks.** Look for delays in approvals, manual handoffs, or duplicate work. Note any parts of the process that rely on outdated systems or informal workarounds.

4. **Evaluate automation potential.** Determine where automation or AI could streamline steps (such as auto-tagging content, routing reviews, or generating reports).

5. **Document findings visually.** Use a workflow diagram to capture your end-to-end process. (Tools like Lucidchart, Miro, or even PowerPoint can help make your findings more digestible for stakeholders.)

6. **Share and validate.** Present your workflow map and findings to key stakeholders for validation. Use their input to refine your understanding and start building consensus around areas for improvement.

These steps lay the groundwork for a stronger, more integrated tech ecosystem that's aligned with L&D needs. Once you have a clear view of how things work today, you'll be better equipped to champion the tools and improvements that will drive future-ready learning.

Step 2. Map Your Data Ecosystem

As L&D professionals, you know that data is not just about metrics. It's also about understanding learners, measuring outcomes, and making informed decisions about how to design and deliver effective learning content. Mapping your data ecosystem involves identifying where your learning data resides, how it flows (or stagnates), and whether it provides the insights necessary to enhance programs, demonstrate impact, and personalize experiences (Figure 5-3).

Figure 5-3. Mapping Your Data Ecosystem

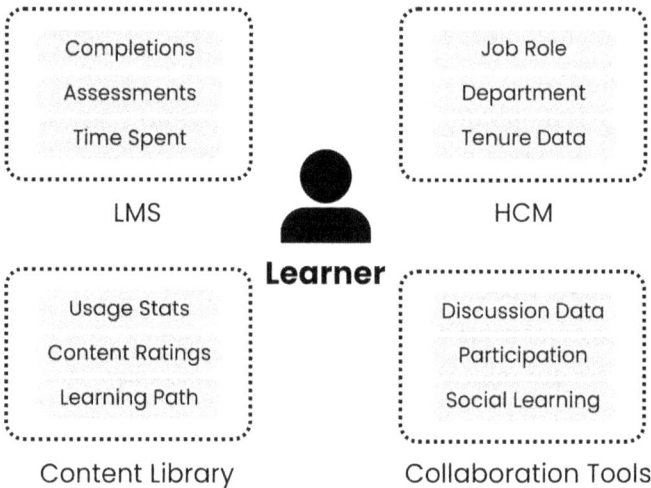

Completions		**Job Role**
Assessments		Department
Time Spent		Tenure Data
LMS	**Learner**	HCM
Usage Stats		Discussion Data
Content Ratings		Participation
Learning Path		Social Learning
Content Library		Collaboration Tools

Whether you are working with an LMS, a learning experience platform (LXP), a content library, or pulling reports from an HR information system (HRIS), this step brings clarity to what can often be a fragmented tech stack. It also sets the stage for using AI to generate meaningful insights later.

Here are six actionable steps for mapping your data ecosystem:

1. **List all systems that influence the learning experience.** Go beyond the LMS. Include content providers, coaching platforms, survey and feedback tools, skills assessments, performance systems, and even communication platforms like Microsoft Teams or Slack. Ask yourself where learning is happening and where learner data is being captured.

2. **Follow the learner data journey.** Select a typical learner or group and track the progression of their data across various systems. How is engagement measured? What gets recorded during and after learning programs? Where does the data go, and where does it stop?

3. **Identify data silos.** Look for systems that are not integrated, duplicated learner profiles, or platforms that require manual exports. These are often the areas that block a full view of the learner experience.

4. **Assess the availability of insights.** Can you answer core questions using the data you currently have? Are learners applying what they've learned? Which programs have the most significant impact on performance? Are you closing any skills gaps? If the answers are unclear, your data may not be working hard enough for you.

5. **Visualize the ecosystem.** Create a basic diagram that shows how data flows between systems. Keep it learner-centered, and use it to start discussions with IT, HR, and program stakeholders. You do not need technical tools to do this—PowerPoint or whiteboard apps work just fine.

6. **Consider AI readiness through an L&D lens.** Could AI help you uncover learning patterns, recommend resources, or connect learning to performance? If your current systems do not allow that kind of insight, use this map to support your case for improving integration and alignment.

Mapping your data ecosystem is not a technical chore, but a strategic opportunity to position L&D as a data-driven function that is ready to evolve and scale.

Step 3. Build a Pilot Use Case

Once you have a handle on your workflows and data, it's time to turn insight into action. As an L&D professional, you are well positioned to spot processes that are repetitive, resource-intensive, or just plain inefficient. These are prime candidates for a small-scale AI or an automation pilot program. The goal is not to overhaul everything at once. Instead, focus on a single, well-scoped use case that solves a real problem and helps demonstrate value quickly.

Pilot programs give you a low-risk way to test new tools, validate assumptions, and build internal momentum for broader change (Figure 5-4). They also help you learn what is needed—technically, operationally, and culturally— for AI to work within your learning function.

Figure 5-4. Building a Pilot Use Case

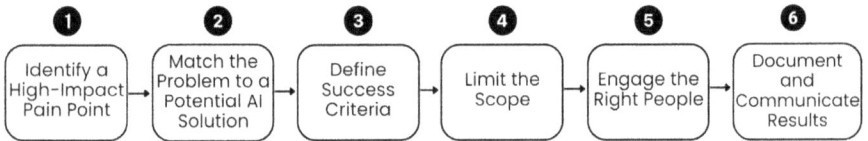

❶	❷	❸	❹	❺	❻
Identify a High-Impact Pain Point	Match the Problem to a Potential AI Solution	Define Success Criteria	Limit the Scope	Engage the Right People	Document and Communicate Results

Here are the six actionable steps for building a pilot use case:

1. **Identify a high-impact pain point.** Look for a recurring challenge in your learning operations. This might be managing SME content updates, answering common learner questions, tagging and organizing content, or manually pulling reports. Focus on something you or your team deal with frequently.

2. **Match the problem to a potential AI solution.** For example, if your team spends hours updating course content from SMEs, you might explore AI tools that assist with content summarization or version control. If learner questions are repetitive, a chatbot could help with automated support.

3. **Define success criteria.** Be clear about what success looks like. Will it save time? Improve learner satisfaction? Reduce manual errors? Even in a pilot program, having measurable outcomes will make it easier to assess results and build your case for next steps.

4. **Limit the scope.** Choose one course, content type, or team to test. A narrow focus helps reduce risk, keep timelines short, and make

it easier to manage expectations. You are testing a concept, not launching a new platform.

5. **Engage the right people.** Involve the team members who are closest to the problem. This might include instructional designers, platform admins, SMEs, or facilitators. Their input will help shape a realistic, usable solution and build buy-in from the start.

6. **Document and communicate results.** Capture what worked, what didn't, and what you learned along the way. Translate your findings into language that matters to stakeholders—whether that's improved efficiency, cost savings, or learner impact.

A successful pilot program is not about proving technology. Instead, it's about establishing value for your organization. As an L&D professional, your ability to frame that value in terms of learning outcomes, workforce readiness, and business alignment is what turns a pilot test into a path forward.

Step 4. Partner With IT

To build a modern, scalable learning ecosystem, L&D must collaborate closely with IT. While your expertise lies in how people develop skills, IT brings the infrastructure knowledge that's necessary to support secure, integrated, and AI-ready systems. A strong partnership ensures that learning goals are considered early in tech planning and that platforms evolve to meet the needs of your learners (Figure 5-5).

Figure 5-5. Partnering With IT

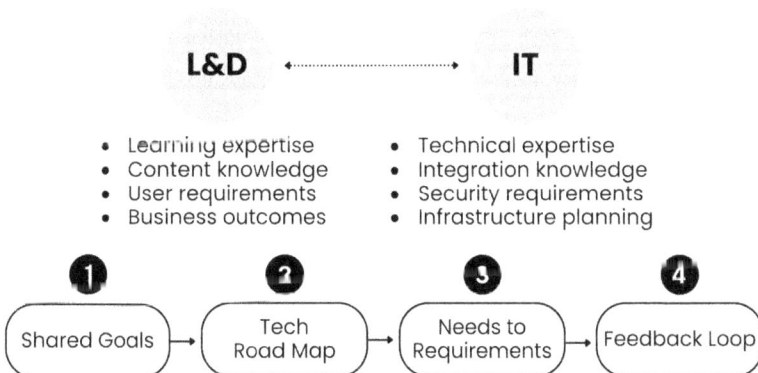

L&D ←·····→ **IT**

- Learning expertise
- Content knowledge
- User requirements
- Business outcomes

- Technical expertise
- Integration knowledge
- Security requirements
- Infrastructure planning

1 Shared Goals → **2** Tech Road Map → **3** Needs to Requirements → **4** Feedback Loop

Let's review the four actionable steps for partnering with IT:

1. **Start with shared goals.** Frame the conversation around business outcomes, not just platform requests. For example, instead of requesting new features, discuss reducing onboarding time or enhancing compliance tracking. This helps IT see L&D as part of the bigger picture.

2. **Understand the tech road map.** Ask about planned system upgrades, data initiatives, and integration projects. You may find opportunities to align L&D improvements with existing efforts, saving time and resources.

3. **Translate learning needs into system requirements.** Be clear and specific. Rather than saying you need better engagement, explain that you need role-based content recommendations or easier content versioning. Precision makes collaboration more effective.

4. **Establish a regular feedback loop.** Invite IT into your planning conversations and ask to join any relevant tech discussions. Ongoing collaboration—not just one-off requests—helps both teams move more efficiently and effectively.

A strong L&D–IT partnership does more than fix problems. It also lays the foundation for innovation and ensures your learning platforms can scale with the organization's evolving needs.

Step 5. Create a Platform Evaluation Rubric

The market is filled with so many tools promising to transform learning that it's easy to get swept up in potential features. A well-crafted evaluation rubric helps L&D stay focused on what matters: how a platform supports learning effectiveness, scalability, and alignment with business goals. Creating a rubric also enables you to compare options objectively and advocate clearly when technology decisions are being made. Figure 5-6 offers an example.

Here are four actionable steps for creating a platform evaluation rubric:

1. **Anchor your criteria in learning goals.** Start by identifying what your team needs to deliver impact—including things like content versioning, skills framework integration, learner experience data, data visibility, and scalability. Your rubric should reflect these specific requirements, not just general tech specs.

2. **Include both functional and strategic dimensions.** Evaluate platforms on their day-to-day usability (for example, admin workload and content workflows) as well as their ability to support future growth, AI capabilities, and integration with other systems.

3. **Use a scoring model to guide decisions.** Assign a weight to each criterion based on priority. For example, content management and learner analytics may carry more weight than cosmetic interface features. This helps keep decisions grounded in L&D needs, not vendor promises.

4. **Involve the right voices.** Co-create or validate the rubric with instructional designers, admins, facilitators, and other key users. Their insights will reveal real-world needs and help avoid blind spots in your evaluation.

Figure 5-6. Example Platform Evaluation Rubric

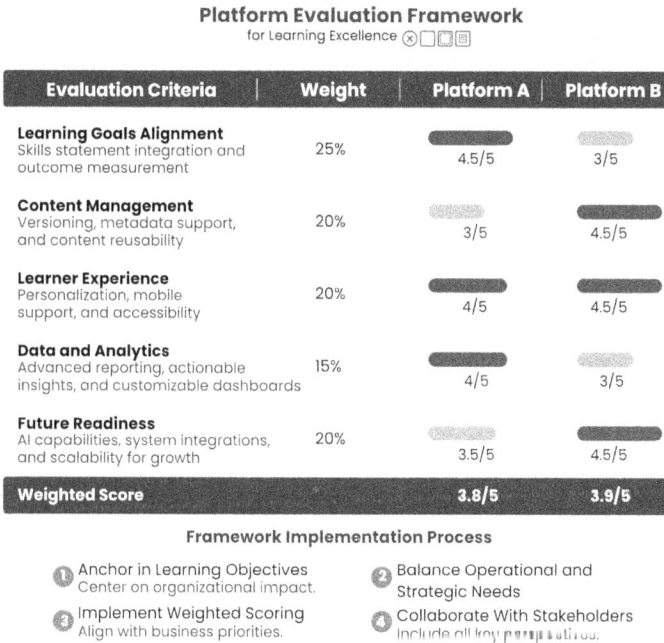

Platform Evaluation Framework
for Learning Excellence

Evaluation Criteria	Weight	Platform A	Platform B
Learning Goals Alignment Skills statement integration and outcome measurement	25%	4.5/5	3/5
Content Management Versioning, metadata support, and content reusability	20%	3/5	4.5/5
Learner Experience Personalization, mobile support, and accessibility	20%	4/5	4.5/5
Data and Analytics Advanced reporting, actionable insights, and customizable dashboards	15%	4/5	3/5
Future Readiness AI capabilities, system integrations, and scalability for growth	20%	3.5/5	4.5/5
Weighted Score		**3.8/5**	**3.9/5**

Framework Implementation Process

1. Anchor in Learning Objectives Center on organizational impact.
2. Balance Operational and Strategic Needs
3. Implement Weighted Scoring Align with business priorities.
4. Collaborate With Stakeholders Include all key perspectives.

A strong rubric shifts the conversation from selecting the coolest tool to determining how best to support your learners and programs. It positions L&D as a thoughtful, strategic partner in platform decision making.

ϙϙϙ

By working through these five steps, you can build a strong foundation for future-ready platforms and systems that enable learning. This process puts L&D in the driver's seat, ensuring that technology choices are informed by real learning needs and positioned to support long-term success.

But platforms alone are not enough. Even the best tools cannot deliver value without the right content and expertise flowing through them. This is where knowledge management comes in.

As organizations grow and evolve, capturing and sharing internal expertise becomes essential to scaling learning and performance. The next step in building a modern learning strategy is to focus on how your team enables access to knowledge, allowing people to learn not only from courses but also from one another.

Knowledge Management

Modern knowledge management systems, such as ServiceNow, transform the way organizations manage information. While traditional systems often become digital graveyards where information is stored but rarely used, these platforms create centralized knowledge bases, automate document categorization, and track content usage and effectiveness. And now they're adding AI capabilities for intelligent search, automated content updates, and personalized recommendations.

AI-powered knowledge management represents a transformative force for L&D professionals, offering unprecedented capabilities to enhance workforce training, personalize learning experiences, and drive organizational knowledge sharing. L&D teams can now create knowledge ecosystems that understand user needs, speak their language, and deliver precisely what's required at the moment of need, without asking employees to become search experts or navigate complex information hierarchies.

Research from MIT shows that integrating a knowledge base into language models enhances output quality and reduces inaccuracies, underscoring the symbiotic relationship between AI and knowledge management (Colon-

Hernandez et al. 2021). AI transforms organizational knowledge repositories into dynamic, accessible resources by:

- Enabling intelligent search that understands natural language queries
- Automatically organizing and categorizing content
- Personalizing knowledge delivery based on user context and needs
- Breaking down information silos across departments

For example, a FinTech startup implemented Knowmax's AI-powered knowledge management platform to address challenges with dispersed information, creating a unified knowledge base that streamlined access for customer-facing teams and increased customer satisfaction scores by 28 percent (Knowmax 2024).

L&D professionals are uniquely positioned to lead knowledge initiatives because we already understand how people learn and apply knowledge, translate complex information into accessible formats, and connect learning experiences to business performance. By positioning ourselves at the center of knowledge management initiatives, L&D professionals can evolve from course creators to true organizational knowledge architects, driving both individual performance and broader business transformation. Figure 5-7 illustrates how this happens.

Figure 5-7. L&D as Knowledge Ecosystem Architects

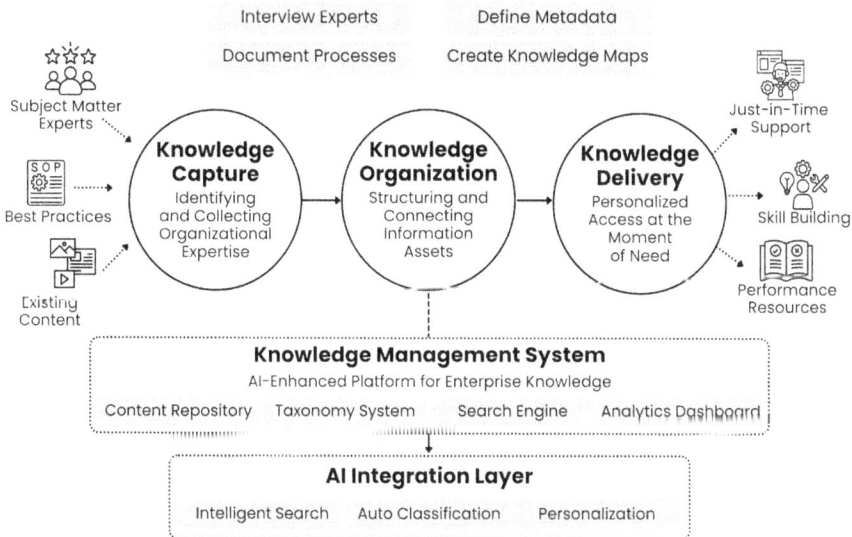

Reimagining How Knowledge Flows in Your Organization

L&D professionals orchestrate a knowledge management process that includes knowledge capture, knowledge organization, and knowledge delivery, supported through an AI-enabled knowledge management ecosystem.

Knowledge Capture

In this initial phase, L&D professionals systematically harvest organizational wisdom from different sources, including:

- **SMEs,** whose specialized knowledge often remains locked in their heads
- **Best practices** developed through years of operational experience
- **Existing content** scattered across the organization in various formats and repositories

L&D's critical role involves interviewing experts to extract tacit knowledge and documenting processes to create standardized approaches. By formalizing this knowledge capture process, L&D ensures that valuable organizational expertise doesn't remain siloed or disappear when employees leave.

Knowledge Organization

Once captured, knowledge requires thoughtful organization before it can be accessible and useful. L&D professionals can:

- Define metadata structures to categorize and tag content.
- Create knowledge maps showing the relationships between concepts, skills, and resources.
- Apply instructional design principles to structure information for optimal learning.

This organizational layer transforms raw information into structured learning assets that can be easily discovered, understood, and applied by employees.

Knowledge Delivery

The ultimate goal is getting the right knowledge to the right people at the right time. L&D professionals design:

- Personalized learning paths that adapt to individual needs and roles
- Microlearning assets for just-in-time performance support
- Contextual knowledge delivery that integrates with the workflow

This ensures that organizational knowledge doesn't just exist in a repository but actively supports employee performance when and where it's needed.

The Technology Platform

Underpinning the knowledge ecosystem is an integrated knowledge management system with four key components:

- **Content repository** that securely stores all knowledge assets in a centralized location
- **Taxonomy system** that organizes information through consistent categorization schemas
- **Search engine** that allows employees to find relevant information quickly
- **Analytics dashboard** that provides insights into knowledge usage and effectiveness

The AI Integration Layer

The most transformative aspect of modern knowledge management is the AI integration layer, which includes:

- **Intelligent search** that can understand natural language queries and the intent behind them
- **Auto-classification** that automatically tags and categorizes new content as it's added
- **Personalization**, which delivers customized knowledge based on an employee's role, history, and context

This AI foundation creates a self-improving system that becomes more intelligent and responsive over time, which reduces the manual effort required from L&D teams while improving the employee experience.

ᛂᛂᛂ

By embracing this knowledge ecosystem architecture, L&D professionals can elevate their strategic value beyond course creation and drive measurable performance improvement across the organization. As organizational knowledge continues to grow in volume and complexity, L&D professionals who master these knowledge management capabilities will become indispensable business partners in building intelligent, adaptive organizations.

Knowledge Graphs

Think of a knowledge graph as your organization's "brain map." Just as our brain's neurons connect through pathways that strengthen with use, a knowledge graph links information in ways that become smarter over time.

Unlike traditional databases that store information in separate tables or folders and act as digital filing cabinets, knowledge graphs create a web of interconnected information that mirrors how humans naturally think and learn—through associations and relationships.

In simple terms: A knowledge graph transforms your organization's scattered information into an intelligent network in which every piece of content knows how it relates to other content, people, skills, and business goals.

When an employee searches "customer objection handling" in a knowledge graph system, they don't just get documents with those keywords. They receive resources aligned with specific objectives, relevant product knowledge, expert colleagues who excel in this skill, upcoming training sessions, and real-world examples from successful sales conversations.

Let's use a food analogy to break down how a knowledge graph functions (Figure 5-8).

Figure 5-8. The Knowledge Graph Recipe

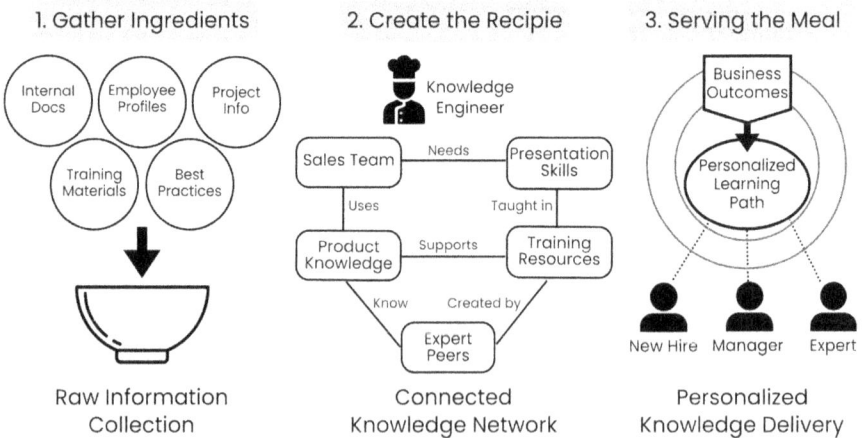

1. Gather Ingredients	2. Create the Recipie	3. Serving the Meal
Internal Docs, Employee Profiles, Project Info, Training Materials, Best Practices	Knowledge Engineer; Sales Team —Needs— Presentation Skills; Uses; Taught in; Product Knowledge —Supports— Training Resources; Know; Created by; Expert Peers	Business Outcomes; Personalized Learning Path; New Hire, Manager, Expert
Raw Information Collection	Connected Knowledge Network	Personalized Knowledge Delivery

1. Knowledge Base Creation: Gathering the Ingredients

The knowledge graph begins by integrating information from across your organization, including:

- **Internal documents**—policies, procedures, and product specs
- **Employee expertise profiles**—skills, experience, and certifications
- **Project information**—goals, teams, outcomes, and lessons learned
- **Training materials**—courses, videos, assessments, and learning pathways
- **Best practices**—documented processes and success patterns

Think of this as collecting all the ingredients before cooking a meal—everything needs to be available before you can create something cohesive.

2. Semantic Connections: Creating the Recipe

Step 2 is where the magic happens. The system doesn't just store this information—it connects it through meaningful relationships. In other words, it uses:

- **Entity identification.** The system recognizes important things (entities) like people, skills, content pieces, projects, and products.
- **Relationship mapping.** It then establishes how these entities relate to one another:
  - *Person X* has *customer service* skills.
  - *Training module Y* teaches *customer service* skills.
  - *Customer service* skills are required for the *sales representative* role.
  - *Document Z* explains *customer service* best practices.
  - *Person A* is an expert in *customer service*.
- **Metadata enhancement.** Each entity and relationship is enriched with additional context like proficiency levels, timestamps, or relevance scores.

3. Intelligent Applications: Serving the Meal

With this rich network of connections, knowledge graphs enable transformative learning applications. Here are some hypothetical examples:

- **Personalized learning journeys.** The system understands an employee's current role, skills, performance, and career aspirations. It can then recommend precisely what they should learn next—and not just generic courses, but specific resources tailored to their needs. For example, when a new manager accesses the system, it could automatically suggest leadership resources that are relevant to their specific team's challenges, their industry, and their previous experience level. Or, when an employee from sales searches for "presentation skills," the system could prioritize sales-focused presentation resources over generic ones.

- **Skills ecosystem management.** Knowledge graphs create a dynamic map of an organization's capabilities, illustrating how skills are connected to roles, projects, and business objectives. For example, as your company pivots toward digital transformation, the knowledge graph could visualize the current skills landscape, identify emerging skills gaps, and recommend development pathways to bridge those gaps.

- **Expert discovery.** By understanding who knows what across the organization, knowledge graphs connect learners with the right experts at the right time. For example, an employee struggling with a specialized customer issue could immediately find colleagues who have successfully resolved similar problems, access their documented approaches, or schedule virtual mentoring sessions.

- **Contextual performance support.** The system delivers learning in the flow of work by understanding what employees are doing and identifying the knowledge that would help them succeed. For example, if a service representative fills out a warranty claim form, the system could proactively suggest relevant policy updates, similar case examples, and quick tutorial videos based on the specific product and issue being reported.

- **Knowledge exploration.** Employees can navigate intuitively through connected information, following their curiosity and discovering related concepts. For example, a developer researching a programming language could easily explore how it connects to frameworks, identify which internal projects have successfully used it, locate communities of practice within the company, and discover how this skill relates to career advancement paths.

Real-World Technology Foundations

Knowledge graphs are built on established technologies you may already be using. For example:

- **Microsoft's Graph API** interconnects data across Microsoft 365 applications and understands relationships between people, content, and activities. This means that your SharePoint documents, Teams conversations, and Outlook communications can already be integrated into a knowledge graph.
- **Google's Knowledge Graph** powers its search capabilities, enabling it to understand that when you search for "apple," you may mean the fruit or the company, depending on the context. This same contextual intelligence can be applied to your learning content.

Both platforms offer application programming interfaces (APIs) and development tools that allow you to build custom knowledge solutions that are tailored to your organization's learning needs.

Implementation: Starting Your Knowledge Graph Journey

L&D teams should establish a strategic partnership with IT when implementing knowledge graph solutions. While IT brings the technical infrastructure and integration capabilities, you contribute crucial insight into how knowledge flows through the organization and how employees actually learn and apply information.

The collaboration should begin with joint discovery sessions in which L&D maps existing knowledge assets, taxonomies, and learning pathways while IT assesses technical requirements and integration points with existing systems. Regular co-creation workshops can help maintain alignment, with L&D focusing on content structure, metadata standards, and learning use cases and IT addressing scalability, security, and performance considerations.

A cross-functional approach ensures the resulting knowledge graph truly enhances organizational learning rather than becoming another underused technical solution.

And let me leave you with this: Implementing a knowledge graph doesn't require overhauling your entire learning ecosystem overnight. You can take a pragmatic approach with these steps:

1. **Start with clear business objectives.** Identify specific learning or performance challenges that would benefit from connected knowledge and establish a cross-functional team with both L&D and IT stakeholders to ensure alignment.
2. **Map your existing content landscape.** Collaboratively catalog existing information sources. L&D should provide insight into knowledge assets, taxonomies, and learning pathways, while IT handles the technical requirements and integration points with existing systems.
3. **Begin with a focused use case.** Select a specific department or skill area that would benefit from better knowledge connections and deliver immediate value, and then conduct joint discovery sessions to understand both the learning needs and technical considerations.
4. **Define governance structures.** Create a shared responsibility model determining who will maintain the knowledge graph. L&D should focus on content structure and metadata standards, while IT handles scalability, security, and performance considerations.
5. **Establish embedded roles.** Identify L&D specialists who understand enough technology to translate learning requirements into technical specifications and IT specialists who understand learning design principles to facilitate ongoing collaboration.
6. **Measure impact through concrete metrics.** Track improvements in time-to-competency, search effectiveness, and knowledge discovery, with regular co-creation workshops to review progress and refine the implementation strategy.

The future of organizational learning depends on how effectively we manage knowledge. By embracing knowledge graphs, L&D can evolve from content creators to knowledge architects, building neural networks of organizational intelligence that continuously adapt and grow smarter with use.

This isn't just a technological shift—it's a fundamental reimagining of how learning happens in organizations. And it positions L&D at the center of business transformation.

But knowledge is only part of the equation. As AI begins to influence every facet of the employee life cycle—from hiring to onboarding, development, and retention—L&D professionals must also expand their focus beyond learning systems and into the evolving world of human capital management.

Human Capital Management Systems

Back in 2021, at a multibillion-dollar supply chain company where I worked, I stood beside the VP of talent management while she launched the organization's first AI-driven job assistant. It was a modest beginning: a chatbot designed to help candidates navigate the hiring process by matching them with open roles based on a few basic questions. My part was to help with the chatbot's personality. It wasn't a revolutionary leap. The chatbot, Tessa, was a deterministic system integrated into our human capital management (HCM) platform to solve a specific problem: helping applicants find the right opportunity faster.

"What do you think?" she asked, watching the chatbot process its first live interaction.

"It's useful," I replied. "But it's just the first step."

Little did I know how prophetic those words would prove to be. Six months later, the vendor that supported the chatbot evolved that simple matching tool into an AI agent that conducted initial screening interviews, answered candidate's questions, provided personalized feedback, and guided prospects through the entire application journey. As L&D professionals, we've been here before. We survived the e-learning revolution. We adapted to mobile learning. We embraced microlearning. But the AI transformation in HCM is fundamentally reshaping our role in the organization.

The HCM and LMS Consolidation Reality

The tech landscape is constantly shifting. A book might not seem the place to discuss vendor mergers and acquisitions, but it's less about the individual deals and more about what they suggest. HCM and learning tech vendors are merging and acquiring one another at unprecedented rates. Cornerstone acquiring SumTotal, Degreed buying Learn In—these aren't random business deals but signals of a fundamental restructuring.

Standalone LMS platforms are vanishing; they're transforming into comprehensive HCM systems that support the coexistence of learning, performance management, skills tracking, and payroll under one roof. The demarcation lines between HR tech and learning tech are blurring beyond recognition.

This integration unlocks capabilities that seemed like fantasy just years ago. Modern HCM platforms index skills across the entire workforce with uncanny precision—and not just formal qualifications, but subtle capabilities revealed through project contributions, communication patterns, and learning behaviors. The AI models connect learning investments directly to performance indicators with a statistical rigor that makes previous ROI attempts seem primitive. The skills intelligence embedded in modern HCM suites turns hunches into hypotheses and instincts into insights.

However, this means that technology decisions now involve unfamiliar stakeholders and competing priorities. When organizations select new HCM suites, the learning module might lack features considered essential in previous LXP platforms. L&D must advocate forcefully for learning requirements during enterprise software decisions.

AI's Impact on Human Capital Management

As AI is rapidly transforming human capital management, there are now unprecedented opportunities to optimize how organizations attract, develop, and retain their most valuable asset: people. Let's review several key areas where AI is making a significant impact in human capital management.

- **Recruitment and talent acquisition:**
  - Automating resume screening and candidate sourcing
  - Conducting initial interviews through chatbots
  - Analyzing social media profiles for a comprehensive candidate assessment
  - Reducing bias in the hiring process
- **Employee engagement and retention:**
  - Providing personalized experiences and timely initiatives
  - Using AI-powered chatbots as virtual HR assistants
  - Identifying areas of concern with sentiment analysis tools
  - Forecasting potential turnover with predictive analytics

- **Performance management:**
  - Providing real-time feedback and performance analysis
  - Offering data-driven insights for more accurate and unbiased assessments
  - Identifying patterns and offering suggestions for performance improvement
- **Workforce planning:**
  - Forecasting future talent needs
  - Predicting attrition rates
  - Recommending talent acquisition and retention strategies
  - Identifying skills gaps

Let's use onboarding as an example to unpack the potential of AI in HCM. While the onboarding process was once the domain of L&D and HR professionals, it's now shared with AI agents that never sleep, never forget a detail, and scale across global enterprises.

Consider what these agents can already do:

- Generate personalized welcome videos in which executives appear to speak directly to each new hire, without recording hundreds of individual messages.
- Create custom learning pathways by assessing each employee's existing skills and knowledge gaps.
- Serve as 24/7 virtual assistants that can answer questions about benefits, culture, and protocols at any hour.
- Automate administrative tasks like document verification and orientation scheduling.
- Offer realistic simulations for new employees to practice skills in a risk-free environment.

I recently observed a sales trainee practicing customer interactions with an AI-generated scenario. The simulation adapted to her responses, challenged her assumptions, and provided immediate feedback. She completed more practice scenarios in two hours than traditional role plays would have allowed in two days. The quality of her interactions also improved visibly with each iteration.

This isn't the future. It's happening right now in organizations worldwide.

豤豤豤

The integration of AI into HCM systems is advancing at a breathtaking speed. Yesterday's innovations have become today's baseline expectations. And new L&D roles continue to materialize as the field transforms. Human-machine performance analysts orchestrate connections between AI-curated content and human-led experiences. They interpret complex patterns in engagement data, recommending targeted initiatives when the AI identifies potential disengagement. Understanding these new AI capabilities in HCM systems is paramount to advancing human and machine performance.

Skills data, which is abundant in our new HCM system monoliths, has emerged as the new currency of talent development. According to the World Economic Forum's *Future of Jobs Report 2025*, employers expect 39 percent of workers' core skills to change by 2030. This creates both a dizzying urgency and unprecedented opportunity, which leads us into our next topic: text mapping and skills indexing.

Optimizing Workflows Through Task Mapping and Skill Indexing

Remember when tracking employee skills meant maintaining endless spreadsheets and hoping managers remembered to update their team's competency matrices? Those days are ancient history now. The revolution in people analytics has transformed how we understand, develop, and deploy talent across our organizations.

Traditional approaches to employee task and skills management, if performed at all, rely heavily on manual tracking, periodic assessments, and often outdated job descriptions. This static view creates blind spots in our understanding of organizational capabilities. AI-driven people analytics provides a dynamic, real-time view of who performs specific tasks and how skills are distributed throughout the organization. The implications for learning strategy are far beyond simple automation.

Human-Machine Task Mapping

Tasks form the fundamental building blocks of work in modern organizations. Yet what we consider a task must evolve as AI reshapes work. A task no longer exists in isolation as a purely human or mechanical endeavor. Instead, it exists on a spectrum of human-machine collaboration, and each one requires different levels of cognitive effort, creativity, and technical precision.

AI has transformed how we train individuals to do their day-to-day tasks. Traditional task analysis focused primarily on human capabilities and limitations. Now, we must consider the interplay between human expertise and machine intelligence. In chapter 2, I introduced my Human–AI Task Scale framework and how it relates to your tasks as an L&D professional and intersects with AI (see Figure 2-3). You can also apply that logic to the tasks employees perform across the organization.

To understand human-machine task enablement, you must analyze tasks through the lens of complementary capabilities. Humans excel at contextual understanding, creative problem solving, and emotional intelligence. On the other hand, AI systems bring speed, consistency, and the ability to process vast amounts of data. This collaboration extends beyond simple task division. Effective human-machine partnerships create feedback loops that enhance both human and machine performance. The key lies in understanding the task's characteristics. Complex decisions that require empathy or ethical judgment remain primarily within human domains. Routine data analysis and pattern recognition, on the other hand, often suit AI capabilities. The most powerful results emerge when you design workflows that leverage both.

To implement effective human-machine task enablement, you can:

- Audit existing workflows to identify tasks suitable for collaboration.
- Map task characteristics to human and AI strengths.
- Design clear handoff points between human and machine components.
- Establish feedback mechanisms to improve both human and AI performance.
- Create guidelines for task ownership and escalation paths.

EXERCISE

Imagining Task Enablement

Start with small, well-defined tasks and document any successes and failures. Then, gradually increase complexity as team members become more comfortable with human-machine collaboration.

To get started, consider a routine task in your L&D role that consumes significant time. Ask yourself:

- How might this task benefit from human-machine collaboration?
- What aspects require human judgment?
- Which aspects could leverage AI capabilities?

Now, imagine redesigning this task to create a more effective partnership between human insight and machine efficiency.

Task mapping reveals the intricate dance between human capability and technological potential. I once collaborated with a team struggling to implement an AI-enabled learning platform. Their challenge wasn't technical. However, they hadn't broken down their complex training workflows into discrete, manageable components. This experience crystallized a fundamental truth: Successful automation begins by understanding the atomic units of work.

Organizations waste countless resources automating the wrong things. Clear task mapping creates the foundation for meaningful automation and skill development by transforming abstract concepts into concrete, actionable steps.

From Tasks to Skills

Tasks represent discrete actions, but *skills* encompass the capabilities required to perform these actions effectively. This distinction matters profoundly in the age of AI. A professional might possess excellent analytical skills but struggle with specific compliance documentation tasks. AI can support task completion while humans develop broader skill sets.

The relationship between tasks and skills flows both ways. Tasks require specific skills, while skill development occurs through task completion. Understanding this dynamic can help you design more effective learning initiatives against the backdrop of human–AI collaboration on task completion.

Real-world implementation requires systematic documentation. Start with high-level processes. Break them into component tasks and identify the required skills for each task. Then, you can map potential automation opportunities. Figure 5-9 shows a simple framework.

Figure 5-9. Optimizing Workflow With AI

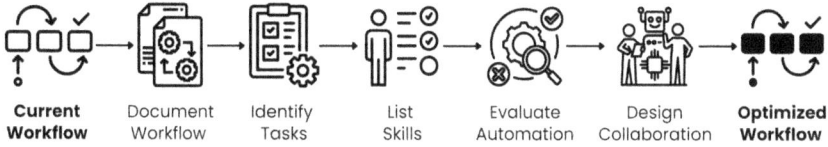

| Current Workflow | Document Workflow | Identify Tasks | List Skills | Evaluate Automation | Design Collaboration | Optimized Workflow |

EXERCISE

Task Mapping

Earlier, I asked you to think about a routine task in your L&D role. Now, consider your most complex project. Ask yourself:

- What tasks consume most of your time?
- Which tasks truly require human creativity?
- Where might AI augment your capabilities without replacing human judgment?

The answer may surprise you and reveal unexpected opportunities for innovation.

Task mapping and skills analysis set the foundation for more sophisticated technological interventions that improve how the business performs and operates. In the era of rapid technological change and evolving job roles, understanding and managing the skills within your organization has never been more crucial.

Skills Indexing

Like with task mapping, skills indexing can be a laborious process if you attempt it manually. And, it often results in outdated data by the time you've finished collecting and analyzing it. *AI-powered skills indexing*, on the other hand, means using AI to automatically identify, categorize, and quantify the skills present within an organization, creating a dynamic, real-time view of the skills landscape. It can continuously scan multiple data sources your company already has, including performance reviews, project management tools (like Jira or Asana), completed courses in your LMS, internal communications, and even resumes and external profiles (such as those on LinkedIn).

Using sophisticated NLP, the AI tool reads between the lines. It doesn't just look for keywords; it understands the context. It identifies the skills people are actually using and even infers which skills they've developed, based on the projects they've tackled.

Crucially, this isn't a static snapshot. The AI tool learns and updates constantly, building a rich, evolving "skills taxonomy"—which is, essentially, a structured library of skills relevant to your business and industry that adapts as roles and technologies evolve.

What Are the Possibilities?

Forget generic training programs or struggling to justify L&D budgets. AI-powered skills indexing can enable:

- **Laser-focused development.** Finally, you can see the real skills gaps—individual, team, and organizational. This means moving beyond one-size-fits-all training to truly personalized learning paths that address specific needs and career aspirations. Imagine recommending the perfect course before an employee even realizes they need it.
- **Smarter internal mobility.** How many times have you seen great internal talent leave because they couldn't find the right opportunity inside the organization? This tech acts like an internal talent scout, matching existing employees' (sometimes hidden) skills to open roles, boosting retention and engagement.
- **Data-driven strategy.** Instead of guessing where your company needs to upskill, you can leverage concrete data. You can demonstrate leadership by clearly understanding where the workforce stands, anticipating future needs based on market trends identified by AI, and developing proactive training strategies. This helps plan for succession and ensures the organization is ready for whatever comes next.
- **Boosting recruitment effectiveness.** Partner with HR to use these skills insights to craft more effective job descriptions and screen candidates more accurately based on the skills that truly matter for success.

Consider Sarah, a project manager, who recently worked on a complex machine learning initiative, analyzing project reports and team communications. Through this experience, she's developed valuable Python and data analysis skills—skills not formally listed in her job description.

Weeks later, someone with exactly that skill set is needed to work on a new AI project. The system instantly identifies Sarah as a strong internal candidate. (Bonus: You've facilitated internal mobility and potentially saved recruitment costs.)

The AI also notices that even though Sarah's Python skills are solid, she lacks experience with neural networks, a key area for advancement in AI. As a result, it automatically suggests she complete specific modules in your LMS or external courses. (You're providing personalized, relevant upskilling directly tied to career growth and organizational needs.)

When a critical strategic project launches a few months later and requires a mix of skills (such as Sarah's Python expertise, a strong data visualization specialist, and a cloud expert), the system helps managers assemble the optimal team quickly. (You're enabling agility and better project outcomes through skills-based team composition.)

Getting Started: Your First Steps

So, what does this actually mean for L&D professionals, and how can you start leveraging it without getting overwhelmed? Here are five steps to get started:

1. **Define one clear goal.** Identify a specific L&D challenge that AI skills indexing could realistically address in the next six to 12 months. What's your biggest pain point right now? Is it filling a specific skills gap? Improving internal mobility for a key department? Start there. Don't try to implement everything at once.

2. **Talk to your people (and IT).** Schedule exploratory meetings with your organization's IT, HR, and legal department leads this quarter. What data do you already have? Is it accessible? Partner with IT to understand the landscape. Crucially, involve your HR and legal teams early to navigate privacy and ethical considerations.

3. **Explore, but don't commit blindly.** Identify two to three potential vendors and request demos that are focused on your chosen objective.

Look at different AI tools and platforms. Many integrate with existing HR systems. Ask for demos focused on your specific goal. Prioritize vendors that are transparent about their AI and data practices.

4. **Pilot small, think big.** Consider running a pilot program in one department or for one specific skill cluster. You'll need to decide which team, skills, and data sources to test. Learn from the experience, gather feedback, and demonstrate value before scaling.

5. **Keep humans in the loop.** Reiterate to your team that any new tech is a tool to support, not supplant, their expertise. Remember, AI provides insights; humans make decisions. Use the data to inform your strategies, personalize recommendations, and guide conversations—not replace them.

AI-powered skills indexing is no longer science fiction. It's a tool that, when used thoughtfully, can significantly enhance our ability to develop people and build more agile, capable organizations. And it fuels the topic of the next section: targeted performance support.

Supporting Performance

Performance support no longer has to mean reviewing the dusty manual on a shelf or a clunky knowledge base that was always slightly out of date. AI-powered business platforms can facilitate dynamic, personalized, and proactive performance support.

Let's look at how this might play out in a day in the life of Isaiah, a project manager:

- **9 a.m.** As Isaiah starts his day, his AI assistant provides a summary of key project updates and flags potential issues that have emerged overnight.
- **10:30 a.m.** During a client call, Isaiah needs some specific information. He whispers a question to his AI assistant, which instantly retrieves the relevant data and displays it on his screen.
- **1 p.m.** Isaiah's working on a complex scheduling problem. The AI assistant analyzes the constraints and suggests several optimal solutions, explaining the tradeoffs of each.

- **3 p.m.** The AI assistant notices that Isaiah has been struggling with a new project management tool. It offers a quick, personalized tutorial that focuses on the features he hasn't mastered yet.
- **4:30 p.m.** As Isaiah prepares for tomorrow's team meeting, the AI assistant suggests an agenda based on the project's current status, team member availability, and upcoming deadlines.

You can think of an AI-powered performance support platform as a Swiss Army knife for productivity. It's a multifaceted tool that's always at your fingertips, ready to help you perform at your best. Ultimately, AI-powered performance support revolutionizes the way we work, learn, and perform. By providing personalized, contextual, and proactive support, AI enables employees to reach new heights of productivity and effectiveness.

As we refine these systems and address the associated challenges, we're moving toward a future in which every employee, including yourself, has a mighty AI co-pilot ready to help them navigate the complexities of the modern workplace.

But where do you begin?

EXERCISE

Build Your AI Readiness Canvas for Performance Support

Use this activity to help you or your team identify where AI can make the most meaningful difference in supporting performance. Start to design small, smart experiments that move the needle.

The goal is to stop thinking of performance support as static documentation or reactive help desks and start designing it as a living system that's proactive, personalized, and intelligent. When you use AI to meet people in their moment of need, support becomes invisible but powerful. It's always there, always helpful, and always learning.

1. Map the Moments of Need
Look across a typical day or workflow. Where do people:
- Struggle to remember key info?
- Need guidance to complete a task?
- Get slowed down by complexity?
- Spend time searching for answers?

Write down four to five of these common moments.

2. Identify the Gaps

For each moment, ask yourself:

- What kind of support exists today?
- What's missing or outdated?
- What's the influence on performance?
- What could AI help with?

3. Layer in AI Opportunities

Now match each gap to the potential AI capabilities in Table 5-1.

Table 5-1. AI Opportunities and Compatible Tools

AI Opportunity	Example Capability or Tool
Contextual assistance	**Moveworks** is an AI platform that uses natural language understanding to resolve workplace requests by analyzing and fulfilling them through integrations with other software applications.
Predictive guidance	**Altair's HyperWorks With PhysicsAI** uses geometric deep learning to deliver simulation results significantly faster, enabling predictive modeling and real-time simulation in engineering workflows.
Personalized learning	**BetterUp Grow** is an AI-based coaching tool that provides real-time, personalized coaching tailored to an individual's role, behavior, and company culture, enhancing professional development.
Workflow optimization	**EYQ AI Platform** is part of EY's suite of AI tools designed to improve efficiency and quality in auditing by automating administrative tasks, reducing staff burnout, and allowing auditors to focus on risk assessment.
Intelligent search	**Microsoft's Copilot** integrates with Microsoft 365 to provide AI-powered search and assistance, retrieving relevant information across documents and emails using natural language queries.
Virtual collaboration	**Tidio AI** is an AI chatbot platform that enhances customer support by automating conversations and providing 24/7 assistance, facilitating more effective collaboration.
Performance analytics	**15Five** is an AI-powered performance management tool that uses robust metrics to help managers identify strengths and weaknesses, providing insights for performance reviews and similar conversations.

4. Prioritize and Prototype

Choose one opportunity that is low risk but could be highly influential. Ask yourself:

- What tool could help? (Do you already use it?)
- What's the smallest way to test it?
- Who should be involved?

Sketch out a 30-day pilot test.

You should consider a few things when beginning your implementation. Start with security—your data matters. Choose platforms with robust protection. Implement clear usage policies. Train your team on safe practices.

In addition, address ethical concerns early. AI can show bias and affect jobs. Create guidelines for responsible use. Monitor outcomes regularly. (Review chapter 4 for more suggestions!)

Finally, success requires proper training. Your team needs to understand AI capabilities. They need practice with new tools and time to develop new workflows.

Conclusion

The transformation happening across business platforms represents a fundamental shift in how organizations capture and distribute collective intelligence.

The implications for organizational learning are profound. Knowledge no longer needs to be formally documented and distributed through training programs to be useful. It flows continuously through AI-enabled systems that capture insights in real-time, connect them to existing knowledge repositories, and push them to the people who need them at the moment of need.

The skills that have always made L&D professionals valuable—understanding how people learn, connecting learning to performance, and aligning both with business outcomes—remain essential. What's changing is the tool set at your disposal and your expanded influence across your organization.

Your AI co-pilot is ready. When it transcribes your next meeting, summarizes key points, assigns action items, and emails participants without your input, you'll experience firsthand how these technologies free us from administrative burdens to focus on what matters most: designing environments where human potential flourishes, supported by increasingly intelligent systems that make knowledge flow effortlessly through our organizations.

AI is no longer a futuristic concept on the edge of your workflow; it's now embedded directly into the systems you use every day. That brings us to a new challenge and opportunity: understanding how learning platforms themselves are evolving with AI at their core. In the next chapter, we'll explore this shift in depth—from the transformation of the LMS to the emergence of LXPs and the powerful AI features driving smarter, more personalized learning experiences.

CHAPTER 6

AI-Enabled Learning Platforms

In This Chapter
- The AI-enhanced capabilities in modern learning platforms
- Criteria for implementing and evaluating in learning platforms

I've been in L&D for long enough to remember when an LMS was the pinnacle of corporate learning tech. Back then, they were essentially digital filing cabinets that were great for tracking compliance training and ensuring everyone had checked the required boxes. Honestly, it often felt like checking a box was all an LMS could accomplish. Learners would slog through mandated modules, we'd record scores and completion rates, and that was that.

Over the past decade, however, I've watched a fascinating evolution: the rise of the learning experience platform (LXP). LXPs can provide personalized learning experiences and social learning, as well as focus on the user experience with things like mobile-first delivery. LMS and LXP platforms often share similar functions, which can cause confusion in the marketplace, and GenAI adds to the mix of capabilities.

In this chapter, we'll explore how LMSs and LXPs are leveraging GenAI capabilities and discuss some real-world stories of companies that have successfully harnessed AI-powered platforms to boost engagement and performance. We'll also review how AI can help you analyze learner engagement data, going beyond traditional metrics (such as time spent or "click next") to improve content and delivery strategies. Another game-changer we'll cover is AI-driven personalized learning paths, which can enable every employee to embark on a learning journey tailored specifically to them.

At the end, I'll outline an implementation framework for AI-driven learning management, including some tools and best practices I've picked up, and key considerations for vendor selection when you're in the market for AI-enhanced learning systems.

The Current State of Learning Platforms

Let's start with a quick refresher on what a traditional LMS is (or was, some might say). It's essentially an administrative hub for learning—the place where L&D teams assign courses, track completions, and manage compliance. In my early days, I used an LMS to roll out annual compliance modules, onboard new hires with standardized courses, and keep records for audits. The focus was very much on administration and control.

The LMS kept meticulous records about things like who took what course, when, and whether they passed a quiz. That capability was (and still is) crucial for things like compliance and certifications.

Around the mid-2010s, many L&D practitioners began to feel the limitations of the check-the-box LMS approach. In response, LXPs were designed to not just manage learning, but to deliver a rich learning experience. So, what does that mean in practice?

First, LXPs look and feel different to the learner. People often compare an LXP's interface to Netflix. In other words, the platform presents content in a modern, visually engaging way with lots of recommendations and personalization options. Instead of a static list of courses you have to take, an LXP might greet you with suggested learning content based on your interests, role, or past activities, much like Netflix suggests the next binge-worthy show for you to watch (Figure 6-1).

Figure 6-1. The Evolution From LMS to LXP

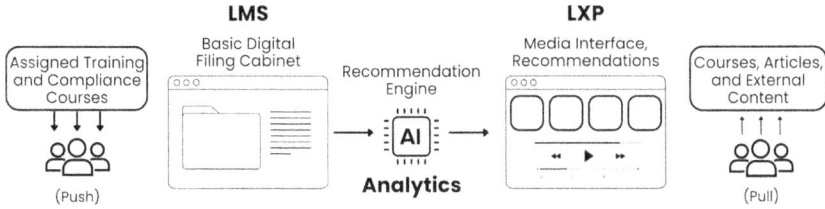

Let me illustrate the contrast with a simple scenario. Imagine the difference between compliance training and a personal development course. In an LMS, compliance training is king. These platforms excel at assigning mandatory courses (such as ethics and codes of conduct) to every employee and then tracking who has completed it. It's a top-down process that ensures everyone meets a requirement (which is important for business).

Now, consider personal development. If an employee wants to learn about data visualization to improve their presentation skills, they'll have to search for it on their own, unless the LMS includes a formal course called "Data Visualization 101." With an LXP, one the other hand, the employee could search the platform for data visualization and find a curated list of resources, including a mix of internal courses and external content, as well as a link to a community forum on the topic.

LXPs empower self-directed learning by employing a *pull model* (learners pulling in what they need) instead of a *push model* (the organization pushing out what learners must do) like an LMS. It's not that one is better than the other; they serve different needs.

As the marketplace has matured, some platforms even offer integrated LMS and LXP capabilities, providing administrative tracking and a great user experience in one system. AI has also begun to have an effect. Under the hood, machine learning algorithms can analyze each user's profile and learning history, as well as compare them to similar learners to recommend relevant, personalized suggestions. Some LXPs can also leverage machine learning to create quiz questions at various levels of difficulty and recommend them based on historical data.

With this context in mind, let's examine some real-world examples of how organizations are using AI in their learning platforms. These case studies not only show what's possible but also provide reassurance that this is happening in practice.

EXERCISE

LMS vs. LXP

Think about the primary learning platform used in your organization. Does it function more like a traditional LMS (administrative focused) or an LXP (experience focused)? Where do you see the biggest limitations or opportunities for improvement based on the descriptions in this section?

Now, list two to three specific learning scenarios in your organization (for example, onboarding, skills development, or compliance training). For each, describe how an LMS and an LXP might handle it differently.

Unilever: Global Personalized Learning at Scale

Unilever, the global consumer goods giant, undertook a significant learning transformation in the early 2020s. With more than 100,000 employees, the company required more than just a traditional LMS to reskill and upskill its workforce for the future. So, Unilever implemented Degreed—a popular LXP—as its online learning hub and integrated it into an internal employee development initiative called the "Future-Fit Plan."

The results have been impressive. Learners create their development plans so they're aligned with future-fit skills, and the LXP (powered by AI) guides them to personalized learning materials. The AI in Unilever's LXP recommends content based on each employee's role, career goals, and even personal interests, creating a personalized learning path that is relevant to them. According to Unilever (n.d.), employees accessed learning content on the LXP more than 2.4 million times in 2022 alone. This is a staggering engagement figure, showing that learners are voluntarily returning to learn when the content is relevant and engaging. Moreover, the company achieved a 49 percent increase in intrinsic motivation among employees who engaged in purpose-driven learning.

IBM: "Your Learning" Platform and AI Personalization

IBM is another early adopter that has leaned heavily into AI for learning. The tech company has built many of its solutions internally including its enterprise learning platform—Your Learning—which was designed from the ground up to be AI-driven. IBM realized early on that the sheer volume of learning content (including hundreds of thousands of learning assets) required AI to help manage and personalize the platform.

The company used its in-house Watson AI technology for several platform functions. This included AI-powered content tagging (so it's richly described and easier to match to learner needs), a chatbot to answer learners' queries, and most importantly, personalized content recommendations for each learner.

IBM made more than 300,000 learning resources available on its platform, ranging from internal courses to external massive open online course (MOOC) content (Qin and Kochan 2020). Without AI, how could an individual possibly find the most relevant five or 10 learning assets they need at a given time? IBM's approach let AI do the heavy lifting in the background.

The system analyzes each person's role, skill profile, learning history, and even what others are learning to provide personal recommendations. IBM essentially built a digital learning marketplace where supply (content) and demand (learners' needs) are matched by AI.

ϙϙϙ

These examples underscore a common theme: AI in learning platforms is driving higher engagement, faster skill acquisition, and better alignment of learning content with business needs. From consumer goods to tech companies, organizations are finding that AI-powered LXPs and LMSs aren't just nice-to-have innovations; they're delivering real ROI in terms of productivity, quality, and employee retention.

In the next sections, we'll break down how AI makes these outcomes possible by examining specific capabilities, including analyzing learner engagement data, personalizing learning journeys, and conducting skills gap analysis.

AI Functions in Learning Platforms

Whether you realize it or not, the platforms you use to deliver learning content to employees (pushed or pulled) have AI programs built into them or offer AI integration capabilities. And that functionality will only skyrocket as time goes on. These AI-driven functions—including learning analytics, personalized learning paths, and engagement bots—are transforming how you ensure your employees acquire the knowledge and skills your organization needs them to have. By using AI to refine content, provide targeted recommendations, and suggest project-based development opportunities, learning platforms are becoming more adaptive and effective.

Learning Analytics: From Basic Metrics to Deep Insights

AI has transformed learning analytics, moving it beyond basic LMS reports detailing completion rates and quiz scores to reveal deeper patterns in learner behavior. While traditional metrics show what happened, AI-powered analytics can explain why and suggest solutions.

AI systems analyze granular data points about how learners interact with content, which sections they repeat, where they struggle, and how they detect meaningful patterns. For example, language learning apps can identify behaviors that predict when a learner is likely to drop out, enabling early intervention. This shifts the approach from reactive to proactive support.

Beyond surface metrics like clicks and logins, AI tools can measure meaningful indicators of knowledge application and retention (Figure 6-2). They can distinguish between memorization and true understanding by analyzing response patterns over time. If a learner struggles with a concept, studies it, and then succeeds later, AI can recognize this as a learning breakthrough—something traditional systems would miss.

Figure 6-2. Traditional L&D Metrics vs. AI-Powered Insights

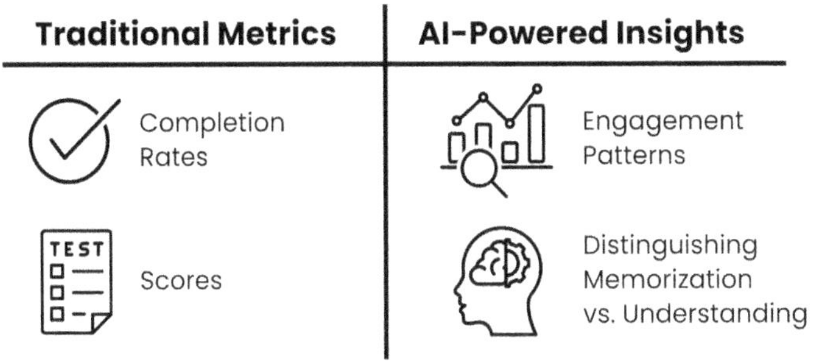

Traditional Metrics	AI-Powered Insights
Completion Rates	Engagement Patterns
Scores	Distinguishing Memorization vs. Understanding

AI-Powered Insights

Consider your current measurement practices. Ask yourself:

- How does your L&D team currently measure learning effectiveness?
- Are you primarily using completion rates and scores, or are you exploring deeper engagement metrics?
- How could AI-powered analytics provide more meaningful insights for your content improvement or learner support?

Now, identify one specific learning program or course in your organization. Brainstorm three to five new data points (beyond completion rates and scores) that AI could potentially track to give you a better understanding of learner engagement and understanding within that program.

Data-Driven Content Improvement

By aggregating learner data, AI analytics provide invaluable feedback for content creators. If most learners replay a specific video segment, this signals either confusion or exceptional value. Similarly, if a quiz question consistently confuses learners, it may indicate unclear instruction or a problematic question design.

Modern AI dashboards offer predictive analytics rather than static charts. They forecast completion rates, predict certification timelines based on current progress, and notify administrators when targets are at risk of being missed. Some systems automatically suggest content additions based on detected learning patterns.

Consider, for example, a digital learning provider that used AI to monitor engagement with a sales training course. It discovered high drop-off rates during a theoretical module. After adding practical examples based on this insight, completion rates rose significantly. The targeted improvement was directed by data, rather than guesswork.

Engagement Bots and Timely Interventions

AI chatbots integrated with learning platforms can monitor participation and provide timely nudges. When a learner hasn't logged in for a while or appears to be stuck, the bot may send a personalized message to offer assistance. These systems can also answer common questions immediately, reducing friction in the learning process.

These analytics capabilities enable L&D leaders to make more informed decisions. They can use the data to justify program changes, allocate budgets more effectively, and present executives with evidence of how learning affects business KPIs, including correlations between training engagement and sales performance.

Personalized Learning Paths

I think personalization is one of AI's most exciting applications in L&D. While one-size-fits-all training has always been a compromise, truly individualized learning was previously feasible only for select employees or through costly one-on-one coaching. AI now enables personalization at scale.

A personalized learning path curates a sequence of experiences, such as courses, articles, videos, and projects (Figure 6-3). Each is tailored to an individual's goals, role, skills gaps, and learning preferences. A personalized learning path functions like a career GPS—mapping your journey from current skills to target competencies with appropriate learning milestones.

Figure 6-3. AI-Curated Learning Assets

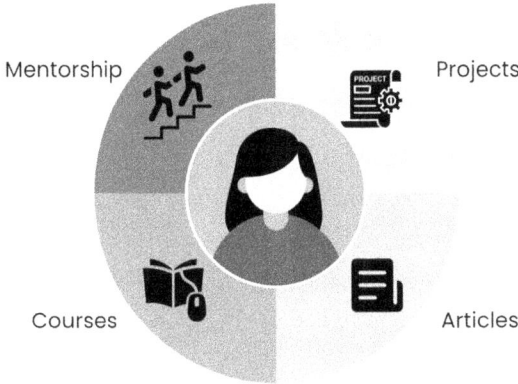

Mentorship

Projects

Courses

Articles

Recommendation Engines and Adaptive Learning

AI personalizes learning using several techniques. Recommendation engines analyze profiles and behaviors to suggest relevant content, much like how consumer platforms recommend products or entertainment. If you are proficient at Excel, the system might suggest content on advanced data analysis next; if you struggle, it might offer a fundamentals refresher.

Adaptive learning platforms assess performance in real time and adjust content accordingly. In a coding course, someone who masters syntax quickly but struggles with object-oriented concepts could receive an accelerated path through the basics, along with expanded instruction on challenging topics, perhaps with alternative teaching approaches. The content adapts to the learner rather than forcing everyone through identical sequences.

Beyond Courses: Comprehensive Development

Personalization extends beyond formal courses to include recommendations for experiences like projects, mentorships, and other developmental activities. Advanced platforms may suggest taking on assignments that require specific skills or matching employees with internal mentors who possess the desired expertise. *I can't emphasize enough how important this functionality is.* Employee AI usage at work could potentially erode the relationship between an expert and a novice (Beane 2024).

AI-powered learning journeys can continuously update to reflect company priorities, promotions, or role changes. When organizational strategy shifts (like suddenly prioritizing cloud computing, for instance), recommendations can adapt to emphasize newly critical skills. NLP tools can even provide conversational support through AI tutors that answer questions in real time.

ꙮ

AI has transformed the long-held L&D dream of individually tailored learning into reality. By leveraging learner data and intelligent algorithms, it creates unique journeys that boost engagement and efficiency, allowing people to learn what they need, when they need it, and in a way that they'd prefer. As an L&D professional, seeing an AI system do this heavy lifting is both a relief (fewer individual learning plans to create manually!) and a delight (happier, more skilled learners).

Evidence suggests that personalized learning significantly boosts engagement, with some companies reporting a 30 percent increase after implementing AI-driven personalization (Vorecol 2024). This makes sense because relevant, tailored learning is inherently more engaging than generic content. Personalization also reduces wasted time if learners can skip familiar material while ensuring critical gaps are addressed.

EXERCISE

The Opportunities and Challenges of Personalized Learning

How significant is the need for personalized learning paths in your organization? What are the potential benefits and challenges of moving away from a one-size-fits-all approach?

Sketch out a hypothetical personalized learning path for a specific role or skill transition within your company (for example, moving from customer support to sales). List at least five different types of learning resources or experiences (such as courses, articles, projects, and mentorships) that AI could curate for this path.

But, implementing personalized paths doesn't mean creating hundreds of custom courses. Often, it involves intelligently leveraging existing content and external resources, with AI assembling appropriate combinations for each person. The L&D team's role is to feed the system with quality content options and define competency frameworks. Initial assessments or preference surveys help the AI effectively personalize learning paths from the start. We'll explore implementation tips in the next section.

Implementing AI for Learning Management

If your organization is like most, you aren't starting from a blank slate. You probably have an LMS (or several) that's been around for years, containing a trove of historical training data and serving critical functions like compliance tracking.

Now, you're adding AI-driven tools or an LXP into the mix. Integration between new and old systems can be one of the toughest hurdles, but it's a solvable one with the right approach. I've gone through a couple of these integration projects, so I'll share a common challenge I encountered along with how I tackled it.

The Challenge of Data Silos and Incompatibility

Legacy LMSs often have their own data schema and may not easily export all the data you want. For AI to analyze learner profiles and engagement, it ideally needs access to past learning records (such as courses completed and scores) and ongoing updates from the LMS (like new completions).

A significant challenge arises when the LMS isn't designed to share data in real time or it uses a proprietary format. I've seen this firsthand: My team's old LMS could export reports but not automatically sync with external systems.

Here's a solution: Leverage middleware or APIs if available (check out the sidebar on the next page). Many modern LMSs (even older ones) have at least some form of API or they support standards like SCORM or xAPI (experience API) for interoperability (Figure 6-4).

Figure 6-4. Integrating an LMS with an LXP

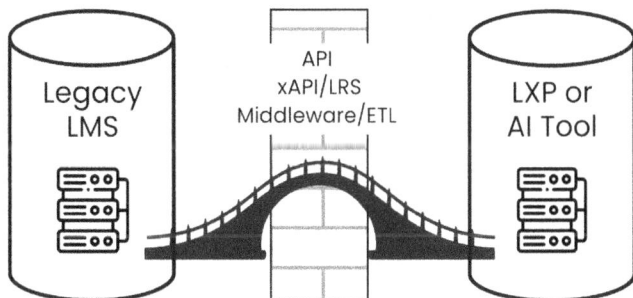

Specifically, xAPI is great for capturing learning experiences from different sources in a unified way. You can set up a learning record store (LRS) to accumulate records from your existing LMS and new LXP or AI tool. If direct integration is not possible, you may want to consider scheduled data dumps (for example, a nightly export of key data from the LMS to the LXP). It's not real-time integration, but it's better than nothing. One time, my team built a simple extract-transform-load (ETL) process that pulled data from the LMS database and fed it into the LXP each night. It wasn't elegant, but it kept the two in sync enough to ensure the AI had recent data.

Using APIs and Plugins

Before diving into the technical details, it's worth stepping back to understand why APIs and plugins matter. As we think about the future of AI agents and their role in education, one of the key questions is how they could actually interact with an LMS. For AI agents to be effective in learning environments—whether to support learners, automate tasks, or personalize content—they need to be integrated into the systems educators already use. That's where APIs and plugins come into play.

There are several ways this kind of integration could potentially happen, each with its own advantages and challenges. While the specifics vary based on the LMS and organizational needs, there are three general pathways to consider when imagining how AI agents might connect with an LMS:

- **Direct API integration.** APIs allow your existing LMS to communicate directly with AI services. Using this approach provides flexibility but requires technical expertise. My team recently integrated an AI content recommendation engine using REST APIs, maintaining complete control over the user experience while leveraging powerful AI capabilities.
- **Plugin-based solutions.** For organizations with limited technical resources, plugins offer a more accessible path to AI integration. Major LMS platforms like Moodle offer specific plugin types for AI integration, including AI service plugins and AI model plugins. These prebuilt solutions reduce implementation complexity while still delivering substantial benefits.
- **Custom development.** Some organizations require tailored solutions that integrate with unique business processes or legacy systems. Custom development allows for precise control over AI functionality but demands significant resources and expertise.

A colleague once asked me about AI integration in their LMS, but their eyes started to glaze over when I mentioned APIs and machine learning models. I stopped, smiled, and instead took a different approach to identifying their biggest training headache. Success in AI integration depends heavily on choosing the right approach, however, and that requires some basic understanding of APIs and plugins. Thankfully, many LMS providers offer APIs and plugins that enable seamless connection with AI-powered tools.

Integration pathways illustrate the foundational work required to bring AI agents into educational ecosystems. While still hypothetical, they highlight the practical steps that would make such integration possible. As the capabilities of AI agents continue to evolve, understanding how they can technically integrate into learning environments is a crucial step toward envisioning their future role in training.

Selecting an AI-Enhanced Learning System

Choosing a learning platform with AI capabilities is a significant decision, and there are numerous options available, each with distinct strengths. As an L&D professional, I've been involved in several selection processes, and it boils down to evaluating both the vendor and the platform features while considering your organization's needs. Let's discuss 10 key considerations and some guidance on what to look for (and ask for) when making your choice.

1. Alignment With Learning Strategy and Needs

First, the system should fit your purpose. Are you primarily looking to add AI-driven personalization to an existing LMS? Or do you need a full LXP to drive a new learning culture? Clarify your use cases and ensure the vendors on your shortlist address them. For example, if personalized learning and skills development are top priorities, look for a platform that explicitly offers AI-driven content recommendations and skills mapping. Many LXPs market this, ask for concrete examples of how their AI recommends content or identifies skills gaps.

A good practice is to share a sample scenario like this with the vendor: "Suppose we have a marketing specialist who wants to become a data scientist.

How would your platform guide their learning journey?" Then, you can determine if the functionality aligns with your vision.

2. AI Capabilities and Transparency

Because AI is the differentiator here, scrutinize those features. Key AI capabilities may include personalized recommendations, adaptive learning paths, predictive analytics (such as predicting who might churn or fail a course), AI-generated content (such as quizzes or flashcards), chatbots for Q&A, and skills inference. Not all platforms offer every feature, so prioritize which ones matter to you.

Also, consider AI transparency. Does the vendor explain how its AI makes decisions? A reputable AI vendor should be transparent about its algorithms and data usage (for instance, using machine learning and collaborative filtering for recommendations or an NLP for skill extraction). You might ask, "On what basis does the system recommend content? Can admins finetune the recommendation logic?" If the AI can be tuned or if it learns from feedback, that's a plus.

Additionally, find out whether the AI has been trained on data that's relevant to your industry or if you'll need to train it. Some vendors have prebuilt AI models (for example, an AI that already knows common career paths or skill-adjacent ones in specific domains), which can jumpstart value. Others might require a cold start, in which the system learns as your employees use it; in that case, ask about the volume of data needed to achieve accuracy.

3. Integration and Compatibility

As we discussed earlier, your new system must integrate seamlessly with your existing technology stack. When reviewing your options, verify the integration capabilities. Do they have open APIs? Out-of-the-box connectors for common HR systems or LMSs? Support for standards like SCORM, xAPI, and learning tools interoperability (LTI)? For instance, if you use Workday for HR, can the learning platform pull worker data from Workday and push back learning completions?

Integration is often a "table stakes" criteria that can eliminate options that won't fit your environment, so don't take vendor claims at face value. If a vendor says, "We integrate with any LMS," ask for references from clients who have integrated it with a system similar to yours. Additionally, consider data export options. You want to own your data, so make sure you can get reports or raw data off the platform for analysis in your own business intelligence tools if needed.

4. User Experience (UX)

Engagement hinges on a great user experience. The interface should be modern, intuitive, and preferably customizable to your branding. Features like a mobile app or mobile-responsive design are crucial, especially if you have a workforce that's not desk-bound. Because we're talking about L&D pros here, you might want to involve some actual end-users when evaluating UX via trials.

Also, consider the content discovery experience: Is it easy for users to find what they need? Is there a powerful search (possibly AI-driven) that can interpret queries? Some platforms even personalize the user interface (UI); for example, showing different homepage banners based on user role or interests. If you value social learning, check the UI for community features (such as discussion boards or user content sharing). Essentially, put yourself in the learner's shoes and see if the platform makes learning easy and enjoyable.

5. Content Curation and Libraries

An AI learning system is only as good as the content it can provide. Find out what content sources the platform can support. Does it come with a content library or marketplace? Can it pull in free content from the web or integrate with content providers like LinkedIn Learning or Coursera? Many LXPs excel at aggregating content from multiple sources. If you have a lot of proprietary content, ensure it can ingest that (for example, support for various media types or bulk uploads).

You should also look at the content curation tools. Can the platform's AI curate external content for you? For example, can it filter and suggest relevant articles from the internet on a given topic? This can save time for L&D teams and keep learning fresh. On the flip side, check if it has robust content governance—you need to ensure that the recommended content is high quality, so some admin oversight or a filtering mechanism is good to have (perhaps the AI can be guided to trust certain sources over others).

6. Analytics and Reporting

We've lauded analytics and the potential of AI to derive new insights. Now, ensure the platform delivers the data you need. Look for dashboards that show skills metrics, engagement stats, and ROI indicators. Can you easily see what content is performing well, which skills are trending up or down, and how different groups are engaging? Ideally, the system should provide both high-level insights for leadership (for example, "The overall skills gap index improved 20 percent this quarter") and the ability to drill down (for example, by department, individual, and content).

If a vendor says, "Our AI is a black box, but trust us; it works," look out because that's a red flag. You need to be able to measure and justify the investment. You should also ask whether it's possible to export data to combine it with HR data (for example, to correlate learning with performance or retention).

7. Scalability and Performance

Consider the size of your user base and growth. The platform should handle peak loads (like everyone rushing to complete required training programs at the end of the year). If you're global, check how it performs in different regions, and whether the vendor has data centers or content delivery networks (CDNs) that minimize latency worldwide.

You should ask, "What's your largest deployment in terms of users?" and "Have you had any outages or slowdowns during critical periods?" Also, if you plan on uploading large files like videos, make sure the platform can handle streaming well.

8. Vendor Support and Expertise

The system is only half the story; the vendor's partnership is the other. Evaluate its customer support, implementation assistance, and L&D expertise. Is the vendor just a software provider, or does it understand learning? If so, will it consult on best practices?

For AI, you might need ongoing tuning. Does the vendor offer a customer success manager or AI specialist who can help? Ask about support service level agreements (SLAs), response times, and escalation paths. It's wise to also inquire about its road map: What AI features is it developing next? The field is evolving, so you want a vendor that is investing in innovation and aligned with your needs (for example, more advanced AI or new integrations).

Vendor stability is important too. Is the company financially stable? Does it have a decent market presence or is it very new? (Startups can be great but they come with risks.) Check references or case studies in your industry. If the vendor has success stories with organizations like yours, that's reassuring.

9. Data Security and Privacy

Given that AI systems handle a lot of employee data (including learning history and skills profiles), ensure the vendor follows strong security practices. This includes data encryption, regular backups, and compliance with regulations (like GDPR if you operate in Europe, for instance). If the AI tool uses any personal or sensitive data (like analyzing communication patterns), confirm that it's within acceptable use.

You might also ask if the vendor allows employees to opt out of certain data processing (especially in Europe, where employees may have rights to not be subject to purely automated decisions). Additionally, clarify who owns the data (it should be you). If using the cloud (most are SaaS now), check their certifications (such as ISO 27001 or SOC 2).

10. Cost and ROI

Finally, evaluate the cost structure. Some platforms charge per user; others charge per usage or by modules or features. AI features might also be premium add-ons. Calculate the total cost of ownership, including implementation services, the potential need for additional IT infrastructure (although most are cloud-based, so that's minimal), and any ongoing costs. Then, gauge the expected ROI. If the system can reduce manual work and improve retention, are you able to estimate those benefits financially? For example, if real-time skills gap analysis helps avoid one costly bad hire by upskilling an internal person, that might save your organization tens of thousands of dollars. Or, if personalized learning cuts onboarding time by 20 percent, what's the productivity gain? Calculating ROI helps you justify the purchase and compare vendors. (However, remember it's not an apples-to-apples comparison; a pricier system might deliver higher ROI through better results).

Vendor Scorecard

It might be useful to create a vendor scorecard with these criteria. For instance, list each consideration, weight them, and then score each vendor. Sometimes, one vendor will shine in AI analytics but have weaker integration, while another might have great content partnerships but a less elegant UI. Your specific priorities (which you set in alignment with strategy) will tell you which tradeoffs to make. For many L&D teams, the ability to integrate and an AI tool's effectiveness (proven by use cases) might outweigh having every possible feature.

To present some of these considerations in an organized way, Table 6-1 shows the key vendor selection criteria along with why each is important, some things to look out for, and questions to ask.

Using such criteria, you can score vendors and have in-depth discussions to make an informed choice. Remember, no system will be perfect in every category, so identify your must-haves and nice-to-haves. For instance, you might accept a slightly less flashy UI or UX if that vendor's AI analytics are far superior (or vice versa).

EXERCISE

Assessing Learning Platform Vendors

Consider your organization's current learning technology stack. Ask yourself:
- What potential integration challenges (data silos or incompatible systems) might you face when introducing an AI-enhanced platform?
- Which integration solutions (such as APIs, xAPIs, or middleware) seem most feasible for your context?

Next, review the vendor selection criteria. Which three considerations would be the absolute most critical for your organization when choosing an AI-enhanced learning system? Why did you choose them?

Using the scorecard in Table 6-1, draft an additional two to three questions specific to your situation, and ask a potential vendor your questions about AI transparency and integration capabilities.

Table 6-1. Key Vendor Selection Criteria and Scorecard

Criteria	Why It Matters	What to Look For	Questions to Ask	Score (1–5)
AI capabilities	Determine how well the system personalizes learning and provides insights. You want mature, effective AI that aligns with your needs (e.g., recommendations and skills analysis).	• A list of AI features (e.g., recommendations, adaptive learning, analytics, or chatbots) • Demos and success metrics • Ensure the AI can handle your content volume and diversity	• What AI-driven features does your system have, and how do they improve learning outcomes? • Could we see a demo of the recommendation engine adapting to a user over time?	
Integration and compatibility	Integration is essential for a seamless learning ecosystem. A system that can't integrate will create silos and extra work.	• Support for APIs (xAPI, LTI, and SCORM standards) • Prebuilt connectors (e.g., to your LMS or HRIS). • Client examples of integration scenarios similar to your case	• Can your platform integrate with our LMS and HR systems? • Can you show an example or reference of this integration in action?	
User experience (learner and admin)	High adoption and engagement depend on an intuitive, pleasant UX. Admins also need a good experience for managing content and interpreting data.	• A modern, easy-to-navigate interface • Mobile support • Personalized dashboards for learners • Clear dashboards and simple content management for admins • Determine if the vendor allows some branding customization	• How do you help drive user adoption? • Do you have resources or playbooks for change management in L&D for your system?	

Table 6–1. (*continued*)

Criteria	Why It Matters	What to Look For	Questions to Ask	Score (1–5)
Content support and curation	The platform should enrich learning with diverse content and make curation easier.	• Ability to support various content types (e.g., videos, PDFs, and courses) • Integration with content libraries (e.g., LinkedIn Learning) • AI curation of external content, and tools for SMEs to contribute content easily	• How much can we configure the skills frameworks or recommendation rules? • Can the AI be tailored to our competency model?	
Analytics and reporting	Demonstrate the value of L&D and help refine programs with rich analytics that ensure you can track progress and ROI.	• Visual dashboards (for skills gaps and engagement) • Exportable reports • Predictive analytics (e.g., who might need training) • Ability to set and track KPIs (e.g., learning completion vs. performance)	• What analytics do you provide on the backend? • Can we create custom reports or dashboards for our leadership?	
Vendor expertise and support	A knowledgeable vendor will guide you in how to best leverage the system. Good support ensures issues don't derail usage.	• Strong implementation support (including training and migration help) • Ongoing customer success check-ins • L&D expertise (do they consult on learning strategy or just tech?) • References praising support responsiveness	• What support do you provide during and after implementation? • What new AI features are you planning in the next year?	

Table 6–1. (*continued*)

Criteria	Why It Matters	What to Look For	Questions to Ask	Score (1–5)
Security and compliance	The system must protect data and comply with laws, especially if you're working in a regulated industry or region. Security policies can also build trust with IT and employees	• Data encryption • Region-specific data handling • Certifications (such as ISO 27001 and SOC 2) • Features like role-based access control (e.g., managers only seeing their team's data) • The vendor's privacy policy regarding user data and AI (it should include no misuse of personal info)	• How does your platform ensure data privacy and compliance with regulations like GDPR or SOC 2? • Can you share documentation of your certifications and how you handle user data in AI models?	
Scalability and performance	The system should accommodate your entire target audience without performance issues, now and as you grow.	• Cloud infrastructure robustness (e.g., uptime guarantees and load testing results) • References from companies of similar or larger size that are using it • Multilanguage or localization support (if you operate globally)	• Can your platform support our expected user volume as we grow? • What are your uptime guarantees and load testing results for clients of similar scale?	
Cost and flexibility	The platform needs to fit your budget and show value. Flexible licensing can help you start small and grow.	• A transparent pricing model (e.g., per user or tiered) • What's included and what's extra (e.g., some vendors charge extra for advanced AI modules) • The ability to test or do a phased rollout licensing • Estimated implementation cost and time • ROI case studies or tools to help calculate impact	• What results have your clients seen after implementing your AI features (e.g., engagement uplift or reduction in skills gaps)?	

In my experience, involving a cross-functional team in the selection process is beneficial, so include IT for integration and security aspects, a couple representative end-users for the UX perspective, HR for alignment with talent processes, and, of course, L&D for core functionality. This way, you won't overlook a critical requirement.

By carefully considering these factors, you'll improve the chances that the platform you select will truly deliver on the promise of AI in L&D—making your life easier and your learning programs more effective—rather than becoming an expensive experiment.

Conclusion

AI is reshaping the world of learning platforms. What began as administrative tools designed to track compliance and manage course completions have evolved into something far more dynamic. The rise of LXPs, powered by AI, marks a fundamental shift in how organizations think about L&D. These platforms are no longer just training material repositories; they are intelligent ecosystems that adapt to each learner's needs, behaviors, and goals.

AI brings new capabilities to the learning platform table, such as predictive analytics, adaptive learning, and skills gap analysis. It enables platforms to go beyond surface-level engagement metrics and instead identify what learners actually need in real time. We are now able to intervene before someone falls behind, recommend the right content at the right moment, and track how learning translates into improved performance.

Of course, implementing AI into existing learning environments is not without its challenges. We discussed the often tricky work of integrating legacy LMS systems with newer, AI-enhanced platforms. From managing data silos to selecting the right vendors, these behind-the-scenes decisions often determine the success or failure of an AI-driven learning strategy. Practical tips—from leveraging APIs to evaluating AI transparency—help ensure that the technology works for you, not the other way around.

Ultimately, the promise of AI in learning is not just about automation or scale, but about restoring a human-centered approach to development at a time when organizations are more complex and fast moving than ever. AI, when thoughtfully applied, can help people learn what they need to know, when they need to know it, and in a format that resonates with how they learn best.

This chapter laid the groundwork for understanding what AI can do within modern learning platforms. In the next chapter, we will turn our focus to the content development capabilities (creation, curation, and adaptation) these learning platforms and tools can facilitate and enhance.

CHAPTER 7

Content Development Powered by AI

In This Chapter
- The content development experience with AI
- The role of content curation and adaptation in your content management strategy
- Ways to implement AI avatars in your learning experiences

I once delivered a presentation to a group in Saudi Arabia using an AI-powered video avatar. The content of my talk was important, but how I delivered it truly stunned the audience. I don't speak Arabic, but at that moment, it looked and sounded like I did.

Leveraging an advanced avatar platform, I created an introduction video in which I spoke fluent Arabic using my voice, perfect lip-syncing, and natural expressions. The bilingual attendees, who were accustomed to switching languages, were shocked to see me deliver this flawless introduction in Arabic. It was a striking demonstration of the world we live in—one that has seen AI shatter language barriers in ways we could barely imagine just a few years ago. Today, it's just another Tuesday in L&D.

Reflecting on the experience, it's clear that technology has redefined the boundaries of language and communication, allowing us to reach new heights in L&D. The content creation landscape has fundamentally shifted. We've moved beyond the binary choice of either expensive, high-quality, and customized content or generic, off-the-shelf solutions. AI tools enable us to create and deliver personalized, scalable content that maintains human connection while leveraging technological efficiency. The challenge is how to implement it thoughtfully and effectively.

This chapter explores the practical implementation of AI in L&D content creation and curation through three primary lenses. First, we'll examine AI-powered authoring tools and their influence on instructional design workflows. Then, we'll look at content curation systems that can help you organize and personalize learning experiences. Finally, we investigate the role of AI avatars in creating engaging, human-centered learning experiences.

By the end of this chapter, you will possess practical strategies for implementing AI-powered content creation and curation tools in your L&D practice. You'll understand how to evaluate, select, and implement AI solutions that enhance learning experiences while maintaining instructional quality and ethical considerations.

Content Creation: Tools and Engines

GenAI tools have revolutionized how we approach learning design. During my first GenAI project, which involved supporting an environmental, social, and governance (ESG) program, I faced a familiar challenge: creating engaging content for 5,000 associates across multiple regions.

Traditional methods would have required weeks of development and numerous SME reviews. However, AI tools transformed this process. I leveraged platforms like ChatGPT for initial content development and an AI-powered LXP to personalize delivery. The results surprised even my most skeptical stakeholders. My development time decreased by 70 percent, and only 4 percent of the content I created required an update after SME reviews.

The pressing need for AI-powered content creation stems from three converging factors in L&D:

- The volume of required learning experiences continues to grow. Organizations must deliver more training across more topics to more learners than ever.

- Learner expectations have evolved dramatically. They demand personalized, engaging content that respects their time and addresses their needs.
- L&D teams face constant pressure to reduce development costs and time-to-deployment while maintaining or improving quality.

Recent industry data reveals that traditional content development approaches can no longer keep pace. A typical hour of custom e-learning content requires 65 to 115 hours of development time (Defelice 2021). Multiply this across hundreds of training modules, and the resource requirements become unsustainable. Gen AI tools offer a compelling solution. They automate routine content creation tasks, enable rapid multilingual adaptation, and facilitate personalization at scale.

The transformation of content creation through GenAI encompasses several key dimensions that L&D professionals must understand. Let's examine each component and its practical application in learning design:

- **Automated content generation.** Modern AI model platforms like ChatGPT, Claude, and Gemini don't simply reconstitute existing content. Through reasoning, they analyze learning objectives, target audience characteristics, and subject matter to generate contextually appropriate material. These tools excel at creating initial drafts of learning content, practice scenarios, and assessment items.
- **Dynamic content adaptation.** Tools like Synthesia and D-ID transform static content into engaging video presentations featuring AI avatars. These platforms support multiple languages, varied presentation styles, and different cultural contexts. One of my global manufacturing clients used this capability to create safety training videos customized for facilities in 12 countries. Each version maintained consistent core messages while adapting to local cultural norms and regulatory requirements.
- **Rapid content iteration and improvement.** Machine learning algorithms analyze learner interaction data, identifying areas where content fails to engage or communicate effectively. This feedback loop enables continuous refinement of learning materials.

The implementation process requires careful attention to several critical factors, and content quality control becomes paramount. While AI generates initial content quickly, human expertise remains essential for ensuring accuracy, appropriateness, and alignment with learning objectives. Successful organizations establish workflows that combine AI efficiency with human oversight.

Picture a master chef using advanced kitchen technology. The tools enhance efficiency and consistency, but the chef's expertise determines the final quality. Similarly, AI content creation tools amplify L&D capabilities while relying on professional judgment for optimal results. The technology handles routine tasks, freeing learning designers to focus on strategy and creativity.

The L&D landscape is rapidly evolving as AI reshapes content creation. Traditionally, instructional designers, educators, and media developers relied on manual workflows using tools such as Adobe Photoshop, Premiere, Audition, and various e-learning authoring platforms. These powerful tools require significant human effort, time, and expertise.

Today, a hybrid content creation model is emerging—one that blends local manual creation with cloud-based, AI-driven automation (Figure 7-1). By leveraging GenAI and multimodal models, you can scale content production, personalize learning experiences, and reduce development time.

There are three primary workflows for this hybrid model: local content creation, remote AI-powered asset generation, and hybrid AI-assisted learning content development. Let's discuss each in more detail.

Figure 7-1. Learning Experience Development With GenAI

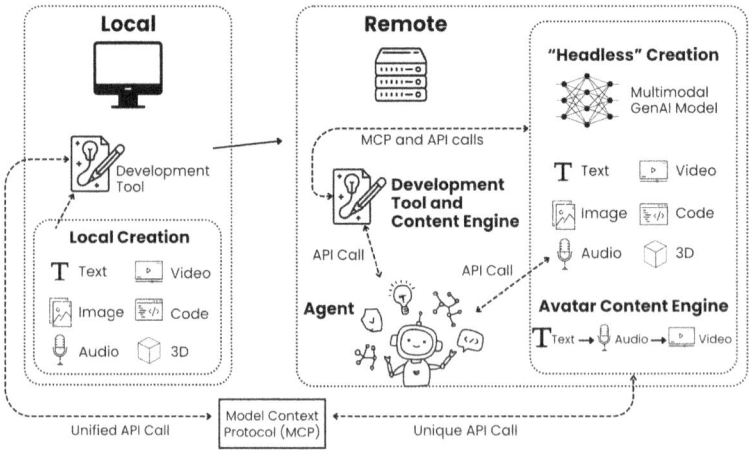

Local Workflow: Traditional Content Creation

In traditional instructional design, content is often crafted manually using specialized software tools that enable L&D professionals to create high-quality learning materials, but they come with constraints in terms of time and scalability. The process involves significant human effort and expertise, requiring instructional designers to plan, design, and produce educational content meticulously.

Manual workflows encompass a variety of tasks, such as writing detailed scripts for lessons, developing comprehensive assessments, and designing visually engaging graphics and user interface elements. Audio production is another critical component that involves recording and editing voice-overs and sound effects to enhance the learning experience. Additionally, video editing is essential to content creation. Training videos and animations should be carefully crafted to ensure clarity and engagement.

Moreover, developing interactive simulations and gamified experiences often requires coding skills and the use of tools like Articulate Storyline, Unity, or programming in JavaScript. In addition, 3D modeling software (such as Blender or Unreal Engine) is indispensable for those creating immersive learning environments.

L&D professionals can rely on a variety of local tools to develop different learning assets, including:

- **Text.** Use Microsoft Word, Google Docs, or Notion to write scripts, create lesson plans, and develop assessments.
- **Images.** Use Adobe Photoshop, Illustrator, or Canva to design graphics, UI elements, and instructional visuals.
- **Audio.** Use Adobe Audition or Audacity to produce voice-overs and sound effects.
- **Video.** Use Adobe Premiere Pro or Final Cut Pro to edit training videos and animations.
- **Code.** Use Articulate Storyline, Unity, or JavaScript programming to develop interactive simulations, branching scenarios, and gamified experiences.
- **3D models.** Use Blender or Unreal Engine to create immersive learning environments.

While these tools offer full control, they present key challenges. For one, creating assets from scratch takes extensive effort. Reproducing variations for personalized learning is also challenging. And above all, they require skilled professionals and software licenses.

This is where AI-powered remote workflows come into play.

What Is the Model Context Protocol?

The *model context protocol* (*MCP*) is an open standard that allows AI systems—like Claude or ChatGPT—to connect seamlessly with external tools, APIs, and data sources without requiring custom integrations.

As illustrated in Figure 7-1, the MCP acts as a bridge between locally created learning content and remotely hosted, AI-driven creation engines.

On the left, we see a traditional desktop setup where an L&D professional uses local tools to build content (such as text, images, audio, code, video, and 3D content). On the right, the "headless" remote services—such as avatar engines, generative AI models, or multimodal toolkits—creates or transforms content via API.

At the center is the MCP, which is shown as the connector that enables standardized communication between these worlds. Instead of building a unique API connection for every tool, the MCP layer handles discovery, permissions, and structured exchange, allowing content and context to flow smoothly between agents, tools, and services.

For L&D, the MCP unlocks:
- Real-time content adaptation using live data
- Integration of AI video, TTS, and code tools into existing workflows
- Scalability and consistency across platforms and formats

Bottom line: The MCP is like a universal remote that lets AI talk to your learning tools—both locally and remotely—making your design process faster, smarter, and future-ready.

Remote Workflow: AI-Powered Content Generation

AI has enabled cloud-based, multimodal content creation, allowing L&D professionals to generate learning assets dynamically without traditional manual processes. With generative AI, organizations can now efficiently produce content, such as instructional scripts, quizzes, summaries, illustrations, info-graphics, voice-overs, videos featuring synthetic avatars, interactive learning modules, and VR and AR assets.

This transformative approach ensures scalability and personalization with unprecedented ease and effectiveness. Organizations can use AI-driven tools for generating:

- **Text.** Use GPT-based models to create AI-generated instructional scripts, quiz questions, and summaries.
- **Images.** Use Stable Diffusion, MidJourney, or DALL-E to create AI-generated illustrations and infographics.
- **Audio.** Use ElevenLabs or WellSaid Labs to create AI-generated voice-overs in various languages and accents.
- **Video.** Use Synthesia, Colossyan, or HeyGen to create AI-generated videos featuring synthetic avatars.
- **Code.** Use GitHub Copilot or OpenAI Codex to develop AI-assisted interactive learning modules.
- **3D models.** Use Meshy AI or 3D AI Studio to generate AI-assisted VR and AR assets.

A key enabler of an AI-powered workflow is the AI agent, which acts as an intermediary between the development tool and content engine and the multimodal AI services. The AI agent can perform various functions—including managing API requests to generate diverse assets—integrating those assets seamlessly into workflows and ensuring that content is adaptable to multiple learning contexts and individual preferences. This automation allows organizations to effortlessly create, personalize, and deploy learning materials that are both high-quality and engaging.

The AI agent can:

- Generate assets based on API requests from an LMS or a remote development content engine.
- Dynamically fetch and integrate AI-generated content without human intervention.
- Personalize learning materials based on learner analytics and adaptive learning models.

Another key aspect of AI-powered workflows is the *headless content creation*, which involves interacting with AI models via API calls, rather than graphical user interface (GUI) software. This allows you to:

- Automatically generate text-to-speech (TTS) narration.
- Integrate AI-generated scripts into text-to-avatar video pipelines.
- Dynamically adapt content for personalized learning paths.

For example, an AI agent can create a video about food safety by going through these steps:

1. Create or use a stored prompt. (For example, the video prompt: "An avatar explains the importance of food safety. Cut in footage and images of a kitchen and restaurant patrons.")
2. Input the prompt into a large language model.
3. Create a video script. (For example, "Scene 1. Close-up of the avatar smiling and saying, 'Welcome! Today, we're diving into something super important: Food safety! It's more than just keeping things clean; it's about keeping you safe.'")
4. Convert the script into AI-generated audio.
5. Apply that audio to an animated avatar.

This process can create a complete learning video without human intervention. The avatar content engine enables this transformation, ensuring a seamless flow from text to audio to video, ultimately delivering high-quality, AI-generated training experiences.

This is only one of many learning content pipelines that can be enhanced with GenAI. As multimodal GenAI matures, you will see more learning experience automation features for media creation. But what about the times when content creation benefits from a mix of human involvement and AI assistance?

Hybrid Workflow: Combining Manual and AI-Powered Creation

Until multimodal GenAI can create complete learning experiences remotely, L&D professionals will participate in hybrid workflows, in which AI enhances traditional desktop-based development tools rather than replace them. In this model, local L&D tools handle the complex information navigation and interactions that require human oversight, while AI-powered tools organize knowledge and generate the media that will be placed inside the local development tool.

One of the most significant advantages of a hybrid workflow is reducing production bottlenecks. By leveraging GenAI to fill in content gaps and handle repetitive tasks, you can focus your talents on making strategic decisions and quality control—areas in which human insight remains irreplaceable.

In practice, you may already be incorporating AI tools into your workflows with a hybrid model. Remember that these tools work best when given clear parameters. So, develop detailed prompt templates that specify learning objectives, target audience characteristics, and desired outcomes (this is the focus of chapter 8). Train your team to think of AI as a collaborative partner rather than a replacement for human expertise.

EXERCISE

Consider Your Current Content Development Process

Where do repetitive tasks consume time that is better spent on strategic activities? Which aspects of your learning programs would benefit most from rapid iteration and personalization? The answers to these questions will guide your approach to AI tool implementation.

If you're considering leveraging AI tools, you should:

- **Choose the right tool for the job.** AI tools have different strengths and weaknesses. Select the one that best suits your specific needs and content creation goals.
- **Use AI to enhance—not replace—human creativity.** You should see AI as a tool to assist human creators, not replace them entirely. Use AI to automate tasks, generate ideas, and improve efficiency, but maintain human oversight and creativity in the content creation process.
- **Be mindful of ethical considerations.** Address concerns about bias, fairness, transparency, and authenticity when using AI in content creation.

- **Stay informed about AI advancements.** The field of AI is constantly evolving. So, you need to keep up to date with the latest advancements and new AI tools to make the most of this technology.

And, while AI offers many benefits for content creation, you must also consider its challenges and limitations, including:

- **Lack of creativity and originality.** AI-generated content can be repetitive or lack the unique perspective of human creators. AI may struggle to develop truly original ideas or capture the nuances of human creativity. You should not present AI-generated content as human-created, and you should be mindful of potential plagiarism issues. While AI can generate original content, ensuring that it doesn't inadvertently copy existing works is essential.
- **Difficulty with context and tone.** AI models may struggle to understand the nuances of human language and may produce inappropriate or tone-deaf content. For example, an AI tool might misinterpret sarcasm or humor, leading to unintended consequences.
- **Dependence on data quality.** The quality of AI-generated content heavily relies on the training data quality. The AI model may produce inaccurate or misleading content if the training data is incorrect or incomplete.
- **Bias and fairness.** AI models can perpetuate biases in training data, leading to unfair or discriminatory outcomes. For instance, an AI model trained on a dataset of predominantly male CEOs might generate text that implies leadership roles are primarily for men.

EXERCISE

AI vs. Manual Showdown

Compare traditional and AI-assisted instructional design workflows by creating, evaluating, and refining learning content.

Step 1. Choose a Training Topic

Pick a learning topic that can be adapted into multiple content formats. For example:

- **Workplace compliance**—such as cybersecurity awareness, workplace harassment prevention, or safety training

- **Technical training**—such as using Microsoft Excel formulas or software troubleshooting
- **People skills development**—such as conflict resolution or leadership communication

Step 2. Define the Learning Assets

Create two versions—one manually and one using AI-powered tools—of the following assets:

- **Text-based content.** Create a microlearning lesson or a set of quiz questions.
  - *Manual approach:* Write the content yourself using Microsoft Word, Notion, or Google Docs.
  - *AI-powered approach:* Use ChatGPT or another AI tool to generate the same content.
- **Visual learning asset.** Create an instructional infographic or UI element for an e-learning module.
  - *Manual approach:* Design it using Canva, Adobe Photoshop, or Adobe Illustrator.
  - *AI-powered approach:* Use DALL-E, MidJourney, or Stable Diffusion to generate an image.
- **Audio or video component** (optional but recommended). Create a short 30-second video lesson or voice-over narration.
  - *Manual approach:* Record and edit a voice-over using Adobe Audition, Audacity, or your phone.
  - *AI-powered approach:* Use ElevenLabs, Descript, or Synthesia to generate an AI-assisted voice-over or video.

Step 3. Evaluate and Compare

After creating both versions, analyze them based on the criteria in Table 7-1.

Table 7-1. Evaluation Criteria

Criteria	Manual Creation	AI-Generated	Observations
Time required			
Ease of use			
Quality and accuracy			
Scalability			
Personalization			
Creative control			

Step 4. Reflection

Consider the following questions:

- Which method was faster?
- Which approach allowed for more creative control?
- Where did AI enhance the process? Where did it fall short?
- How could you integrate AI into your real-world instructional design workflow?
- How might AI affect the role of instructional designers in the future?

Step 5. Refinement

Now that you've compared your AI-generated and manual content, refine the AI-generated assets to enhance accuracy and instructional quality. Identify where human expertise is essential in improving clarity, engagement, and training effectiveness.

As vendors increasingly integrate generative AI capabilities for text, image, audio, and video creation into their platforms, L&D professionals must develop new skills to critically evaluate these tools against standalone alternatives. The most successful learning organizations will be those that strategically leverage the right AI tools for specific content development needs rather than assuming that integrated solutions are automatically superior or that external models are worth the additional workflow complexity.

Content Management

I had some insightful discussions with Lynda Weinman during the evolution of Lynda.com (what would become LinkedIn Learning in 2015)—particularly about the challenges of managing and organizing an ever-expanding library of video content. Weinman's journey from distributing three VHS tapes to curating thousands of online courses is a testament to her visionary approach to digital education.

As Lynda.com grew in the early 2000s, the need for an efficient content management system (CMS) became paramount. Implementing a robust CMS allowed the site to seamlessly organize, retrieve, and update content, ensuring users could easily navigate the extensive library on their own. Eventually, Lynda.com decided to build its own CMS from the ground up. This system facilitated content curation and enhanced the user experience by providing intuitive access to relevant courses.

It can be challenging for employees to navigate learning content platforms like LinkedIn Learning due to their extensive array of content. To address this, many organizations integrate these platforms with their existing LMS, allowing L&D professionals to assign specific courses that are aligned with individual development plans. Additionally, curated learning paths and personalized recommendations help learners focus on relevant content, making the vast number of resources more manageable and tailored to their needs.

The Content Proliferation Challenge

Content proliferation presents a paradox in corporate learning. Organizations invest heavily in learning resources, yet associates struggle to find relevant materials when needed. Traditional content management approaches falter under the sheer volume of available information. A typical enterprise learning ecosystem now contains thousands of assets across multiple platforms, making manual curation unsustainable.

As a result, employees spend significant time searching for learning content and information at work, and employee engagement suffers when valuable content remains buried in overwhelming repositories. What's more, employees are so frustrated with having to search across every company app or service for this information that nearly half (43 percent) would consider leaving a job if there wasn't an efficient or easy way to access it (Glean 2022). AI curation addresses these challenges through intelligent content organization, personalized recommendations, and dynamic adaptation to employee needs.

This growing disconnect between content abundance and accessibility demands a paradigm shift in how organizations manage their learning resources.

Today's learning landscape is characterized not by a scarcity of resources but by an overwhelming abundance. A client recently confided to me that finding relevant materials on their learning content platform felt like "searching for a specific drop of water in an ocean." This challenge represents two distinct but interconnected opportunities for L&D professionals: intelligent content curation and strategic content adaptation.

Content curation leverages AI to discover, organize, and deliver the right content at the right time, while *content adaptation* employs AI to transform existing materials through translation, format conversion, summarization, and personalization (Figure 7-2). Together, these capabilities create a dynamic learning environment that maximizes the value and influence of organizational knowledge assets.

L&D teams face a dual imperative: they must efficiently organize and recommend the most relevant learning resources from vast repositories (curation), while ensuring existing high-value content can be transformed to meet diverse learning needs (adaptation). AI technologies offer powerful solutions to both challenges, fundamentally changing how organizations manage their learning ecosystems.

Figure 7-2. The Role of AI in Content Management

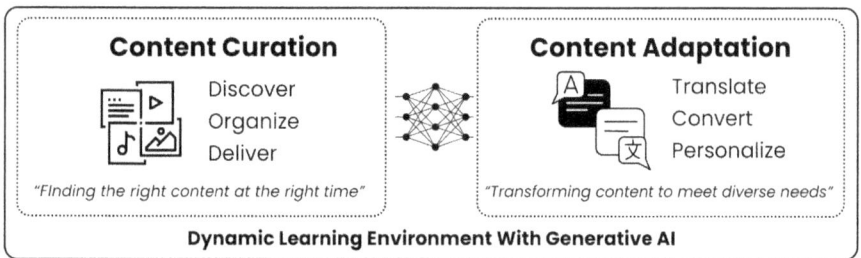

Content Curation	Content Adaptation
Discover	Translate
Organize	Convert
Deliver	Personalize
"Finding the right content at the right time"	*"Transforming content to meet diverse needs"*

Dynamic Learning Environment With Generative AI

Let's first explore how AI content curation is revolutionizing how organizations manage their learning assets before examining how AI content adaptation transforms static resources into dynamic learning experiences tailored to individual needs.

Content Curation

Content curation involves selecting, organizing, and presenting content relevant to a specific audience or topic. When reviewing learning content platforms (like LinkedIn Learning, Pluralsight, and OpenSesame), you'll notice a distinct pattern regarding how they leverage AI to support users. They layer functions like digital coaches and personalization on top of their existing content platforms.

AI algorithms can analyze vast amounts of data from various sources—including user preferences, browsing history, and even Slack activity—to identify relevant content. This allows AI-supported platforms to personalize content recommendations, ensuring users are presented with information that aligns with their interests. AI can also analyze content for quality, relevance, and credibility, filtering out low-quality, outdated, incorrect, or irrelevant information. This helps ensure that the curated content remains current and reliable.

AI-powered content curation tools can automate several tasks, such as:

- **Content discovery.** AI algorithms can scour the web for relevant content, using keywords, semantic analysis, and other techniques to identify valuable pieces.
- **Content analysis.** AI can analyze content to understand its topic, sentiment, and relevance to a specific audience.
- **Content organization.** AI can categorize and tag content, making it easier to find and manage.
- **Content recommendations.** AI can provide personalized content recommendations to users based on their interests and preferences.

How It Works

Figure 7-3 shows how AI-driven content curation operates as an interconnected system: A digital coach collaborates with GenAI to deliver personalized content tailored to the user's learning needs. This system functions across three key processes—analysis, adaptation, and optimization—ensuring an intelligent and dynamic learning experience.

Figure 7-3. The AI-Driven Content Curation Process

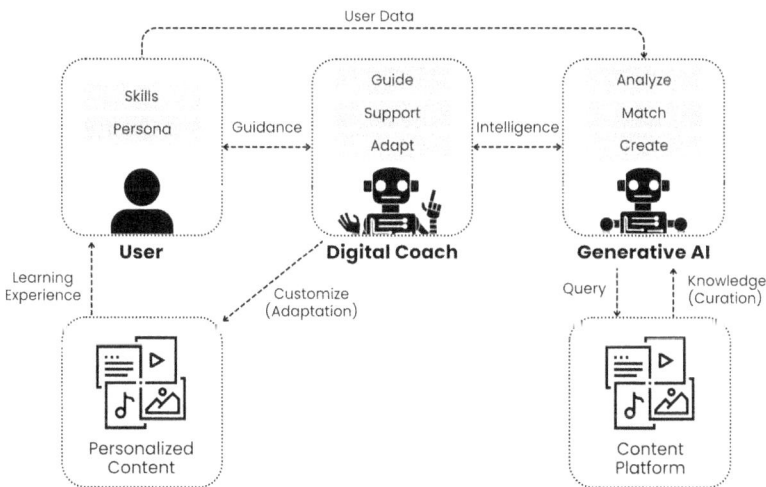

During analysis and intelligence, the GenAI system analyzes, matches, and creates content by examining metadata, usage patterns, and contextual relationships. It understands deeper connections beyond keywords—such as linking a video on emotional intelligence to leadership, conflict resolution, and team management—enabling smarter content discovery. The AI queries a content platform for additional knowledge and then curates relevant resources for learning.

During guidance and personalization, the digital coach bridges the gap between AI and the user, employing guidance, support, and adaptation to create tailored learning experiences. It considers user data to personalize recommendations, including skills, role requirements, and career aspirations. For example, a junior developer who's exploring leadership would receive different content than a seasoned manager who's updating their technical expertise. As the user interacts with content, the digital coach dynamically refines its recommendations to ensure continuous learning adaptation.

During the optimization and content effectiveness feedback loop, the system tracks engagement metrics, completion rates, and learning outcomes to determine whether the recommended content was effective. High-impact resources gain greater visibility, while underperforming content is modified or retired. The digital coach customizes the learning experience based on real-time insights, ensuring the ecosystem remains fresh and relevant.

This integrated AI-powered system provides users with intelligent, personalized, and continuously optimized content, enhancing their learning journey with relevant and engaging materials.

Picture a skilled librarian who knows every book, understands each reader's interests, and anticipates their future needs. AI curation systems serve as that librarian—organizing vast knowledge repositories and guiding employees to valuable resources.

Implementing an Internal Learning Content Platform

When considering what type of custom video or learning content platform to integrate into your organization, you're making a strategic decision similar to Lynda.com's approach to building one internally.

While vendor solutions may not always align with your specific business needs or user support requirements, advances in AI technology have made custom implementation more feasible. However, success depends on meticulous attention to data quality, system configuration, and ongoing maintenance. Based on my experience implementing multiple content management systems, I've organized some key considerations into five implementation phases:

1. **Configure baseline metadata standards.** Establish clear metadata standards and content evaluation criteria for your organization's business objectives. Implement regular audits to ensure the AI receives accurate signals for effective content curation decisions.

2. **Deploy an initial AI analysis of your existing content.** Begin with a comprehensive content audit to understand your current learning ecosystem. Analyze how learners discover relevant resources and identify patterns in their search behavior. These insights will highlight opportunities for AI-driven curation to streamline learning experiences. Document all content types, formats, and existing metadata structures, and establish governance guidelines for consistent content tagging and organization.

3. **Establish personalization parameters.** Define the factors driving personalization in your system, such as learner roles, skill levels, learning history, and career development paths. Configure your AI to balance personalized recommendations with organizational learning priorities.

4. **Monitor and refine recommendation algorithms.** Regularly analyze system performance and user engagement metrics to fine-tune recommendation algorithms. Adjust weights and parameters based on learner behavior and feedback to improve relevance and learning outcomes.

5. **Implement feedback loops for continuous improvement.** Develop clear success metrics focused on measurable learner outcomes. Track engagement rates, time-to-competency improvements, and learner satisfaction scores. Use these insights to refine curation strategies and enhance system effectiveness continuously.

Implementing a custom learning content platform requires careful planning and execution across these five phases. As you consider your content management strategy, it's important to think about how the learning content will adapt to changing needs.

In the next section, we'll explore integrating adaptive learning principles into your content management strategy to maximize learning effectiveness and engagement.

Content Adaptation

I remember one afternoon when I was staring at my YouTube analytics dashboard, which showed modest but respectable numbers for the latest 30-minute deep dive I'd posted on my online show, *Brainpower*, about learning content ecosystems. Putting together these live shows was a labor of love and expertise that I'm proud of, yet I'd always ponder new ways to leverage those videos into other formats.

Then, I heard about Google's NotebookLM.

Curious but skeptical, I decided to give it a shot. After all, content adaptation wasn't new to me—I'd been manually repurposing my videos into blog posts and social media snippets for years. But the process was always time consuming and (if I'm being honest) creatively draining.

Using the NotebookLM interface, I pasted the link to my video on learning content ecosystems. After tinkering with some features, I gravitated to one that got my attention: the audio overview. What happened next can only be described as AI magic. The system began processing the content, extracting not just my words but also the intent, structure, and essence of my ideas.

As I put on my headphones and pressed play, I was greeted not by my own voice, but by two engaging radio hosts—one male, one female—introducing a conversation about learning content ecosystems. They bantered naturally, asked insightful questions of one another, and took turns explaining concepts that had taken me weeks to articulate in my video.

"Today, we're exploring how organizations can build adaptive learning ecosystems that respond to both learner needs and market demands," the male host began, his tone conversational yet authoritative.

"Exactly, and this isn't just theoretical—we've got practical frameworks to share," his female co-host responded.

I sat back in my chair, mouth slightly agape. This wasn't a verbatim transcription with different voices. This was a completely reimagined presentation of my content, restructured for the audio medium, with a natural conversational flow that maintained all the key points from my video. They elaborated on my framework with the perfect balance of detail and simplicity. They used the analogies I had mentioned but developed them further. They even inserted thoughtful pauses and moments of reflection that made the content more digestible than my somewhat dense video explanation.

After listening to the entire 12-minute conversation without once reaching for the pause button (something I rarely experience with podcasts), I came across another feature labeled "interactive mode (BETA)."

I clicked it and started the podcast again. A few seconds in, I was able to join the session. The hosts stopped mid-conversation, as my microphone became enabled. I asked, "How important is a prompt when creating an AI agent?"—referring to a concept in the video.

I waited, expecting perhaps a simple response. Instead, the female host began speaking directly to me, and her co-host also joined in. Here's what they said:

> **Female host:** Oh, great question! It's so central to how agents work.
>
> **Male host:** As we were just saying, the speaker in the video really emphasizes this point.
>
> **Female host:** Yeah, he said an agent is only as good as its prompt.
>
> **Male host:** Think of it like giving instructions to a really capable assistant.
>
> **Female host:** The clearer and more specific your instructions, the better the outcome.
>
> **Male host:** Exactly. The prompt tells the agent what task to perform and how to do it.
>
> **Female host:** So, a well-designed prompt is like a blueprint for the agent's actions
>
> **Male host:** And if the prompt is vague or poorly written—
>
> **Female host:** Then, the agent might not do what you expect, right?

Male host: Precisely. It might produce irrelevant or inaccurate results.

Female host: So, even though AI is getting smarter, those initial instructions are key.

Male host: They really are the foundation for getting value out of AI agents.

Female host: Does that help clarify things for you?

Male host: Now, picking up where we were . . .

My jaw dropped. I spent the next 15 minutes in this surreal dialogue, pausing and unpausing, asking questions that ranged from clarifying basic concepts to probing the edges of some advanced ideas. Each time, the hosts responded thoughtfully, maintaining their distinct personalities and the natural cadence of radio professionals. They weren't just regurgitating information; they were expanding on it, contextualizing it, and responding to my specific questions with perfect relevance.

This wasn't just content adaptation with GenAI. This was content evolution—a responsive transformation of my ideas that could grow and develop through interaction. I had created a video, but NotebookLM had given me conversation partners who understood my subject matter as well as I did, and who were infinitely patient and available.

Reflecting on what I'd experienced, the true power of NotebookLM's AI content adaptation became clear. This wasn't just a tool for repurposing content—it was a paradigm shift in how we conceive of content and format it in the first place.

I began to see how the AI algorithms had analyzed my original content, identifying key elements such as tone, style, and target audience. Then, it had used that information to adapt my content for an entirely different purpose. This was exactly what experts had described as the full spectrum of AI-powered content adaptation:

- **Translate content.** While my content didn't need to be translated into a different language, I could see how the same algorithms could accurately translate text and even adapt it to the cultural nuances of a target audience.

- **Summarize content.** The podcast hosts had masterfully summarized complex sections of my video, generating concise explanations that made my ideas easier to consume in an audio format.
- **Repurpose content.** This was the most obvious transformation—the platform took my video script and converted it into a completely different format: a conversational podcast.
- **Personalize content.** The system had somehow understood the needs of podcast listeners versus video viewers, tailoring the information to match the expectations of an audio audience.
- **Generate different content formats.** Beyond simply converting my words to audio, the platform had restructured everything into a new format with two distinct voices, transitions, and audio-friendly pacing.
- **Automate content creation.** Most impressively, NotebookLM had generated entirely new elements—questions between hosts, conversational transitions, and even light banter—that weren't present in my original video.

For years, I had been thinking of my YouTube videos as the original content and everything else as derivatives. But NotebookLM had shown me that the true value was in the ideas themselves, not their initial format. My video wasn't the content; it was merely one expression of it. In addition, the podcast version (or the concise executive briefing, in-depth study guide, and interactive FAQ I created later) wasn't a derivative; it was another equally valid expression of the same core ideas, optimized for a different context, a different medium, and a different moment in a person's day.

This revelation transformed how I thought about my entire content strategy. What if my ideas could exist simultaneously in multiple forms, each designed for optimal impact in its native medium? What if adaptation wasn't an afterthought but a parallel process? The same can apply for the L&D content and experiences that you and your organization create.

The implications for learning content are particularly profound. Simply uploading one piece of content can lead to a transformation that allows it to be experienced through multiple modalities, supporting different learning needs. And you aren't required to manually recreate everything—a process that I know from experience is exponentially more time-consuming than the initial content creation (Figure 7-4). The hours you previously spent reformatting and rewriting can now be directed toward developing new ideas that flow effortlessly into whatever channels will reach audiences most effectively.

Figure 7-4. Content Adaptation With Multimodal AI

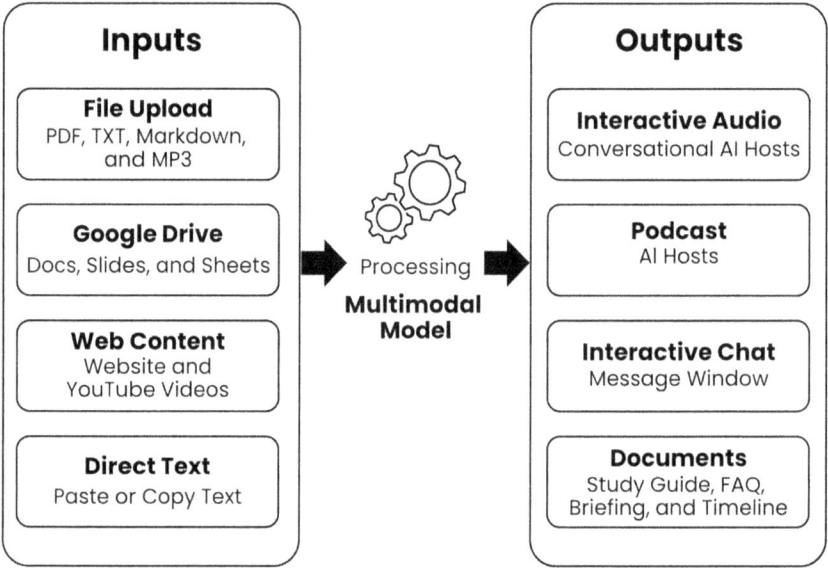

This isn't just efficiency—it is efficacy. A podcast version can reach people during their commutes who would never sit down to watch the video. A study guide can serve learners who need to engage more deeply with the frameworks. An FAQ can help practitioners quickly find answers to specific implementation questions.

Not to gaze too deeply into my crystal ball, but I'd bet these transformations will soon be available within learning content platforms and LMS and LXP environments. Imagine uploading a single piece of source content that automatically adapts into multiple formats tailored to different learning paths. A technical procedure could simultaneously exist as a step-by-step guide for methodical learners, an interactive simulation for hands-on learners, and a conceptual overview for big-picture thinkers.

LXPs could leverage this technology to dynamically adjust content based on learner behavior. A struggling learner might receive more scaffolded explanations, while an advanced learner could get accelerated content with deeper dives into complex topics. And this would all happen automatically without requiring instructional designers to manually create multiple versions.

This integration promises to democratize personalized learning at scale. Content adaptation isn't just about maximizing reach or efficiency. It's about respecting the many ways people learn and consume information, meeting them where they are and in formats that work best for their context.

That first experience of hearing my video transformed into an engaging radio conversation was a glimpse into the evolving relationship between AI and human creators, in which technology amplifies our creative instincts, leading to more personalized, relevant, and engaging content experiences.

EXERCISE

The "Content Chameleon" Challenge

Choose a piece of content you know well. It could be a blog post you wrote, a presentation you gave, a chapter from this book, or even a favorite informative video or podcast episode. (It doesn't have to be work related!) Now, imagine you have access to an advanced AI tool like the one described earlier (NotebookLM).

Follow these steps:

1. **Select your source content.** Clearly identify the piece of content you'll be working with. Note its original format (for example, a 10-minute video, a 1,500-word article, or a 45-minute webinar).

2. **Identify the core ideas.** What are the essential messages or takeaways from your source content? (Remember: The true value lies in the ideas themselves, not their initial format.)

3. **Brainstorm adaptation formats.** Thinking about the capabilities we've mentioned (such as translate, summarize, repurpose, personalize, generate different formats, or automate creation), brainstorm at least three radically different formats that you could use AI to adapt the core idea into. Push beyond simple repurposing! Some examples include:

- An interactive Q&A chatbot based on the content
- A short, conversational podcast episode between two AI hosts discussing the key points
- A personalized microlearning module that adjusts based on the user's role (such as manager versus individual contributor)
- An executive summary tailored for a specific C-suite role
- A visual infographic summarizing the key statistics or steps
- A "choose your own adventure" style learning scenario based on the concepts

4. **Describe the transformation.** For each new format you brainstormed:
   - Briefly describe what it would look and feel like.
   - Identify the target audience for this specific format.
   - Determine how this format could leverage AI adaptation capabilities (such as personalization, summarization, or generation of new elements like dialogue).
   - Identify the unique value this adapted format offers compared to the original (including accessibility, engagement, different learning preferences, or specific use cases like commuting).

5. **Reflect on the potential.** Consider the NotebookLM example in which I interacted with the AI hosts. How might adding interactivity to your adapted formats change the learning experience? What possibilities excite you most about this approach for your own work or organization?

Want more inspiration? Collaborate with an LLM (like ChatGPT or Gemini). Describe your content and ask for more adaptation ideas. Take it further by asking how these AI transformations technically work (for example, ask, "How could AI turn my article into an interactive Q&A?"). This can spark fresh concepts and demystify the AI processes involved.

Creating Avatars

It's getting more and more difficult to determine whether video and audio avatars are AI. And, by the time you're reading this book, it will be increasingly challenging to tell an AI avatar from a human.

I'm choosing to focus on video and audio avatars in this chapter because they are the most disruptive forms of AI-generated media. Unlike AI-generated text and images (and even more so than the AI-generated podcast adapted from my video), avatars can mimic human presence in a way that feels immediate and real. Their nuanced expressions, natural dialogue, and lifelike responsiveness make them far more convincing. And our moments of interaction with them reveal a fundamental truth about learning technology: Success hinges not on technological sophistication but on human connection.

Traditional video-based training faces persistent limitations. Production costs restrict personalization, fixed content becomes outdated quickly, and global deployment requires extensive localization. Meanwhile, these digital AI instructors can adapt dynamically to learner needs, speak multiple languages fluently, and maintain consistent quality across iterations. Figure 7-5 shows an example of my AI avatar speaking in Arabic (built using Synthesia).

Figure 7-5. Example of My AI Avatar

مرحبًا بكم مجددًا في الورشة!

Consider a scenario for a multinational company that needs to deliver a compliance training program in 12 distinct regional languages. In a traditional approach, this could require engaging various SMEs who are proficient in one of the target languages. Consequently, you would need each SME to record the training module separately, or write 12 transcripts for a voice professional, resulting in 12 different recordings.

In contrast, a single AI avatar is capable of delivering the same core content fluently across all 12 languages, while also adapting tone and examples for different regional contexts.

Looking forward, the use cases for AI avatars will only grow. Consider these possibilities:

- **Seamless collaboration with human facilitators.** Avatars could collaborate with human teachers and instructors to share the workload and responsibilities of teaching. Avatars could lead breakout sessions, provide individualized tutoring, or even co-teach alongside human educators. The goal would be to create a fluid and complementary partnership in which human and avatar educators work together to maximize student learning.

- **Real-time performance support.** Avatars could offer immediate and personalized feedback to learners during tasks or assessments. This might involve providing hints, suggesting resources, or adapting the difficulty of a task in real time, based on the learner's performance. This type of instant and targeted support could significantly enhance the learning experience and improve outcomes.

- **Adaptive teaching styles based on emotional recognition.** Avatars with emotional recognition technology could analyze learners' facial expressions, tone of voice, and other cues to gauge their emotional state. The avatar could then use this information to adapt its teaching style, tone, or pace to better meet the learner's needs. For example, if a learner appears frustrated, the avatar could offer encouragement or suggest a different approach. This level of personalization could foster a more supportive and engaging learning environment.

Implementing Avatar-Based Solutions

Avatar technology in learning encompasses three critical dimensions:

- **Emotional resonance** stems from sophisticated neural networks that analyze and mirror human interaction patterns. Modern audio-based avatars detect subtle engagement cues through voice patterns and interaction data and adjust their presentation style accordingly. A learner showing signs of confusion triggers more detailed explanations, while signs of mastery lead to advanced content progression. Video adaptations of these functions are forthcoming.

- **Adaptive instruction** leverages real-time processing capabilities. Avatars integrate natural language understanding with learning science principles. They respond to questions contextually, maintaining coherent dialogue threads across complex topics and creating genuinely interactive learning experiences.
- **Scalable personalization** represents the transformative potential of avatar technology. Each learner interacts with a uniquely tailored instance of the avatar instructor. Cultural backgrounds and professional contexts shape the experience. For example, a manufacturing team could receive safety instructions with industry-specific examples. Sales professionals could encounter customer interaction scenarios relevant to their markets.

Understanding these elements helps learning professionals effectively implement avatar-based solutions. Additionally, successful avatar implementation follows a structured approach. Begin with carefully selected pilot programs and focus on content areas in which personalization and interactivity drive significant value. Think about your most effective human instructors: What qualities make their teaching memorable? How might AI avatars replicate these characteristics while adding unique technological advantages?

Your insights will guide the thoughtful integration of avatar technology into your learning programs. I've created the following exercise for you to go through as you consider implementing audio or video avatars.

EXERCISE

Implementing AI Avatars in Your Learning Strategy

Once you complete these steps, you will have a clear plan for integrating AI avatars into your training programs.

Step 1. Identify Opportunities for AI Avatar Integration

Thoroughly examine your existing L&D programs to identify learning experiences that you could enhance with AI avatars. Consider which programs could benefit from personalized guidance, role-playing scenarios, simulations, or 24/7 support provided by an AI avatar.

Review your current learning programs and answer the following questions:
- What types of training do you offer? (For example, compliance training, leadership development, or customer service training.)
- Where do learners struggle most? Could an AI avatar assist with engagement, practice, or support?
- Identify at least three areas where you could use avatars to enhance learning content.

Step 2. Assess Technical Infrastructure

Evaluate your hardware and software capabilities, network bandwidth, and data storage needs to ensure seamless avatar deployment and performance.

Conduct a quick assessment of your organization's tech capabilities by answering these questions:
- Do you have the hardware and software to support AI avatars?
- Is your network bandwidth sufficient for real-time avatar interaction?
- Who in your IT department can help evaluate technical feasibility?

Step 3. Build a Business Case

To secure buy-in and resources for AI avatar implementation, develop a strong business case outlining potential benefits and ROI. Use concrete metrics (such as improved learner engagement, knowledge retention, skill development, and performance outcomes) to demonstrate the value of avatar integration.

Draft a one-paragraph justification for incorporating AI avatars into your learning programs. Use these questions to get started:
- What problem will AI avatars solve?
- How will you measure success? (For example, increased engagement, faster training completion, or improved retention.)
- What ROI metrics will resonate with leadership?

Step 4. Design a Pilot Program

Before a full-scale implementation, launch a pilot program to test the effectiveness of AI avatars in your specific learning environment. Define clear success criteria and KPIs to measure how the avatars influence learner outcomes and satisfaction. Pilot programs that demonstrate the value and feasibility of AI avatars will foster buy-in from stakeholders, paving the way for wider integration within the organization.

To run a small-scale test before full implementation, start by answering these questions:

- Which learning module or audience will you test first?
- What are the KPIs? (For example, learner feedback or knowledge retention scores.)
- What will success look like?

Step 5. Develop Avatar Usage Guidelines
Establish clear guidelines and best practices for using AI avatars in your learning programs. Make sure the avatar's role, interactions, and content align with your learning strategy and objectives. Your avatar selection should also reflect your organization's values.

To define the role and personality of your AI avatar, start by answering these questions:

- What tone and style should the AI avatar have? (For example, should it be formal or conversational?)
- Should it have a specific look to match your brand?
- How should it interact with learners?

Step 6. Plan for Ongoing Evaluation and Improvement
Continuously monitor and evaluate the effectiveness of your AI avatar implementation. Gather feedback from learners and stakeholders to identify areas for improvement and iterate your approach. Regularly update and refine your avatar usage guidelines to remain relevant and effective.

Create a checklist for monitoring avatar performance using these questions:

- How often will you gather learner feedback?
- Who will be responsible for updates and improvements?
- What will you do if learners resist or disengage?

Bringing AI avatars into your learning programs might feel like a big step, but by breaking it down into these actionable exercises, you're already on your way.

The key is to identify where avatars can add the most value, test in a controlled setting, and refine as you go. Remember, technology should enhance learning, not complicate it. Your learners should feel more engaged, supported, and empowered with AI avatars in the mix. So, take it one step at a time, stay open to feedback, and have fun exploring the possibilities. You've got this!

AI Avatar Quick Tips!

AI avatar development is still in its nascent stage at the time of writing this book, so I'll leave you with you some very high-level tips to approach the process the right way, from script preparation to sharing and distribution.

To prepare your script:

- Keep language simple, direct, and focused on viewer value.
- Structure your script with a clear introduction, main content, and a conclusion.
- Use punctuation strategically for pacing (including commas for short pauses).
- Aim for 60 to 120 seconds for microvideos, and up to 4 to 5 minutes for tutorials.

To choose avatars:

- Browse through diverse AI avatar options to find the right fit.
- Select avatars that match your content's tone and purpose.
- Consider creating custom avatars that match your brand or team.

To enhance engagement for video avatars:

- Explore animation options for more dynamic presentations.
- Add animated icons instead of static ones.
- Synchronize animations with spoken words.
- Add text overlays to highlight key points.
- Include captions for accessibility and better comprehension.

To improve your video avatar's background:

- Customize backgrounds with stock media or your own uploads.
- Choose appropriate layout formats, such as landscape for desktop and portrait for social.
- Add screen recordings for tutorials and demonstrations.

To record your custom avatar:

- Film in a quiet space with good lighting and a simple background.
- Include different modes in your recording, such as "listening mode" (silent with engaged expressions), "talking mode" (clear speaking), and "idling mode" (neutral with occasional nodding).
- Maintain consistent body position while you're recording.
- Use higher-quality cameras for better avatar results.

To share and distribute your avatar:

- Generate shareable links or embed codes for websites.
- Use embedded codes to ensure any future video updates appear automatically.
- Enable team collaboration with feedback options.
- Support downloading with or without captions, depending on platform needs.

ᎰᎰᎰ

The most advanced AI avatar technology is only valuable if it effectively supports learners' needs and helps them learn, grow, and perform better in their roles. Always prioritize the needs of your learners and let technology serve those needs rather than the other way around. By strategically focusing on the learner experience and leveraging AI avatars, you can create a more human, adaptive, and engaging learning environment that empowers individuals to succeed.

Conclusion

Our exploration of AI in learning reveals transformative potential and practical challenges. Technology promises personalized learning at scale through intelligent content creation, strategic curation, and avatar-driven instruction. Success requires thoughtful implementation guided by clear ethical principles. The tools augment human expertise rather than replace it.

This vision requires careful cultivation, and our role as L&D professionals is growing more crucial. We can balance technological capability with human insight and ensure learning experiences remain authentic and effective. The tools change, but our core mission endures: facilitating meaningful professional growth and development.

Over the next four chapters, I'll take you along a journey for putting AI to use in L&D and content development effectively, efficiently, and ethically—from designing prompts to building AI-powered workflows to setting up autonomous agents and deploying conversational AI.

CHAPTER 8

Prompt Design

In This Chapter
- Fundamental prompt design principles
- Techniques for structuring effective prompts and methods for evaluating prompt results
- Ways to implement prompt design in various instructional design workflows, from performance consulting to content creation

Let's start with a prompt exercise. Open your favorite large language model (LLM), such as ChatGPT, Google's Gemini, Microsoft's Copilot, or Grok. Type the following prompt into the message window and send it to the model:

> Create learning objectives on customer service skills for retail associates.

What response did you get? Does it meet or exceed your expectations?

The learning objectives may be generic and incomplete depending on the model you used. This is directly related to the quality of the prompt and the training data in the model.

Remember your first attempt at writing learning objectives? Your careful consideration of action verbs, the precise measurement criteria, and the alignment with business goals. Now, imagine asking an AI tool to write those objectives. Would it capture the nuanced understanding of human learning that you've developed over years of practice? The answer might surprise you.

A participant shared her experience at one of my recent AI workshops: "I used to spend hours writing learning objectives for our management training programs. The process was meticulous. Each objective required careful consideration of measurable outcomes, performance indicators, and alignment with business goals." She paused, and then smiled. "Last month," she continued, "I learned about prompt design. With a well-crafted prompt, I was able to generate a complete set of learning objectives in minutes."

The AI tool understood the context, suggested innovative measurement approaches, and identified potential learning gaps. But here's the key: Her expertise guided the LLM. Because of her years of instructional design experience, she knew exactly what to ask for. Prompt design just amplified her capabilities—and it can do the same for you.

Let's try creating learning objectives again, but using a prompt with a very specific request:

> As an instructional designer specializing in retail customer service, your task is to develop a set of learning objectives using the SMART framework; create clear, measurable, and student-centered learning objectives. Incorporate appropriate Bloom's Taxonomy action verbs, ensuring that each objective explicitly states the expected outcomes in areas such as effective communication, problem resolution, and customer engagement, and aligns course content with assessment methods in a way that is specific, measurable, achievable, result-oriented, and time-bound.

What response did you get this time? Are these learning objectives clear and specific? Keep in mind: The words you use in your prompt directly affect the quality of the AI tool's response.

L&D professionals who master prompt design can create personalized learning experiences at scale, generate adaptive content in real time, and build sophisticated assessment frameworks in minutes. And the stakes are high: Organizations investing in AI-powered learning solutions need L&D professionals to craft precise, effective prompts that drive meaningful learning outcomes. This chapter provides the framework, strategies, and practical applications to bridge the gap between traditional instructional design and AI-enhanced learning development. By the end, you will be able to confidently design and implement effective AI prompts for learning applications.

Let's start by exploring how prompt design is reshaping the future of organizational learning.

How Do Large Language Models and Prompts Work?

Prompt design, or prompt engineering, is a relatively new discipline focused on crafting and refining input prompts to effectively use LLMs for various applications and research, including designing and developing L&D experiences. It involves understanding the strengths and weaknesses of different LLMs, selecting the most appropriate model for a given task, and continuously evaluating and refining prompts to optimize their performance.

I prefer the term *prompt design* over *prompt engineering* because it's more approachable to individuals who may think that prompting is complex or requires a programming background. It is neither. Prompts can be long or have programmatic qualities, but anyone can create an effective prompt as long as they have proper frameworks and tactics.

When you submit a prompt to an LLM, the model will give you a response like the examples in Figure 8-1.

Figure 8-1. Example LLM Prompt

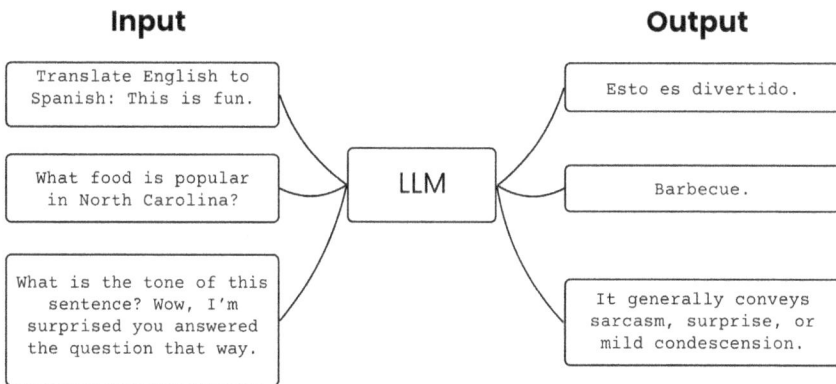

Input		Output
Translate English to Spanish: This is fun.	LLM	Esto es divertido.
What food is popular in North Carolina?		Barbecue.
What is the tone of this sentence? Wow, I'm surprised you answered the question that way.		It generally conveys sarcasm, surprise, or mild condescension.

Before we get into best practices for prompt design, let's review a foundational question: How the heck does this work?

When an LLM receives a prompt, it doesn't "understand" the text in a human sense. Instead, it processes the prompt through layers of learned parameters to predict the most likely words based on the model's training data inside a vector database.

Figure 8-2 shows an example of what happens when you submit the same question ("What is the capital of the state of New York?") to an LLM and a Google search.

Figure 8-2. LLM vs. Google Search

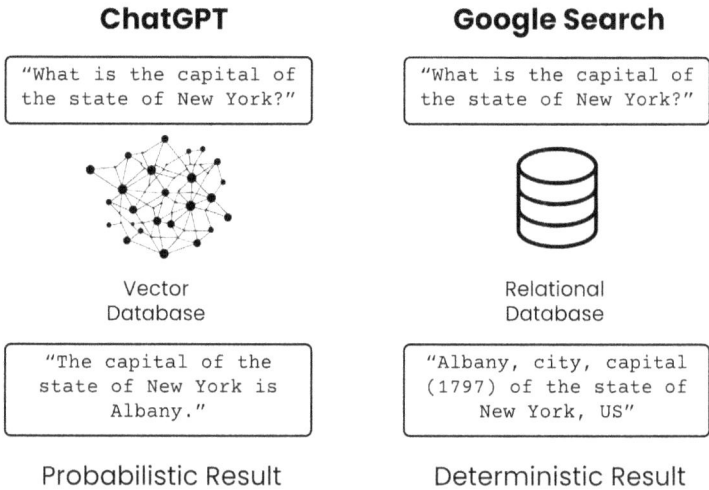

ChatGPT	Google Search
"What is the capital of the state of New York?"	"What is the capital of the state of New York?"
Vector Database	Relational Database
"The capital of the state of New York is Albany."	"Albany, city, capital (1797) of the state of New York, US"
Probabilistic Result	Deterministic Result

The result from the LLM, "The capital of the state of New York is Albany," is all based on probability. If you ask an LLM the same question three times in a row, you could get any of the following results:

- The state capital of New York is located in Albany, New York.
- The state capital of New York is located in Albany.
- The state capital of New York is Albany.

When you perform a Google search, the results are based on information collected from the internet and stored in a database (in this case, text from the Britannica.com website).

This prediction mechanism is why prompt design is powerful and nuanced. An LLM responds to the explicit instructions, implicit patterns, contextual cues, and structural elements within your prompt. This includes multimodal models that produce voice, music, images, and video.

LLM Probability

Using your favorite LLM, try the following prompt:

What is the capital of New York?

What result did you get? Try running the same prompt a few more times. Did the wording of your results change?

Natural Language Processing (NLP) Basics

Before diving into the specifics of prompt design, it's essential to understand the role natural language processing (NLP) plays in LLMs, which have revolutionized how we interact with AI.

NLP is a branch of AI that focuses on enabling computers to understand, interpret, and generate human language. Here are some examples:

- The autocorrect function in text messaging
- Talking to a virtual assistant like Siri or Google Assistant
- Spell check and grammar correct in Microsoft Word, Google Docs, or Grammarly
- Automated customer service phone support

LLMs use several core NLP processes to understand and generate human-like text, making them capable of various tasks, such as translation, summarization, and chatbot conversations (Figure 8-3). These include :

- **Syntactic parsing,** which involves breaking down sentences into their grammatical components (such as nouns, verbs, and adjectives) to understand the syntactic structure of the text.
- **Semantic analysis,** which goes beyond simply identifying words to understand their meaning and relationships within the text, allowing LLMs to interpret context, idioms, and humor.

Figure 8-3. Syntactic Parsing vs. Semantic Analysis

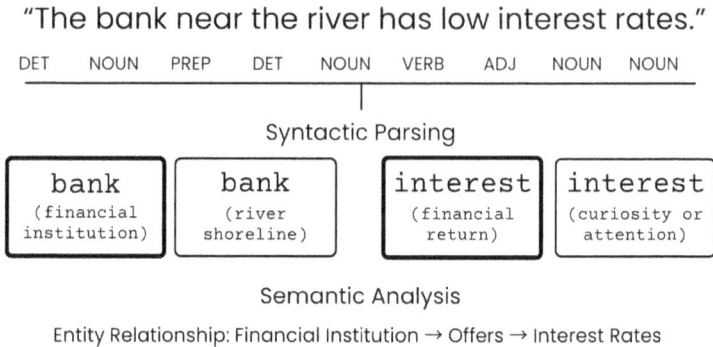

"The bank near the river has low interest rates."

| DET | NOUN | PREP | DET | NOUN | VERB | ADJ | NOUN | NOUN |

Syntactic Parsing

bank	bank	interest	interest
(financial institution)	(river shoreline)	(financial return)	(curiosity or attention)

Semantic Analysis

Entity Relationship: Financial Institution → Offers → Interest Rates

While LLMs like ChatGPT and Gemini represent significant advancements in NLP, it's important to distinguish between these concepts. Traditional NLP systems—like text autocorrect or grammar checkers—rely on explicit rules and linguistic knowledge to process language. They excel in tasks with clear structures, like identifying parts of speech or extracting specific information. However, they may struggle with ambiguity and complex contexts.

In contrast, LLMs learn from massive datasets of text and code, enabling them to handle more nuanced and complex language tasks. They are particularly adept at generating human-like text and can adapt to various language styles and formats. LLMs excel at predicting the next word in a sequence, allowing them to generate coherent and contextually relevant text.

Large Language Model Mechanics

I want to take a moment to briefly walk you through how a prompt eventually becomes a result. (I don't have enough space in this book to review this process's intricate details, and there's also a lot of math involved, so I will skip that too. You can thank me later.)

For this example, I'll use my favorite prompt, which I mentioned in the introduction. I've been using this prompt as a control statement ever since the release of ChatGPT 3.5 in 2022. Whenever a new model is released, I'll input this prompt:

How do I cook a smoked potato salad?

Yep. That's it. Nothing complex. By maintaining simplicity, I can see the nuances and the quality of the outputs for each model. Figure 8-4 breaks down what happens when I enter this prompt in the message window and hit the send button.

Figure 8-4. Smoked Potato Salad Example Prompt

1	Enter the Prompt	`How do I cook a smoked potato salad?`
2	Text Preprocessing	`how do i cook a smoked potato salad`
3	Tokenization	`["how," "do," "i," "cook," "a," "smoked," "potato," "salad"]`
4	Encoding (Embedding and Positional Encoding)	`[[0.25, 0.73, 0.11], [0.81, 0.64, 0.95], ...]`
5	Forward Pass and Self-Attention	`"how" → Low "cook" → High "smoked" → Medium "potato salad" → High`
6	Decoding and Text Generation	`"To make smoked potato salad, first smoke the potatoes, and then mix them with mayonnaise and seasonings."`
7	Postprocessing	`"To make a delicious smoked potato salad, first smoke the potatoes, and then mix them with mayonnaise, mustard, and seasoning for flavor."`

Here's the step-by-step process in more detail:

1. **Enter the prompt** into the message window and send it to the model.
2. **Text preprocessing.** The model cleans the input text by converting it to lowercase, removing unnecessary punctuation, and normalizing its format.
3. **Tokenization.** The cleaned text is broken down into smaller units, such as words or subwords, to prepare it for processing.
4. **Encoding (embedding and positional encoding).** Each token is converted into a numerical vector, and positional encoding is applied to retain word order information.
5. **Forward pass and self-attention.** The numerical representations of the words are processed through multiple neural network layers to detect patterns and relationships. The model then assigns importance to different words in the sentence, ensuring it understands contextual relationships.

6. **Decoding and text generation.** The model predicts the next words based on the learned patterns and constructs a meaningful response.
7. **Postprocessing.** The generated response is cleaned and refined for better readability, grammar, and formatting.

Isn't that a wild process? As you can see, this is very different from pulling a record from a database. Each word is selected based on math and probability.

Large Language Model Characteristics

LLMs exhibit a unique set of characteristics. When it interprets words, the model leverages several functions, including:

- **Context sensitivity.** LLMs interpret new information in relation to the preceding text, making the sequence and structure of information critical.
  - *Example:* If you begin a prompt with "You are an instructional designer with 20 years of experience," all words following this statement will be influenced by "instructional designer" and "20 years of experience."
- **Pattern recognition.** These systems identify and replicate patterns in style, format, and reasoning from the examples provided.
  - *Example:* In the body of your prompt, give examples of the result you are looking for. This could be a learning objective, multiple-choice question, or the introduction to a video script. By providing examples of your output format in your prompt or patterns of reasoning, you can guide an LLM to the desired result.
- **Prior knowledge activation.** Prompts can trigger specific knowledge domains that are embedded in the model's training data.
  - *Example:* Foundation models like ChatGPT, Gemini, Claude, and Grok have an immense amount of training data. The information typically represents any large domain of knowledge, such as how to make chocolate chip cookies, fix a leaky faucet, or have a difficult conversation with an employee. Odds are, if you ask the foundation model about a widely known topic, it will respond with the correct information most of the time.

- **Generalization capabilities.** Models can apply learned concepts to new scenarios that are not explicitly covered in training.
  - *Example:* Imagine you were just hired and are now tasked with developing an employee training program for an industry you know little about, such as a biotech lab specializing in gene editing. You can use the following prompt: "Create a structured training program for onboarding new lab technicians in a gene-editing biotech company." The model will generalize the output based on its knowledge of instructional design principles, training program structures, basic biology and lab procedures, and compliance and safety regulations.

By understanding these capabilities, you can choose specific tasks for you and the AI model to collaborate on and design focused prompts that leverage these functions. For instance, if you don't have access to a SME, but the knowledge or skills are general or public facing, you can leverage a model to be the SME for you. You will eventually need to speak with a human SME to gather nuances that aren't in the model's training data, but this allows you to move the project forward.

Understanding Limitations

While LLMs offer powerful collaboration and knowledge generation capabilities, recognizing their boundaries is equally important. Even as you leverage these models as stand-in subject matter experts or collaborative partners, understanding their limitations will help you design more effective prompts and set appropriate expectations for their outputs.

Let's examine the key constraints that affect prompt design strategy:

- **Catastrophic forgetting.** LLMs may forget previously learned information while fine-tuning for new tasks.
  - *Example:* A model trained to write medical content might lose its ability to generate the accurate legal analysis that it could previously perform. Well-designed prompts can include relevant domain knowledge to help the model access both skill sets.
- **Limited memory and context window constraints.** These technical limitations affect how much information an LLM can process at once.

- *Example:* When analyzing a 60-page document, the model may forget details from earlier pages when responding about later sections. Prompts that include strategic summarization or chunking techniques help manage these constraints.
- **Challenges with numerical data analysis.** LLMs are primarily trained on text data and may struggle with numerical predictions.
  - *Example:* An LLM asked to forecast sales trends might generate plausible-sounding but mathematically inaccurate projections. Prompts that explicitly request step-by-step calculations or specific formatting of numerical outputs can improve accuracy. (Note: Reasoning models that excel at math and programming are now accessible in the marketplace and will eventually remove this limitation altogether.)
- **Need for continuous monitoring.** LLM outputs require regular evaluation to ensure reliability.
  - *Example:* A chatbot deployed for customer service might gradually drift in tone or accuracy over time. Implementing evaluation prompts that check outputs against benchmarks helps maintain quality.

Foundations of Prompt Design

Now that you understand how an LLM works, as well as its superpowers and limitations, let's discuss some best practices to keep in mind when designing a prompt:

- **Be clear, concise, and specific in your language.** Avoid ambiguity and provide as much detail as possible.
- **Use a natural and conversational tone.** The interaction will be more intuitive and user-friendly.
- **Provide context and background information.** This helps the AI model understand the task and generate more relevant responses.
- **Use complete sentences.** The AI engine will better comprehend the input and generate more coherent responses.
- **Avoid using leading or biased language.** Ensure that your prompts are neutral and objective.

- **Acknowledge model limitations.** Be aware of the AI model's capabilities and limitations to avoid unrealistic expectations.
- **Test and iterate.** Refine your prompts based on the AI model's responses and user feedback.

Take a moment to review Table 8-1, which compares the language we used in the first and second learning objective prompts at the beginning of this chapter. Clear language, context, and complete sentences make a considerable difference in the quality of your results.

Table 8-1. Prompt Comparison

Generic	Clear Language and Context
Create learning objectives on customer service skills for retail associates.	As an instructional designer specializing in retail customer service, your task is to develop a set of learning objectives using the SMART framework; create clear, measurable, and student-centered learning objectives. Incorporate appropriate Bloom's Taxonomy action verbs, ensuring that each objective explicitly states the expected outcomes in areas such as effective communication, problem resolution, and customer engagement, and aligns course content with assessment methods in a way that is specific, measurable, achievable, result-oriented, and time-bound.

In addition to using straightforward, concise language, the second prompt illustrates a conversational tone, includes background information, uses complete sentences, and is specific about the output format.

The Evolution of Prompt Design

Prompt design has evolved dramatically since the release of ChatGPT 3.5 in November 2022. Back then, very few professionals had a grasp on how to design effective prompts. Since then, we've witnessed a maturation in the process:

- **Early phase**—simple freeform instructions or questions
- **Current phase**—structured prompts, templates, and sophisticated techniques
- **Emerging phase**—automated prompt optimization

Automated prompt optimization represents a significant advancement in prompt design. When you submit a prompt to a model, a prompt optimization algorithm automatically refines it. These systems reduce the need for manual prompt design, which has implications for how we might interact with AI systems in the future.

Image generation platforms, like DALL-E, are a practical example. Text-based models like ChatGPT automatically reconfigure user prompts with additional descriptive details to improve output quality when creating images.

In the example in Figure 8-5, ChatGPT automatically updated the initial image prompt with details like "rustic bowl," "golden-brown," and "warm and inviting" to generate a better-looking image.

Figure 8-5. Example of Automated Prompt Optimization

Initial Image Prompt	Automated Prompt Optimization	Generated Image
A delicious smoked potato salad.	A delicious smoked potato salad served in a rustic bowl. The dish features golden-brown smoked potatoes mixed with creamy dressing, fresh herbs, and crispy bacon bits. Garnished with paprika and ground black pepper. The background is warm and inviting, with a wooden table and soft natural lighting.	

While automated prompt optimization functions are increasingly common, understanding how to craft effective prompts will give you more precise control over your AI interactions. The automated systems provide a foundation, but the nuanced adjustments—including specific word choices, structural elements, and contextual framing—make all the difference in output quality. Think of it like photography: Automatic settings work for casual snapshots, but professionals manually adjust the aperture, shutter speed, and composition to achieve their vision.

As we move forward, we'll explore how small, intentional adjustments to your prompting approach can translate to substantial improvements in AI-generated content. In the next section, we'll discuss freeform prompting, which follows simple yet powerful patterns. Understanding these templates dramatically enhances your results, allowing you to direct AI systems with remarkable precision rather than relying solely on automated systems to interpret your needs.

Freeform Prompts

Freeform prompts directly interact with LLMs, allowing you to input natural language instructions or questions. They are direct statements you make to the model as if you are having a conversation. Experimenting with different freeform prompts unlocks the model's full potential for creating engaging and compelling learning experiences.

These prompts offer flexibility and can be used for many tasks, including generating creative text formats, brainstorming ideas, and engaging in open-ended conversations. I use freeform prompts to verify whether an LLM can complete a task and determine the initial quality of the result. For most simple tasks, you can get away with using a freeform prompt, like composing an email or generating a summarization. However, these prompts can also produce unpredictable or irrelevant outputs, requiring careful refinement and iteration. This is often the result of prompts with incorrect word choice, a lack of details, or context.

EXERCISE

Freeform Prompts

Here are a few freeform prompts you can try. (You can also find them on the book's website, joshcavalier.ai/ApplyingAIBook.) Replace the words in [*ALL CAPS*] with your content. Examine the quality of the results as you test them. Would you be able to use the information as is? Are edits needed, or is the output unusable?

Create a brand-new chat for each prompt. If you use these prompts in the same conversation, the words you've used and the model's results will influence the probability of words it chooses in the remainder of the conversation.

Generate training materials:

Create a comprehensive training module for [*TOPIC*]. Include learning objectives, interactive exercises, and a knowledge check at the end.

Design learning assessments:

Develop a 10-question multiple-choice quiz to assess knowledge of [*TOPIC*]. Provide an answer key with explanations for each correct answer.

Personalize learning paths:

Based on the learner's profile [*LIST SKILLS, INTERESTS, AND GOALS*], suggest a personalized learning path with relevant courses, resources, and activities.

Facilitate role-playing scenarios:

Simulate a conversation between a manager and an employee who needs to improve their [*SKILL*]. Provide feedback and suggestions for improvement.

Generate creative content:

Write a short story about a character who learns a valuable lesson about [*TOPIC*]. Use this story to illustrate its importance in the workplace.

What did you notice about the quality of the results? They are a start, but to create optimal results, you should give the model more details in each prompt.

It's time to take our freeform prompts to the next level by leveraging a simple framework that adds details. We will focus on three key elements in our prompt: role, task, and details. Table 8-2 breaks down the customer service prompt from the beginning of this chapter by element.

Table 8-2. Role, Task, and Details

Role	As an instructional designer specializing in retail customer service,
Task	Your task is to develop a set of learning objectives using the SMART framework;
Details	Create clear, measurable, and student-centered learning objectives. Incorporate appropriate Bloom's Taxonomy action verbs, ensuring that each objective explicitly states the expected outcomes in areas such as effective communication, problem resolution, and customer engagement, and aligns course content with assessment methods in a way that is specific, measurable, achievable, result-oriented, and time-bound.

Role

By assigning a specific role to the model, such as an "instructional designer specializing in retail customer service," the prompt guides the platform to choose words based on this relevant expertise. LLMs generate better responses when they understand the intended perspective, tone, and depth required.

Assigning a role improves outputs when:

- Expertise is required (for example, instructional design, legal writing, or medical explanations).
- A specific tone or professional approach is needed.
- Different viewpoints would lead to different recommendations (for example, a customer versus a business owner).

Without a defined role, the model may provide a more general or less nuanced response.

Task

Stating the task explicitly (such as "develop a set of learning objectives using the SMART framework") gives the LLM a precise purpose. Without a well-defined task, the model may provide broad or unrelated responses.

Stating the task improves outputs when:

- A specific outcome is needed (for example, a list, a structured framework, or step-by-step instructions).
- The model could otherwise generate something too general or unfocused.
- Following a structured methodology (like SMART goals or Bloom's Taxonomy) is crucial for quality output.

Vague tasks like "help with learning objectives" might lead to generic, loosely structured suggestions.

Details

Adding details refines the model's output by incorporating necessary constraints and guidelines. In the example prompt, specifying "measurable and student-centered learning objectives," "Bloom's Taxonomy action verbs," key focus areas such as "communication" and "problem resolution," and assessment alignment ensures relevance and completeness.

Including details improves outputs when:

- Precision is required (for example, defining clear learning outcomes instead of broad suggestions).
- Using frameworks that require specific structures (such as SMART goals or Bloom's Taxonomy).
- Ensuring responses align with real-world application (like training retail employees).

Without these detailed constraints, the model might generate outputs that lack depth, structure, or specificity.

ʕʕʕ

LLMs perform best if the prompts are structured with a role, a clearly defined task, and detailed constraints. This approach minimizes ambiguity, aligns responses with user expectations, and ensures the output is accurate, relevant, and actionable.

When working with LLMs, applying these elements strategically can make the difference between a generic response and an expert-level answer.

EXERCISE

Role, Task, and Details

I've updated the sample freeform prompts from the previous exercise with a role, a clear task, and details. Try them out and see how the results change. Remember, for now, create a new conversation with each prompt.

Generate training materials:

As an experienced instructional designer specializing in corporate training, your task is to develop a comprehensive training module for [TOPIC] that enhances learner engagement and retention. The module should include clearly defined learning objectives using Bloom's Taxonomy action verbs to ensure measurable outcomes. It should also incorporate interactive exercises that reinforce key concepts and encourage active participation. At the end, include a knowledge check with multiple-choice, short-answer, or scenario-based questions to assess comprehension. Ensure the content aligns with instructional design best practices, making it engaging and effective for learners.

Design learning assessments:

As an assessment designer focused on evaluating learner comprehension effectively, your task is to create a 10-question multiple-choice quiz to assess knowledge of [TOPIC]. Each question should be clear, unbiased, and aligned with the learning objectives, ensuring that it accurately measures understanding. The quiz should include plausible distractors to prevent guesswork and truly test comprehension. Additionally, provide a detailed answer key explaining why each correct answer is correct and clarifying common misconceptions. The assessment should fairly represent the breadth of the topic, ensuring that learners are thoroughly evaluated.

Personalize learning paths:

As a learning consultant specializing in adaptive education strategies, your task is to design a personalized learning path tailored to a learner's [LIST SKILLS, INTERESTS, AND GOALS]. The learning path should recommend courses relevant to the learner's skill level and career aspirations, ensuring an optimal progression. Include supplementary resources, such as articles, videos, or hands-on projects, to reinforce learning. Additionally, integrate interactive activities or assessments that provide feedback and measure progress. The learning path should be adaptive, catering to different learning styles and needs, ensuring an effective and engaging learning experience.

Facilitate role-playing scenarios:

As a corporate training facilitator specializing in soft skills development, your task is to simulate a realistic conversation between a manager and an employee who needs to improve their [SKILL]. The scenario should include a workplace context that frames the challenge being addressed. Present a realistic dialogue that captures the dynamics between the manager and employee, reflecting authentic challenges and emotions. The manager should provide constructive feedback with specific, actionable suggestions for improvement. Conclude with a reflection section that allows learners to analyze the interaction and consider alternative approaches. This exercise should encourage professional growth and enhance communication skills.

Generate creative content:

As a workplace storyteller and learning designer, your task is to write a short story about a character who learns a valuable lesson about [TOPIC], demonstrating its importance in a professional setting. The story should feature a relatable protagonist facing a workplace challenge that requires growth or adaptation. Show the character's journey, including struggles, realizations, and the application of newly acquired knowledge. The narrative should highlight the lesson learned and its impact on workplace behavior or success. Make the story engaging and thought-provoking, encouraging readers to reflect on their own experiences and apply the lesson in their professional lives.

Take a moment to compare the results of the first version of the prompt with the second version, which included the role, task, and details.

For some results, it may be hard to discern the differences in quality. For example, the "generate creative content" prompt produces stories; the second prompt guides the model to a specific story format, whereas the first may give you different story structures each time you run the prompt.

This is where your expertise comes in. Validating the quality of your results and refining your prompts dramatically increases your productivity. It's interesting to see how the quality of the results begins to increase as you guide the large language model with additional details. However, depending on the amount of information you add to the prompt, it may become unwieldy to read, edit, and make proper word choices. This leads us to the creation of structured prompts.

Structured Prompts

Unlike freeform prompts, structured prompts use predefined templates or formats to guide an LLM's response. These templates often include specific instructions, context, or examples to help the model understand the desired output.

Structured prompts offer several advantages, including:

- **Improved accuracy.** By providing clear words, instructions, and context, structured prompts produce more accurate and relevant responses.
- **Consistency.** Templates ensure prompt structure and content consistency, leading to more predictable outputs.
- **Reusability.** Templates can be reused for similar tasks, saving time and effort in prompt creation.

Let's explore how to transform a freeform prompt into a structured one. First, here's a simple freeform prompt to create a video script:

Create an educational video script on [*TOPIC*].

Due to the lack of details in the prompt, the results will contain various script structures and an inconsistent tone of voice, which likely won't produce the best example for the topic.

Next, let's add a role, task, and details to the prompt.

As a skilled instructional designer and scriptwriter, your task is to create a detailed educational video script on [*TOPIC*] that is engaging, informative, and well-structured. The script should include a clear introduction that captures the audience's attention and outlines key learning objectives. The main content should be structured logically, using concise explanations, real-world examples, and storytelling or scenario-based learning, if applicable. Ensure that the tone is appropriate for the professional target audience. Conclude with a summary reinforcing key takeaways and, if relevant, include a call to action for further learning or reflection.

This prompt will produce an educational video script with more details and a consistent structure. However, as the prompt increases in size, it becomes laborious to parse out keywords, instructions, or other information that may need to be updated as you experiment.

Note: Two roles are mentioned at the beginning of this prompt (instructional designer and scriptwriter). This prompt technique is called *role stacking*. Using more than one role increases the probability that related words associated with these roles will appear in the results.

Here's an example of my favorite template for a structured prompt that will create that same educational video script. When you try this prompt, replace the [*TOPIC*] and [*AUDIENCE DETAILS*] with your information. (Note: After you replace [*TOPIC*], the word TOPIC appears in ALL CAPS throughout the rest of the prompt. *TOPIC* is a prompt variable. The value you assign at the top of the prompt is used throughout the rest of the prompt.) Enter the following in your LLM of choice:

Task: Create a compelling educational video script.

TOPIC = [*TOPIC*]

Role: You are an expert instructional designer and scriptwriter specializing in video-based learning experiences. Your tone is friendly and inspiring.

Audience: The target audience consists of [*AUDIENCE DETAILS*], ensuring the content is tailored to their level of expertise and learning needs.

Audience = Viewer.

Create:

Definitions:
- **Focusing objective:** A statement presented to the viewer before encountering the topic, designed to highlight the most important aspects of the subject. This objective helps create an emotional connection, capturing attention and setting the stage for deeper engagement.
- **Performance objective:** A statement presented to the viewer before encountering the topic, outlining the key competencies or skills they will acquire. This objective clarifies what the Viewer should be able to do or understand by the end of the video, ensuring a measurable learning outcome.

Format:
- **Emotional pull:** Using a Focusing Objective, write a strong hook to immediately grab the Viewer's attention and emphasize why the TOPIC matters.
- **Prime:** Using a Performance Objective, provide an engaging overview of the TOPIC, highlighting the key transformation or knowledge the Viewer will gain by watching the video.

- **Content:** Deliver clear instructions on the TOPIC, breaking down key concepts in a structured, easy-to-follow manner. Incorporate real-world examples, practical applications, and engaging story-telling elements to enhance understanding.
- **Reflection:** Summarize the key takeaways from the TOPIC, reinforcing the main learning points.
- **Emotional push:** End with a compelling call to action or inspirational message, encouraging the Viewer to apply what they've learned or take the next step in their learning journey.

Intent: The goal of this script is to educate, engage, and inspire the audience while ensuring the message is clear, actionable, and impactful. The script should be for voiceover narration, making it effective for an engaging video learning experience. Avoid bullet points and maintain narration.

This prompt is a very different way to create an educational video script using an LLM! It leverages a prompt framework called TRACI, which stands for:

- **Task**—defines what needs to be done. It provides clear instructions on the prompt's goal or objective.
- **Role**—identifies who is performing the task. This helps guide the AI model's response style, expertise, and perspective (for example, instructional designer or learning consultant).
- **Audience**—specifies who the content is for. Understanding the target audience ensures the output is relevant, appropriately detailed, and engaging.
- **Create**—outlines how the task should be executed. This section includes the structured guidance, formats, and necessary elements that must be included in the output.
- **Intent**—clarifies why the task is important. It ensures that the content aligns with the overall purpose—whether that's to educate, inspire, inform, or engage.

Based on my experimentation with various prompt frameworks, I've found that TRACI is one of the best for L&D professionals because it provides a structured, outcome-driven approach to content creation. It ensures clarity and precision by clearly defining the task, role, and audience, preventing vague or generic outputs. It aligns content with learning goals and promotes measurable outcomes. With TRACI, you can work with large language models to create effective, structured, and engaging learning experiences that maximize retention and application.

EXERCISE

Freeform to Structured Prompt

Now, it's your turn to create a structured prompt. Create a freeform prompt based on a daily task you perform at work. Start simple:

1. Ask the LLM to help you complete the task.
2. Add your role and task details to your prompt. Start a new conversation with your LLM of choice and try the prompt with the additional details.
3. Finally, convert this prompt into a TRACI prompt by:
   - Bringing the task to the top of the prompt
   - Defining the role of the model
   - Adding any audience information
   - Placing all your task details into the create section
   - Including the purpose of the prompt in the intent section

Verify the quality of the results for each prompt. If it performs well, save it in a Word document or Google Docs file. In the next chapter, I will review the steps for creating a prompt library where you can store your high-impact prompts.

Prompt Design Techniques

Effective prompt design employs various approaches. Some techniques (like the TRACI framework) excel at producing consistent, standardized results, while others guide the model through analytical reasoning processes.

The techniques described in this section will help you design prompts that yield more precise, relevant, and effective learning outcomes for your training programs and educational initiatives. You can employ several techniques together to enhance the effectiveness of your prompts. Try each one and examine the outputs from your preferred model.

Zero-Shot Prompting

Zero-shot prompting involves directly posing questions or tasks to an LLM without including specific examples or instructions. The freeform prompts that only contained the task you attempted earlier in this chapter are all zero-shot prompts. While this technique may have limitations regarding response format and accuracy, it can still yield coherent and relevant answers for straightforward L&D needs.

Here's an example of a zero-shot prompt:

> What are the key components of an effective onboarding program for remote employees?

Few-Shot Prompting

Providing an LLM with a few examples of the desired output can help it understand the task and generate similar responses. This technique is particularly valuable when designing assessment questions or creating consistent training materials across different modules. Note that the last "assessment suggestion" is left blank. The two prior examples help the LLM complete the answer.

Here's an example of a few-shot prompt:

> **Instruction:** Based on the learning goal or objective provided, suggest a relevant assessment strategy that's suitable for an instructional design context.
>
> **Goal:** Learners will be able to list the five stages of the ADDIE model.
>
> **Assessment suggestion:** A multiple-choice quiz or a short-answer question asking learners to list the five stages would be appropriate for assessing recall.
>
> **Goal:** Assess if learners can apply Bloom's Taxonomy to critique a learning objective.
>
> **Assessment suggestion:** Provide learners with sample learning objectives and ask them to identify the Bloom's level and justify their reasoning, or ask them to rewrite a poor objective to meet a higher cognitive level.

Goal: Evaluate a salesperson's ability to handle customer objections effectively during a simulated sales call.

Assessment suggestion:

And here's another:

Instruction: Rewrite the following vague learning goal into a specific, measurable, achievable, relevant, and time-bound (SMART) learning objective that's suitable for a corporate training module.

Goal: Understand basic project management.

SMART objective: By the end of this one-hour module, participants will be able to identify the five phases of the standard project management life cycle and list two key activities within each phase.

Goal: Be better at giving feedback.

SMART objective: After completing the two-hour feedback workshop and role-play session, managers will be able to deliver constructive feedback using the SBI (situation-behavior-impact) model in at least four out of five simulated scenarios, as evaluated by a facilitator checklist.

Goal: Know about the company's safety procedures.

SMART objective:

Chain-of-Thought (COT) Prompting

Chain-of-thought prompting encourages an LLM to reason step-by-step, which makes its thought process more transparent and facilitates deeper learning. This technique is excellent for developing troubleshooting guides or creating decision-making scenarios in leadership development programs. (Note: Some LLMs are *reasoning models* and already have this functionality; they don't require a COT prompt.)

Here's an example of a COT prompt:

A new manager notices a significant drop in team productivity following a reorganization. How should they approach diagnosing and addressing this issue? Let's think step by step.

Tree-of-Thought (TOT) Prompting

Tree-of-thought prompting allows an LLM to explore different scenarios and consider various paths before arriving at a solution, promoting critical thinking and problem-solving skills. It's ideal for creating complex case studies or simulation exercises for management training.

Here's an example of a TOT prompt:

> You're the chief learning officer at a global organization implementing a new learning management system. Adoption rates are lower than expected three months after launch. Let's consider different approaches to improve engagement and usage across the organization.

Role Playing and Persona

Assigning a specific role or persona to an LLM can help create more engaging and realistic learning experiences. This technique works well for designing dialogue-based scenarios for customer service training or creating immersive leadership challenges.

Here's an example prompt:

> I want you to act as an experienced DEI facilitator leading a difficult conversation about unconscious bias. Create a dialogue that demonstrates effective techniques for managing resistance and fostering psychological safety.

Multi-Step Prompting

Breaking down complex tasks into smaller, more manageable steps can improve an LLM's performance and provide a structured learning experience. This technique is perfect for developing comprehensive how-to guides or creating scaffolded learning activities for complex skill development.

Here's an example multi-step prompt:

> **Prompt 1:** Create a 5-minute microlearning script about giving constructive feedback.

> **Prompt 2:** Develop three realistic workplace scenarios in which these feedback principles could be applied.

Prompt 3: Design a reflection activity that helps learners identify their personal feedback style and areas for improvement.

Remember, all prompts and results influence the probability of words as the conversation continues. You may also hear this technique called *prompt sequencing* or *prompt chaining*.

Guiding LLM Outputs With Rails

Guiding LLM outputs with rails involves using predefined boundaries or constraints to guide an LLM's output, ensuring relevance, safety, and factual integrity. This technique is essential for creating compliance training materials or developing content that must adhere to specific organizational policies or industry regulations.

Here's an example prompt:

Create a learning module about data privacy best practices for our sales team. Focus only on GDPR and CCPA regulations. Keep each explanation under 150 words, avoid technical jargon, include a practical example for each principle, and format the content as microlearning segments that could be delivered via mobile devices.

ϙϙϙ

Next, I want to explore a couple more techniques that show how wild working with large language models can be. They involve incorporating programmatic elements and human psychology into your prompts. These tactics will give you flexibility and better results.

Programmatic Prompting

No, you do not need to learn how to program or write base code, but understanding a few programming concepts will improve your prompts. Programmatic prompting involves structuring prompts with code-like syntax and logical operations to achieve highly specific and consistent outputs.

This technique is particularly valuable in L&D contexts that require precision, reproducibility, and systematic approaches. Using conditional statements, variables, and structured data formats within prompts, L&D

professionals can create dynamic learning content that adapts to different scenarios and learner needs.

Programmatic prompts often incorporate elements like:

- **Variables**, which can be replaced with different values to maintain value consistency in the prompt and generate variations of the same content (we used this tactic earlier in the structured prompt example by setting the TOPIC variable)
- **Conditional logic** that guides an LLM to produce different outputs based on specified criteria
- **Iteration instructions** that generate multiple examples or variations of a concept

Programmatic prompting is beneficial for creating adaptive learning paths, personalized assessment tools, or standardized yet customizable training materials across large organizations.

Take a moment and try this example prompt, which contains variables and iteration instructions:

> Generate a leadership development scenario using these parameters:
>
> SCENARIO_TYPE: [*difficult conversation*]
>
> LEADERSHIP_LEVEL: [*middle management*]
>
> INDUSTRY_CONTEXT: [*healthcare*]
>
> CHALLENGE: [*team conflict about resource allocation*]
>
> LEARNING_OBJECTIVE: [*practicing constructive feedback*]
>
> For each SOLUTION_APPROACH, provide:
> - Dialogue script (250–300 words)
> - Key principles applied
> - Potential outcomes
> - Reflection questions for learners
>
> Generate three different SOLUTION_APPROACHES:
> - Directive approach
> - Collaborative approach
> - Coaching approach

In this example, SOLUTION_APPROACHES is the prompt variable, and the statement "For each SOLUTION_APPROACH, provide:" is the programmatic iteration.

Let's now look at a prompt containing variables and conditional logic to create questions at three difficulty levels: beginner, intermediate, and advanced. Each difficulty level also has unique question criteria.

Notice that you can assign a variable value with equal (=) or a colon (:). For clarification, a double equal (= =) operator compares the values of the variables, where equal (=) assigns the value.

CREATE_ASSESSMENT:

TOPIC: [*TOPIC*]

FORMAT: Multiple-choice questions

DIFFICULTY_LEVELS: [*Beginner, Intermediate, Advanced*]

BLOOM_TAXONOMY_LEVELS: [*Remember, Understand, Apply, Analyze*]

QUESTION_COUNT: Three per difficulty level

RESPONSE_OPTIONS: Four per question

CONDITIONAL_LOGIC:

IF DIFFICULTY_LEVEL == "Beginner" THEN
- Focus on terminology and basic concepts
- Use BLOOM_TAXONOMY_LEVELS: [Remember, Understand]
- Include simple, direct scenarios
- Provide more comprehensive explanations in feedback

IF DIFFICULTY_LEVEL == "Intermediate" THEN
- Focus on principles and relationships between concepts
- Use BLOOM_TAXONOMY_LEVELS: [Understand, Apply]
- Include realistic workplace scenarios

IF DIFFICULTY_LEVEL == "Advanced" THEN
- Focus on complex problem solving and decision making
- Use BLOOM_TAXONOMY_LEVELS: [Apply, Analyze]
- Include ambiguous scenarios with multiple variables
- Include research references

FOR_EACH_QUESTION:
- IF assessing "Remember" THEN format as term-definition matching
- IF assessing "Understand" THEN format as scenario interpretation
- IF assessing "Apply" THEN format as case-solution matching
- IF assessing "Analyze" THEN format as a scenario with multiple considerations

INCLUDE_FOR_EACH_QUESTION:
- Learning objective addressed
- Explanation for correct answer
- Common misconception for most plausible wrong answer

Cognitive and Psychological Prompting

Recent advancements in prompt design have revealed significant improvements in the performance of LLMs, which use techniques that leverage human cognitive patterns and psychological principles.

Here are a few statements you can add to your prompts for better results:

- To enhance reasoning, say, "Take a deep breath and think step by step."
- To promote accuracy, say, "Break down the issue into smaller steps."
- To improve quality, say, "I'll tip $200 for a detailed answer."
- To enhance performance, say, "This is crucial for my career."

Researchers and professionals have enhanced AI-generated responses' accuracy, depth, and relevance by structuring prompts to mimic human reasoning, incorporating emotional cues, or introducing artificial incentives.

Try the following prompt, which includes a few of these psychological techniques:

Act as an award-winning educational video scriptwriter with 15 years of experience in corporate storytelling.

Write a compelling 90-second script for a leadership training video aimed at mid-level managers in a Fortune 500 company, designed to improve team performance by 30 percent next quarter.

Open with a relatable leadership challenge to immediately engage viewers and then introduce three key leadership skills that directly affect performance metrics like project completion and retention, using a real-world scenario to demonstrate their effectiveness.

Conclude with a strong call to action that drives immediate implementation, reinforcing urgency and accountability.

Maintain a confident, authoritative tone, ensuring every insight is evidence-based and aligned with corporate KPIs.

Assume the CEO will review the final video, requiring a polished, high-impact narrative.

Write the full script now. ($200 tip upon completion.)

Notice the use of psychological techniques:

- **High-stakes accountability** ("Assume the CEO will review the final video")—This creates a sense of urgency and importance, leading to a more detail-oriented and polished response.
- **Monetary incentive as a motivator** ("$200 tip upon completion")—This signals high value, leveraging reward motivation to drive a more thoughtful and refined output.

It still baffles me that you can increase the quality of your outputs by being kind and motivating the model with your prompt. Therefore, you need to consider doing so when designing prompts.

ꙮꙮꙮ

As for the big takeaway from this section, there are three elements in a well-designed prompt:

- **Words.** The words you choose directly influence the quality of the prompt results.
- **Logic.** Structure and programmatic operators increase the consistency and depth of your results.
- **Motivation.** Leveraging positive statements and motivation improves your prompt results.

By considering these three items when designing your prompts, you can leverage your expertise and effectively collaborate with artificial intelligence.

Iterative Prompt Design and Testing

Creating an effective prompt is not a "one-and-done" process. Prompt refinement is iterative and involves adjusting and improving prompts to achieve your desired output. Here are several techniques for refining your prompts:

- **Self-refinement.** LLMs can be prompted to evaluate and refine output prompts, leading to improved accuracy and coherence. That's right—you can give the model your prompt and ask it to improve the prompt. If you use a reasoning model, get ready to be amazed when you input your updated prompt.

- **Iterative feedback.** This technique involves providing the LLM with feedback on its output and prompting it to generate a revised response. You can incorporate those prompts into the original prompt based on how you interact with the model through conversation.

- **Conciseness.** Keeping your sentences concise and focused can improve an LLM's ability to understand the task and generate relevant responses.

In addition, using an iterative process allows you to fine-tune prompts and optimize them for specific learning contexts and learner needs. Try following these steps:

1. **Create initial prompts.** Start with a clear and specific prompt based on the task or problem you are trying to solve.

2. **Test and evaluate.** Observe the LLM's response and assess its relevance, accuracy, and effectiveness.

3. **Refine and modify.** Based on the evaluation, make incremental changes to the prompt to improve its performance. This could involve adjusting the wording, adding more context, or providing more specific instructions.

4. **Repeat the process.** Continue testing and refining the prompt until it consistently elicits the desired learning outcomes.

Iterative prompt design is a dynamic and evolving process that requires adaptability and careful observation of an LLM's responses. Its output can provide valuable feedback that informs the next iteration of the prompt, leading to continuous improvement.

During the iterative process, it's also worth experimenting with the order of the content you include in the prompt. Rearranging the instructions or information can sometimes affect the LLM's response. For example, in multi-modal prompts that include images or other media, try placing the files before the instructions to see how they influence the output.

As LLMs evolve, prompt design will play an increasingly critical role in shaping the future of AI interaction and development. By staying informed about the latest advancements and best practices in prompt design, you can harness the full potential of LLMs and drive innovation as an L&D professional. Let's now turn to how to write your prompts to create effective learning experiences.

Crafting Effective Prompts for Learning

My first attempt at writing an AI prompt for an ESG (environmental, social, and governance) training program was humbling. I was tasked with creating 80 multiple-choice questions with four difficulty levels that would eventually be added to a learning experience platform.

I began by uploading the prior year's public-facing ESG report to ChatGPT. (No security issues here!) That seemed like a good start, but then I used my first prompt:

> Create 80 multiple-choice questions on ESG based on the
> document. Questions have four levels of difficulty.

The questions ChatGPT created were generic and disconnected from the document—far from the carefully crafted ones I pride myself on delivering. That moment taught me something crucial about prompt design: Technical knowledge of how generative AI models work isn't enough. Success requires a deep understanding of learning science and principles.

I worked on various iterations of that multiple-choice question prompt. As I continued to add details about the question levels and format, the quality of the questions from ChatGPT improved. I didn't know it then, but I was creating my first structured prompt based on best practices for multiple-choice questions.

My final prompt looked like this:

Act like an instructional designer. Create 80 multiple-choice questions on ESG (environmental, social, and governance) based on the document. The audience is professionals who need to understand ESG. Questions follow four different levels:

- **Level 1:** Basic recall questions to test fundamental ESG knowledge
- **Level 2:** Concept application questions to assess understanding of ESG principles
- **Level 3:** Scenario-based questions requiring critical thinking and problem-solving in ESG contexts
- **Level 4:** Strategic decision-making questions related to ESG policies and practices

Ensure an equal distribution of questions across all four levels and explain the correct answer.

Follow these rules when creating questions:
- Avoid double negatives in the question stem.
- Make all distractors plausible.
- Test comprehension, critical thinking, and recall.
- Use simple sentence structure and precise wording for the question stem.
- Mix up the order of the correct answers.
- Keep the number of options to three.
- No trick questions.
- Avoid using "all of the above" and "none of the above" as options.

Notice the difference in the prompts. I added the instructional designer role, defined the question levels, and included all the task rules for creating the multiple-choice questions. The rules included avoiding double negatives, keeping the options to three, and avoiding using "all of the above" and "none of the above." These rules and others are grounded in empirical evidence. As you build your prompts, verify your task details and follow the industry's best practices and learning science.

The result? After reviewing the questions and making some adjustments, I submitted them to the vice president of ESG for review. Only 1 percent of the questions came back with serious issues (either because they didn't align with our ESG initiatives or mentioned an outlier topic). A task that would have taken me 20 to 24 hours was reduced to four hours.

As you craft your prompts, make sure that you follow these steps in the input-output framework (Figure 8-6):

1. **Use clean data for your input.** This means that your source data is valid, the prompt is well-structured (even a freeform prompt), and the prompt is grounded in learning science and best practices.
2. **Use the correct LLM.** Not all models are the same. Some are trained in vast domain information, some are better at coding and math, and others are grounded in learning science, like Google's LearnLM model.
3. **Validate model results.** Does the output complete the task, provide a focused result, and match or exceed the requirements?

Figure 8-6. Input-Output Framework

As you can see, integrating generative AI into L&D tasks requires a methodical approach that respects existing workflows and learning science while enhancing them through strategic implementation.

After working with many learning professionals across different organizations, I've observed a pattern: Those who succeed with generative AI don't simply overlay AI onto their processes; they weave it into the fabric of their work with precision and purpose.

In wrapping up this chapter, let's explore a couple examples to review the thought process for designing effective prompts that support the learning journey. Here are two scenarios:

1. Use generative AI to assist in performance consulting.
2. Design a detailed image creation prompt to support scenario-based training.

Each scenario uses the same input-output framework for designing the prompt. As you read on, consider the following questions:

- What are the required clean inputs?

- What model am I using?
- What is the quality of the prompt's outputs?

Performance Consulting Scenario

Consider performance consulting. Traditionally, an L&D professional serves as a strategic partner who analyzes performance gaps and identifies their underlying causes. This approach examines knowledge and skills deficiencies, environmental factors, incentive structures, tools, resources, and organizational processes.

I learned about performance consulting early in my career and attended week-long training courses, but honestly, as an art director, I thought it was a bore. Experience has made me appreciate the importance of performance consulting, but the work is still methodical. This is where generative AI can be used as a collaborator.

When incorporating generative AI into a performance consulting workflow, there are four critical elements:

- **Systematic data collection (input).** The quality of your investigation directly affects the quality of the prompt results. This includes gathering business metrics, conducting comprehensive needs assessments, interviewing stakeholders across organizational levels, observing work processes, and examining existing systems.
- **Collaborative prompt design.** This is where your craft meets technology. Your prompts must reflect what you want the AI to do and how you want it to support your analytical process. The prompt architecture should align with your methodical approach to front-end analysis, including business impact, performance, cause, and population analysis.
- **Model selection (LLM or multimodal).** Performance consulting might benefit from a reasoning model that can identify patterns across disparate data points. However, you should view AI as your assistant, not a replacement for the consultant's expertise in building relationships and understanding organizational context.
- **Rigorous validation and stakeholder engagement (output).** The prompt output requires testing hypotheses against multiple data

sources and stakeholder perspectives. This collaborative validation process prevents AI automation bias while ensuring the solutions address root causes rather than symptoms.

Let's use one specific task in performance consulting—business metrics analysis—as an example (Figure 8-7):

- **Input:**
  - Quarterly performance reports from three departments
  - Customer satisfaction survey results (past 12 months)
  - Employee turnover rates compared to industry standards
  - Training completion rates and post-training assessment scores
- **Model:** Reasoning model that can analyze data
- **Output:** Actionable analysis report

Figure 8-7. Input-Output Framework: Business Metrics Analysis Example

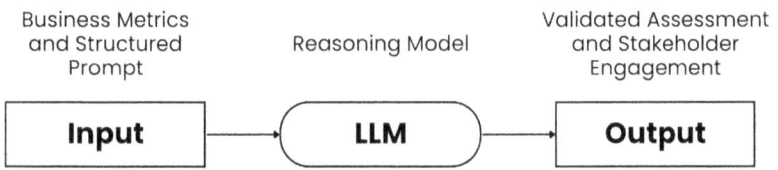

Business Metrics and Structured Prompt	Reasoning Model	Validated Assessment and Stakeholder Engagement
Input	**LLM**	**Output**

Here's a freeform prompt for the task:

Role: Act as a performance consultant with expertise in cross-departmental metrics evaluation.

Task: Analyze these business metrics across departments to identify performance gaps and potential causes.

Details: Consider the relationship between customer satisfaction trends, employee turnover, and training effectiveness. Highlight any significant correlations between metrics and suggest which areas might benefit from further investigation beyond training solutions. Include a preliminary assessment of whether the issues stem from knowledge or skills gaps, environmental factors, incentive structures, or organizational processes.

This initial prompt is just the beginning of the prompt design process. From here, you can expand it using the TRACI framework and be very specific about how the analysis is handled based on the identified business metrics.

After proper analysis, the critical phase of selecting appropriate initiatives is based on identified causes. AI can support but not replace the performance consultant's judgment and stakeholder collaboration in this area. Performance consultants understand how organizational elements interact rather than viewing issues in isolation. Therefore, the performance consultant's expertise must guide how you integrate AI into your L&D practice.

Scenario-Based Training Scenario

Visual elements can dramatically enhance learner engagement and retention when developing scenario-based training. Let's discuss how this works with AI image generators like Midjourney and DALL-E.

Just as with performance consulting, creating compelling training imagery requires understanding the inputs and outputs of your process:

- **Learning objectives analysis.** What specific scenarios need visualization to support learning outcomes?
- **Prompt architecture.** How do you structure prompts to generate images that align with learning needs? What environmental, interpersonal, and situational elements must be present?
- **Model selection.** Which AI image generation model best suits your specific training scenario needs (for example, Midjourney, DALL-E, or Stable Diffusion)?
- **Validation against learning goals.** Does the generated imagery effectively support the intended training scenario?

Let's create an image for a training scenario involving customer service at a bank branch (Figure 8-8):

- **Input:**
  - This scenario involves a frustrated middle-aged customer talking to a bank representative.
  - Image prompts need different information to create realistic images. This includes style, subject, setting, composition, lighting, and any additional information.
- **Model:** Image models like Midjourney, DALL-E, or Stable Diffusion
- **Output:** Image aligned to the training scenario

Figure 8-8. Input-Output Framework: Scenario-Based Training Example

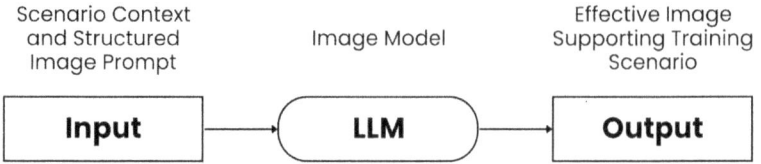

Scenario Context and Structured Image Prompt	Image Model	Effective Image Supporting Training Scenario
Input	**LLM**	**Output**

Here's a prompt you could use to generate a customer service image:

Style: Photorealistic professional photography, 8K resolution, studio lighting, and corporate documentation style

Subject: A visibly frustrated middle-aged customer (furrowed brow and tense posture) and a composed bank representative maintaining professional demeanor at a customer service desk

Setting: Modern retail banking branch with clean lines, professional atmosphere, other customers visible in the background, and security personnel present but not prominent

Composition: Customer and representative positioned across a counter from each other, papers and a smartphone on the counter between them, the customer's hand slightly raised in a gesturing motion, and the representative maintaining eye contact

Lighting: Bright corporate lighting, soft diffused overhead illumination typical of professional environment, and subtle shadows to enhance facial expressions

Additional information: Customer wearing business casual attire, representative in professional banking uniform, digital displays visible in background, and the representative displaying open body language despite tense situation

The resulting image in Figure 8-9 provides a realistic scenario that L&D professionals can use as a visual for discussions around proper de-escalation techniques, body language awareness, and professional responses to customer frustration.

By applying our structured input-output framework to image generation, you can create precisely targeted visual assets that support specific learning objectives rather than settling for generic stock photography that may not align with the training scenarios. To be effective, you must understand the learning design process and communicate your requirements to the AI model through well-crafted prompts.

Note: While AI-generated images can be highly realistic, it's essential to quality check the output for visual anomalies such as distorted hands, extra fingers, inconsistent lighting, or expressions that fall into the uncanny valley. These subtle issues can distract from the learning objective and reduce credibility. Always inspect and, if needed, regenerate or edit images to ensure they maintain visual integrity.

Figure 8-9. Resulting Customer-Service Image

Conclusion

My first attempt at prompt design felt like learning to ride a bicycle: wriggly, uncertain, and full of small failures that led to bigger insights. Now, I watch learning professionals master these skills in days rather than months. As the tools evolve and our expertise grows, and the possibilities expand.

The increasing adoption of AI in L&D highlights the growing importance of prompt design as a future-proof skill for learning professionals. As more organizations embrace AI-powered tools and technologies, the ability to communicate effectively with and guide these systems will become increasingly critical.

This chapter explored the foundations of prompt design for learning. We examined structures that work, discovered patterns that scale, and learned how small adjustments create significant impact.

Looking forward, the next chapter opens new possibilities. We'll explore how prompt libraries streamline development, discover AI tools that automate routine tasks, and examine GPTs that transform workflow efficiency.

CHAPTER 9

AI Learning Workflows and Automation

In This Chapter

- Ways to build and maintain effective prompt libraries tailored to L&D needs
- Strategies for integrating AI workflows into existing instructional design processes
- GPTs, Gems, and Copilots for personalized learning experiences
- Sustainable systems for continuous improvement

Have you ever had to rewrite the same training material for a different audience? I've been there, and it can be painful. The repetitive nature of content adaptation haunts many L&D professionals. We craft similar materials repeatedly, adjusting tone, examples, and complexity. What if this fundamental learning design challenge was key to understanding part of AI's transformative potential in our field?

During a workshop, a senior instructional designer shared her experience managing learning content. She had spent years maintaining a collection of reusable learning templates, scenarios, and assessment frameworks. This curated library streamlined her work but required constant updates and contextual adaptations. She had a difficult time keeping up with changes (like a brand refresh), but she didn't have to recreate the wheel.

In many ways, her approach and its challenges mirror the principles that now drive AI prompt libraries, workflows, and automation. Her systematic method for managing templates foreshadowed the future of AI-enhanced learning design.

Traditional L&D teams often struggle with content scalability and personalization, and waste time adapting existing materials for new contexts. Meanwhile, innovative organizations leverage AI prompt libraries, workflows, and automation to transform single pieces of content into multiple learning experiences (Figure 9-1). The gap between these approaches grows wider every day. The difference lies in whether teams are adopting AI tools and how they're conceptualizing and implementing them.

Figure 9-1. Traditional vs. AI-Enhanced L&D

Traditional L&D
Struggles with scalability
and personalization

AI-Enhanced L&D
Transforms content
with AI tools

Understanding prompt libraries, workflows, and automation requires shifting your perspective. Learning experiences are becoming hyperpersonalized and focused on an individual's needs, and this chapter describes the path to that reality. By examining how AI tools integrate with established L&D practices, we can uncover patterns that reshape our approach to learning design. The future belongs to professionals who grasp the technical foundations and strategic implications of AI-enhanced learning systems.

By the end of this chapter, you will understand how to build and maintain a prompt library, automate key workflows, and leverage GPTs effectively. This will enable you to create more engaging, scalable, and personalized learning experiences while maintaining instructional quality.

Prompt Libraries

In the previous chapter, we explored how to craft effective prompts for an LLM, beginning with freeform prompts and refining them into structured, repeatable formats. But what happens when you have a highly productive prompt and need to scale it across a team or an entire organization? A prompt library is essential. Most learning professionals interacting with AI start by using a trial-and-error approach. They write a prompt, analyze the output, tweak it, and repeat. Over time, they develop effective prompts through experience. But without a way to manage and refine these prompts, organizations run into three major challenges:

- **Inconsistent outputs.** Team members use their own prompts for the same tasks, leading to varied and sometimes unreliable results.
- **Wasted time.** Without a centralized library, teams spend unnecessary hours recreating prompts or troubleshooting unpredictable AI behavior.
- **Scaling challenges.** A great prompt that works once may not work in different contexts or with ever-changing AI models unless it's properly documented and structured for reuse.

A prompt library solves these problems by transforming individual, ad hoc prompt development into a systematic, scalable approach. It ensures that once an effective, structured prompt is developed, it can be stored, shared, and continuously improved rather than being lost in someone's notes or buried in a document.

Are you storing your prompts in Word or a Google Doc? If so, you should consider moving them into a prompt library.

What Is a Prompt Library?

A prompt library is like a well-organized toolbox for generative AI models. It's a curated collection of prompts designed to guide AI systems in generating specific responses or completing tasks. Your prompts can be simple or complex, ranging from straightforward freeform prompts to intricate structured prompts that require AI to analyze information, engage in dialogue, or produce learning content.

Figure 9-2 is a screenshot of my public prompt library for learning professionals created in Notion.

Figure 9-2. Prompt Library Example

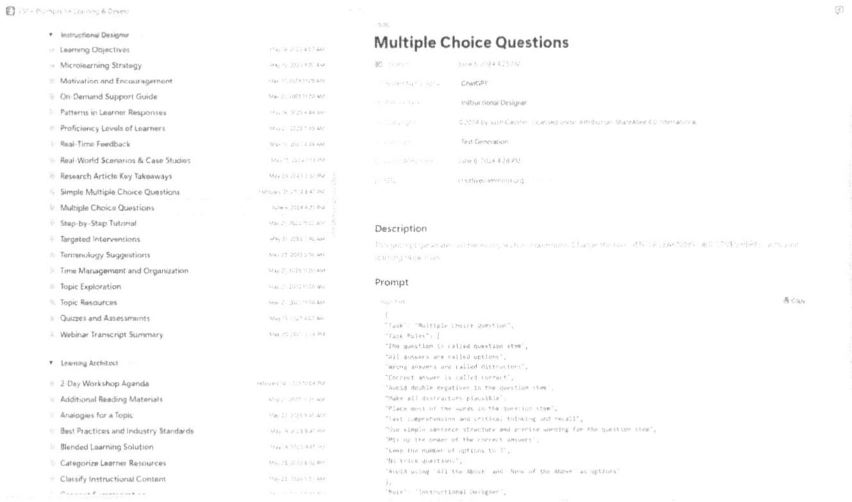

My Prompt Library

You can find instructions for how to access my prompt library on the book's website, joshcavalier.ai/ApplyingAIBook.

Prompt libraries can significantly enhance AI-driven learning initiatives in several ways:

- **Efficiency and productivity.** Prompt libraries save time and effort by providing a readily available collection of standardized prompts for L&D tasks. This reduces redundancy and duplication of effort and allows you to focus on higher-level work, rather than spending time crafting prompts from scratch. Well-organized libraries make it easy to find and access relevant prompts, improving efficiency and scalability.
- **Consistency and quality.** By using predefined and tested prompts, you can ensure consistency in the quality of AI-generated outputs across different learning activities. This leads to more reliable and predictable results, which are essential for maintaining the integrity of learning processes and assessments.

- **Scalability.** Using prompt frameworks (like TRACI) as reusable building blocks allows you to create customized prompts by combining different elements and adapting to specific learning needs and contexts.
- **Collaboration and knowledge sharing.** Prompt libraries are a central platform for storing, organizing, and accessing AI prompts. They enable you and your team to share best practices and learn from one another's experiences. This fosters a collaborative learning environment with your peers where you can work together to improve AI proficiency and develop more effective learning strategies.

EXERCISE

Creating a Prompt Mini-Library

This exercise will guide you through creating an initial prompt library, empowering you to organize, refine, and maximize the efficiency of your AI interactions. By the end of this activity, you'll have created a personalized mini-library of at least six effective prompts, organized clearly to support your most common tasks.

Step 1. Select Your Workspace
Choose a digital workspace to store your prompts. (This could be Google Docs, Microsoft Word, Notion, Evernote, or Excel or Google Sheets.) Create a new document titled "Prompt Library."

Step 2. Brainstorm Prompts
Reflect on your daily, weekly, or routine interactions with AI tools:
- What prompts do you frequently use for writing, editing, brainstorming, researching, coding, summarizing, or performing creative tasks?
- Which prompts consistently provide excellent results or significantly simplify your workflow?

List at least six prompts that you frequently use in your document, leaving space between each one.

Step 3. Clarify Each Prompt's Purpose
For each prompt you listed, briefly describe:
- The exact scenario or task you use it for
- The desired outcome or type of response you expect from the AI model

For example, if your prompt says, "Rewrite this paragraph to be clearer and more engaging," you could note the following scenario and outcome:

- **Scenario:** Editing drafts of blog posts or articles
- **Desired outcome:** A concise, polished, and reader-friendly version of the original text

Step 4. Tag Your Prompts by Category

Create a simple tagging system to categorize your prompts by function. Here are some examples:

- Writing and editing
- Learning design
- Idea generation
- Summarization and analysis
- Technical support and coding
- Marketing and social media
- Personal productivity

Assign each prompt a category tag to enable easy reference in the future.

Step 5. Reflection and Enhancement

Review your initial prompt library and answer the following questions:

- Which area or category currently has the most prompts? Why?
- Are there categories with fewer or no prompts? Would expanding into these areas benefit your workflow?
- Can you identify one prompt to improve? Rewrite it clearly, concisely, and with greater specificity to produce more accurate results.

Add your insights or refined prompts directly to your prompt library.

Congratulations! You've taken the first step toward creating a robust, practical prompt library.

Tools and Platforms for Creating and Managing Prompt Libraries

Now that you've successfully created your initial prompt library in a simple document or spreadsheet, you might notice certain limitations. While helpful initially, tools like Google Sheets and Excel often struggle with extensive prompts due to character limits within individual cells, which makes longer structured prompts cumbersome to store and manage effectively.

Additionally, these tools can be restrictive regarding collaboration, searchability, categorization, and scalability as your library grows. Transitioning to more robust platforms—such as Notion or Monday.com—can help you overcome these challenges, allowing you to manage lengthy, structured prompts seamlessly. These advanced platforms offer intuitive categorization and tagging systems, powerful search functionality, easy handling of long-form content, real-time collaboration, customizable workflows, and automation opportunities. Moving your prompt management to a specialized platform also ensures your growing library remains accessible, organized, and scalable, which can greatly enhance your productivity with AI tools.

Here are some tools and platforms you can use to create and manage your prompt library:

- **Spreadsheet tools** like Google Sheets and Excel offer features like easy categorization via tabs, sharing, and real-time collaboration, making them suitable for individuals and teams. These are good options if you are sticking with shorter, freeform prompts.
- **Database platforms** like Airtable can provide a more robust and flexible database environment for organizing and managing prompts. They may include features like custom views, role-based permissions, and API (application programming interface) access, and are suitable for larger teams and organizations with more complex prompt management needs.
- **Versatile workspaces** like Notion and Monday.com enable you to integrate prompts with other project management tasks. They may provide features like version control, collaboration, and knowledge management, and are suitable for teams that want to manage prompts alongside other project-related information. You can also share your library as a website.
- **Specialized platforms** like PromptLayer, PromptHub, and PromptKnit offer specialized features for prompt management, version control, testing, and evaluation. These platforms often provide advanced functionalities like prompt comparison, performance tracking, and integration with other AI tools.

- **Open-source libraries** like OpenPrompt, Promptify, and PromptFlow provide frameworks and tools for developing and managing prompts for different AI tasks. These libraries offer flexibility and customization options for developers who want to integrate prompt management into their applications and workflows.

Once you've selected the ideal application or platform for managing your prompt library, the next step is determining what additional details you'll need to capture beyond the prompts themselves.

Essential Metadata Fields for a Prompt Library

Simply storing the text of your prompts is a good starting point, but enhancing them with structured metadata—like categories, tags, intended use cases, success ratings, version history, and author or team notes—will significantly improve usability, retrieval, and scalability. Understanding and thoughtfully implementing this metadata layer will transform your prompt library from a simple collection of text snippets into a powerful, strategic resource for your work with AI.

Figure 9-3 shows an example of the metadata for a multiple-choice question prompt in my L&D prompt library.

Figure 9-3. Prompt Metadata Example

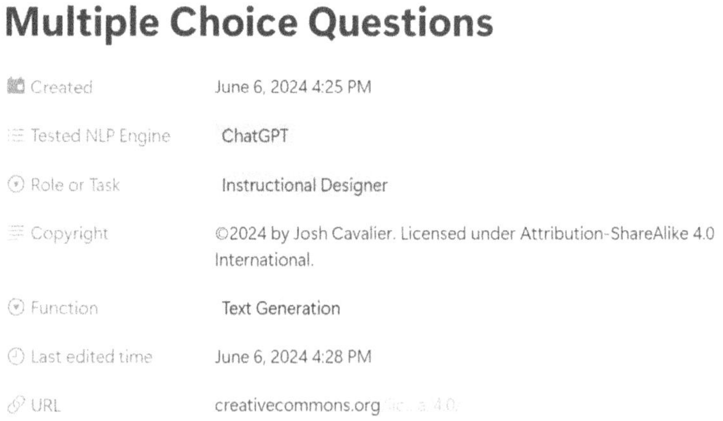

Multiple Choice Questions

Created	June 6, 2024 4:25 PM
Tested NLP Engine	ChatGPT
Role or Task	Instructional Designer
Copyright	©2024 by Josh Cavalier. Licensed under Attribution-ShareAlike 4.0 International.
Function	Text Generation
Last edited time	June 6, 2024 4:28 PM
URL	creativecommons.org

Table 9-1 provides an overview of potential metadata fields that you can use to organize and manage prompts effectively. The specific fields will vary depending on your organization's needs and preferences as well as the individual creating the prompt library.

Table 9-1. Metadata Fields for a Prompt Library

Metadata Field	Description	Example
Prompt	The actual text of the prompt	Write a short story about great customer service.
Category or tag	Keywords or categories that help organize and classify the prompt	• Creative writing • Storytelling • Customer service
Version	The version number of the prompt, allowing for tracking changes over time	v1.2
Date created	The date and time the prompt was created	2025-01-05 12:00:00
Author	The creator of the prompt	John Doe
Function	The intended purpose or function of the prompt (e.g., text generation or summarization)	Text generation
Tested model	Which generative AI models the prompt was tested on	ChatGPT 5, Gemini 3, and Claude 4
Keywords	Relevant keywords that help with searching and filtering prompts	• Customer • Service • Short story
Title	A name for the prompt	"The Customer Service Scenario"
Description	A detailed account of the prompt	This prompt is designed to generate creative learning scenarios.

EXERCISE

Migrating and Enhancing Your Prompt Library

In this exercise, you'll migrate your initial collection of prompts from your basic document or spreadsheet into a more robust platform (such as Notion or Monday.com) while enriching each prompt with helpful metadata.

Step 1. Set Up Your Workspace

Log in to your chosen platform and create a dedicated workspace named "Prompt Library."

- On Notion, create a new database or table.
- On Monday.com, create a new board with groups or items.

Step 2. Define Metadata Fields

Add metadata fields (columns or properties) to help you organize, filter, and use your prompts effectively. Recommended metadata fields include:

- **Prompt text** (long text field)
- **Category** (select field; for example, writing and editing, idea generation, or technical support)
- **Function or use case** (text field)
- **Date created** (date field)
- **Version** (text field)

Step 3. Migrate Your Prompts

Copy and paste your six original prompts into the new platform, populating the "Prompt Text" field.

Step 4. Add Metadata

For each prompt, carefully add detailed metadata:

- Categorize each prompt clearly.
- Describe its exact purpose or use-case scenario.
- Set the creation date as today's date.
- If applicable, include a version number.

Step 5. Organize and Filter

Test the effectiveness of your metadata by using your platform's filtering, sorting, or searching capabilities to quickly locate prompts based on specific criteria.

After completing this exercise, reflect on the following questions:

- How has adding metadata improved your ability to manage and use your prompts?
- Which additional metadata fields might you consider adding as your prompt library grows?

Continue expanding your library by regularly adding new prompts and refining existing ones, maintaining consistent metadata to maximize the value and accessibility of your collection.

Versioning, Testing, and Maintaining Prompt Libraries

Version control and maintenance are essential for ensuring a prompt library's long-term effectiveness and integrity, just like they are for managing assets in your L&D programs.

Even if you're a team of one, chances are you have devised your methods for tracking versions of learning content. But sometimes, an ad hoc approach breaks down when managing an entire organization's L&D portfolio. Here are some best practices to follow:

- **Version control.** Assign clear version numbers or unique identifiers to each prompt iteration. Document key changes and use status labels (such as "draft" or "final") to manage development.
- **History and access.** Preserve previous prompt versions and their metadata, allowing quick rollbacks when needed. Regularly retire outdated or ineffective prompts to maintain a streamlined, relevant library.
- **Regular reviews.** Schedule consistent reviews to integrate new insights and user feedback. Actively seek user input through structured feedback channels like surveys or suggestion boxes.
- **Prompt organization.** Organize prompts logically (by discipline, task, or user role) to enhance usability. Choose a structure that aligns best with your instructional goals and team needs.
- **Performance tracking.** Monitor prompt usage and effectiveness metrics (such as relevance, accuracy, readability, and efficiency) to identify opportunities for improvement. Tools such as LangSmith and DSPy can streamline this process.
- **A/B testing.** Experiment with prompt variations through A/B testing to discover and apply the most effective versions based on performance data.

Integrating these practices helps instructional designers maintain a robust, effective prompt library that continually supports and enhances your content creation workflows.

ǝǝǝ

Prompt libraries are a valuable asset for AI-driven learning initiatives, offering numerous benefits such as improved efficiency, enhanced collaboration, and increased scalability. By following the best practices outlined in this chapter, you can set yourself up to effectively leverage prompt libraries in your L&D workflows.

Streamlining Tasks With Prompt Workflows

The evolution of AI in L&D is ushering in an era of unprecedented efficiency and creativity. While asking a generative AI model to perform a specific, isolated task like generating a quiz question or summarizing an article is useful, this approach often results in fragmented outputs that require significant manual intervention to assemble into a cohesive learning experience.

L&D professionals can move beyond the novelty of single, isolated AI prompts to a more sophisticated approach using *prompt workflows* (also commonly known as *prompt chains*). By leveraging prompt workflows, you can transform materials such as transcripts, summaries, or even existing learning content into formats like:

- **Training guides**—comprehensive guides that expand on key concepts.
- **Microlearning modules**—short, focused bursts of learning for just-in-time knowledge.
- **Interactive video content**—engaging videos with embedded quizzes, polls, and branching scenarios.
- **Simulations and scenarios**—immersive learning experiences that allow learners to practice skills in a safe environment.
- **Assessments**—formative and summative assessments that evaluate learning and identify knowledge gaps.

Now that you understand how to build your prompt library, let's turn to leveraging interconnected prompts to revolutionize content creation, automate complex processes, and ultimately create a more agile and responsive L&D function.

Transitioning From Single Prompts to Prompt Workflows

As a learning professional, you're accustomed to breaking down complex topics into clear, structured steps. Prompt workflows leverage this same principle by connecting multiple prompts sequentially.

Each prompt's output serves as the input for the next prompt, creating a powerful sequence that refines and enriches content at each step. Think of prompt workflows like an instructional design assembly line—each prompt builds on the last, resulting in detailed, targeted, and sophisticated deliverables. A prompt workflow is a single conversation with an LLM. After the model responds to your first prompt, you continue prompting in the same chat.

Figure 9-4 illustrates a prompt workflow for transforming a learning objective into a course outline and video script.

Here's a detailed explanation of the steps and actions in this workflow:

1. **Initial prompt to LLM.** The process begins with a prompt instructing the LLM to "Write a learning objective on handling customer objections for retail associates."
2. **LLM result.** The LLM then generates a clear and detailed learning objective.
3. **Second prompt (course outline).** The next prompt then instructs the LLM to "Write a detailed course outline based on this learning objective."
4. **LLM result (course outline).** The model produces a structured course outline beginning with "Module 1: Introduction to Customer Objections."
5. **Third prompt (video script).** Following the course outline, another prompt requests the LLM to "Write a video script for Module 1: Introduction to Customer Objections."
6. **LLM result (video script).** The model then creates a narrative script intended for a video lesson.

This step-by-step approach to creating content by continuing the prompts with an LLM allows you to leverage the conversation's context. Keep in mind that the words you use in your prompts and the words returned in the result will affect the probability of certain words appearing later in the conversation. Subsequent responses are conditioned on this accumulated context, significantly influencing the probability distribution of words in future outputs.

Figure 9-4. Prompt Workflow Example

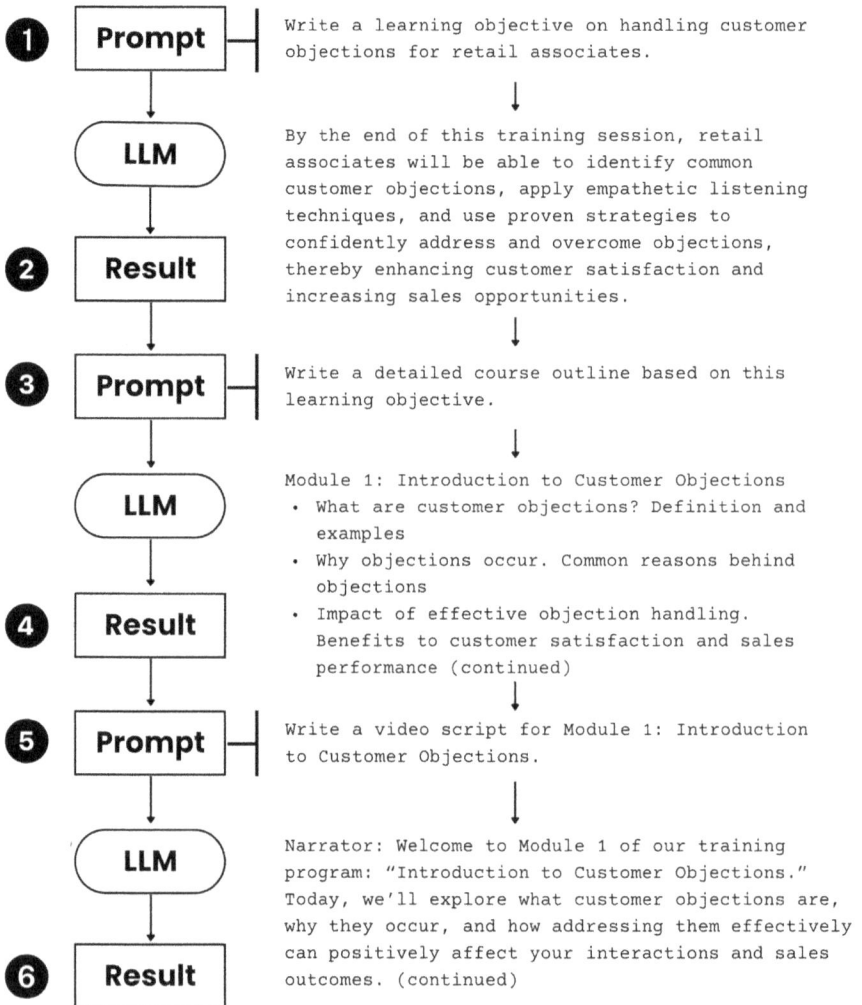

① **Prompt** — Write a learning objective on handling customer objections for retail associates.

↓

LLM

② **Result** — By the end of this training session, retail associates will be able to identify common customer objections, apply empathetic listening techniques, and use proven strategies to confidently address and overcome objections, thereby enhancing customer satisfaction and increasing sales opportunities.

↓

③ **Prompt** — Write a detailed course outline based on this learning objective.

↓

LLM

④ **Result** — Module 1: Introduction to Customer Objections
- What are customer objections? Definition and examples
- Why objections occur. Common reasons behind objections
- Impact of effective objection handling. Benefits to customer satisfaction and sales performance (continued)

↓

⑤ **Prompt** — Write a video script for Module 1: Introduction to Customer Objections.

↓

LLM

⑥ **Result** — Narrator: Welcome to Module 1 of our training program: "Introduction to Customer Objections." Today, we'll explore what customer objections are, why they occur, and how addressing them effectively can positively affect your interactions and sales outcomes. (continued)

Each time you input a prompt and receive a response, that text becomes part of the context window. Based on the previous exchanges, future outputs will weigh words, concepts, and styles more heavily. For example, if a topic, phrase, or particular word is mentioned frequently or explicitly, the model's probability distribution shifts toward repeating or referencing that language again later.

As you can see, single prompts are effective for straightforward tasks, but complex instructional design projects benefit from interconnected prompts that progressively refine content. To recap, prompt workflows:

- Break down complex tasks into manageable steps.
- Enhance accuracy, depth, and relevance through incremental refinement.
- Maintain consistency across instructional materials.
- Leverage quality results from an LLM by maintaining the context window conversation.

Let's walk through a couple examples using freeform, zero-shot prompts to showcase the power of prompt workflows. Note that your results will be stronger if you upload reference documents, web sources, and structured prompts.

EXERCISE

Prompt Workflows

Try these prompt workflows in your preferred LLM to expedite task completion with just a few prompts.

Imagine you need to create an e-learning module on effective communication. A simple three-step prompt chain could look like this:

Prompt 1. Learning objectives:

Generate five learning objectives for an e-learning module on effective communication, targeting employees in a customer service role.

Prompt 2. Video script:

Using the learning objectives from the previous output, write a script for a three-minute video illustrating techniques for handling difficult customer interactions.

Prompt 3. E-learning storyboard:

Based on the video script provided, develop a detailed storyboard for an e-learning module, including scene descriptions, visual elements, on-screen text, and interactive elements.

Or, let's say you have a recorded webinar on a new product launch. You can use a prompt workflow to transform it into multiple learning assets. Start by uploading a webinar transcript (either autogenerated or refined manually).

Prompt 1. Summary:

Create a concise summary of the key product features and benefits discussed in the webinar transcript.

Prompt 2. Training video storyboard:

Develop a storyboard for a five-minute training video explaining the product's value proposition, using the summary provided.

Prompt 3. Quiz questions:

Generate five multiple-choice quiz questions based on the webinar transcript to assess understanding of the key product features.

Prompt 4. Microlearning module outline:

Create an outline for a microlearning module on how to effectively position the product to different customer segments, based on the key benefits identified in the summary.

Integrating With Existing Tools and Frameworks

The beauty of AI workflows lies in their adaptability. You can seamlessly integrate them into your existing content creation processes by linking familiar tools—such as storyboarding software, learning management systems (LMSs), and authoring tools—with AI-generated outputs.

You can integrate a prompt workflow directly into your preferred rapid authoring tool. Start by uploading your raw content (such as a Word document or SME interview transcript).

Prompt 1. E-learning storyboard draft:

Based on the provided document, draft an e-learning storyboard for a module on [TOPIC], including scene descriptions, on-screen text, and interactive elements.

Prompt 2. Visual suggestions:

For each scene in the storyboard, suggest relevant visuals, graphics, or stock footage that could be used.

Prompt 3. Quiz or assessment:

Develop a five-question quiz to assess learners' understanding of the content covered in the module.

Prompt 4. Simulation idea:

Suggest an idea for an interactive simulation that allows learners to apply the concepts learned in the module in a realistic scenario.

The authoring tool will then present this AI-generated storyboard with visual suggestions, assessment questions, and simulation ideas. You can refine and enhance the final product, leveraging your expertise to ensure quality and alignment with your learning objectives.

The growing demand for prompt workflow management has also led to the emergence of specialized AI-driven platforms designed to facilitate seamless prompt chaining. These platforms provide intuitive interfaces for creating and managing complex workflows, often with visual tools that make it easy to see the flow of information between prompts.

Certain advanced AI authoring tools now allow designers to embed prompts directly within an authoring environment. Each prompt acts as a governor, controlling the automatic generation of specific elements within the application.

For instance, one prompt might create video frames with appropriate visuals and on-screen text, while another generates interactive segments with branching scenarios. The cumulative effect of these embedded prompts is a polished, media-rich e-learning module that was developed with a fraction of the time and effort required using traditional methods (Figure 9-5).

Figure 9-5. Dynamic Learning Interaction

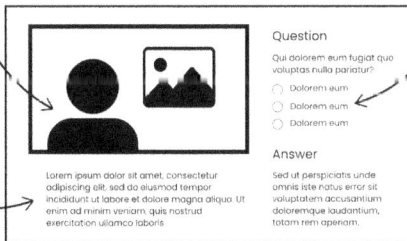

Video Prompt:
An avatar explains the importance of food safety. Cut in footage and images of a kitchen and restaurant patrons.

Text Prompt:
Describe the importance of food safety at a restaurant in one paragraph.

Question

Qui dolorem eum fugiat quo voluptas nulla pariatur?
◯ Dolorem eum
◯ Dolorem eum
◯ Dolorem eum

Answer

Lorem ipsum dolor sit amet, consectetur adipiscing elit, sed do eiusmod tempor incididunt ut labore et dolore magna aliqua. Ut enim ad minim veniam, quis nostrud exercitation ullamco laboris

Sed ut perspiciatis unde omnis iste natus error sit voluptatem accusantium doloremque laudantium, totam rem aperiam.

Question Prompt:
Based on the video transcript, create a multiple choice question with three options. Display the explanation of the correct answer.

Enhancing Efficiency and Personalization

Automating prompt workflows significantly reduces manual effort and dramatically speeds up production time. This newfound efficiency allows L&D teams to update training materials more frequently, ensuring that content remains current and relevant. It also opens the door to greater personalization.

Imagine you need to create training modules for a new software product that's tailored to different departments within your organization. Instead of creating each module from scratch, you can use a single core prompt workflow and simply swap out role-specific prompts within the chain.

- **Core workflow**—a sequence of prompts that generates the basic structure of the module (such as objectives, core content, and assessments).
- **Role-specific prompts**—prompts that tailor examples, scenarios, and terminology to a specific audience (for example, sales, HR, customer support, or engineering).

By swapping out role-specific prompts, you can quickly produce multiple versions of the training module—each personalized to a particular department's needs and context.

Refining and Storing Prompt Workflows

Prompt workflows are not static entities. They are living systems that should be continuously updated and refined. As you gain experience, analyze learner feedback, and observe the performance of your AI-generated content, you can fine-tune your prompts to improve the quality, relevance, and effectiveness of your learning deliverables.

Say you've established a prompt workflow that reliably produces a basic training module on a specific topic. Now, you can refine each prompt to elevate the quality of the output. You might:

- **Enhance engagement.** Modify prompts to include more engaging activities, such as interactive scenarios, gamified elements, or real-world examples.
- **Improve clarity.** Refine prompts to produce clearer narratives, more concise explanations, and more intuitive user interfaces.

- **Strengthen alignment.** Adjust prompts to ensure that the content aligns more closely with specific business goals, performance metrics, or compliance requirements.
- **Incorporate learner feedback.** Based on data from learner interactions and feedback surveys, modify prompts to address areas where learners struggled or expressed confusion.

Prompt libraries play a crucial role in scaling and streamlining these evolving workflows. Systematically organizing your refined prompts within a library ensures that your best practices, insights, and improvements are easily accessible and reusable across your learning initiatives. Platforms like Notion or Monday.com can be invaluable for documenting these workflows because they provide robust tools for capturing the iterative process of prompt refinement.

Figure 9-6 shows an example of my YouTube prompt workflow in Notion.

Figure 9-6. Prompt Workflow Example

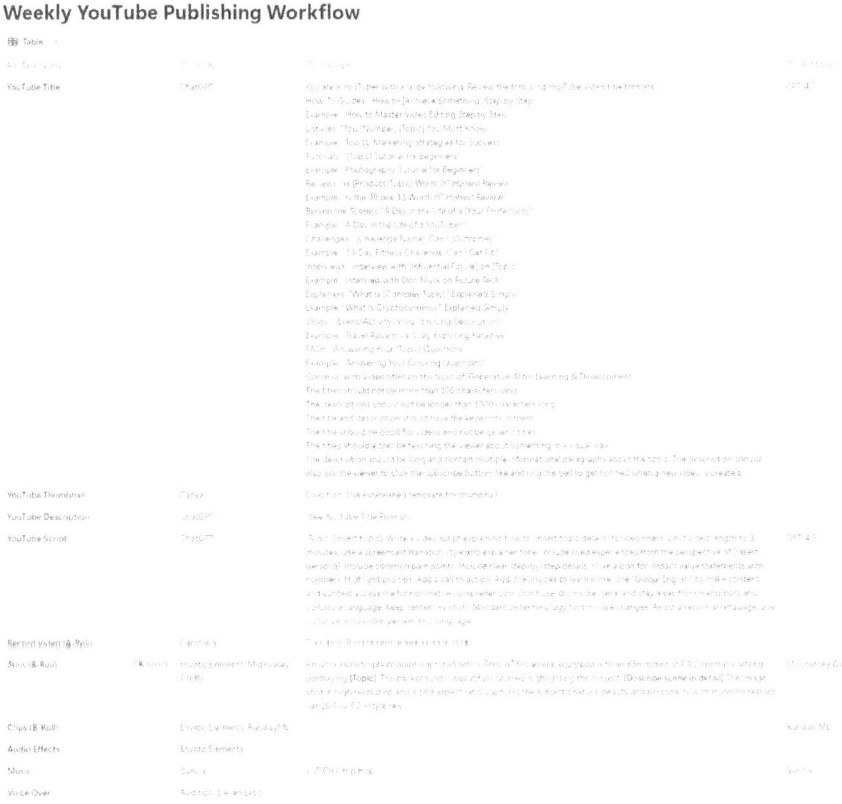

Weekly YouTube Publishing Workflow

Leveraging these tools enhances transparency, promotes collaborative refinement, and ensures your prompt workflows continuously evolve to deliver effective learning experiences.

The shift from single prompts to prompt workflows represents a significant leap forward in the application of AI in L&D. By embracing this approach, you can unlock new levels of efficiency, scalability, and personalization.

As these workflows mature and integrate into a broader ecosystem of AI-powered tools, they will transform the L&D function into a driving force for organizational learning, agility, and success. The future of L&D is intelligent, automated, and interconnected, and prompt workflows are the key to unlocking its full potential.

Using GPTs and Automation to Increase Efficiency

As we explore the AI-driven landscape, we must differentiate advanced AI tools (like OpenAI GPTs, Google Gems, or Microsoft Copilot agents) from traditional automation built using platforms like Zapier, Make.com, or n8n. When I mention GPTs, you can include Google Gems and Microsoft Copilot agents for the rest of this conversation.

GPTs (*generative pretrained transformers*) rely on human-initiated interactions—which are typically conversational prompts—and can reference external knowledge or data via APIs to creatively respond to or intelligently adapt tasks. These tools excel at understanding context, generating human-like text, and facilitating complex workflows through guidance or co-creation with users.

In contrast, *an automation* is triggered by events (such as user actions or system-generated events) that follow systematic, predefined logic sequences to perform tasks. Automations orchestrate multiple tools or models to execute tasks, but they're not autonomous or creative; they strictly follow set instructions and lack independent decision-making capabilities. Figure 9-7 provides a comparison of GPTs and automation.

Figure 9-7. GPTs vs. Automation

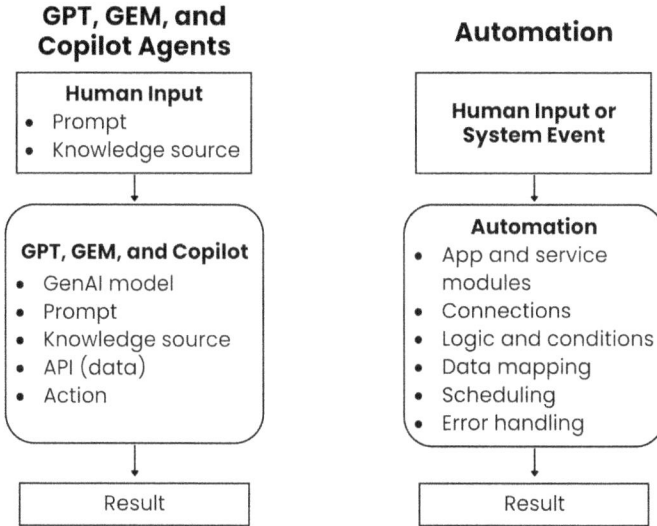

GPT, GEM, and Copilot Agents	Automation
Human Input • Prompt • Knowledge source	**Human Input or System Event**
↓	↓
GPT, GEM, and Copilot • GenAI model • Prompt • Knowledge source • API (data) • Action	**Automation** • App and service modules • Connections • Logic and conditions • Data mapping • Scheduling • Error handling
↓	↓
Result	Result

Essentially, autonomous AI agents go one step beyond automation. They combine the adaptive reasoning and contextual intelligence seen in conversational AI agents with proactive decision making and self-directed task execution. Unlike a simple automation, autonomous agents dynamically navigate complex environments, prioritize actions based on changing circumstances, and independently complete tasks toward user-defined objectives without continual human oversight. Think of them as responsive assistants engaging in intelligent dialogue, whereas automations function like structured workflows, reliably performing predetermined tasks in response to specific events.

I'll discuss AI agents in the next chapter. So, hang tight! For now, let's explore how GPTs can revolutionize your L&D initiatives.

What Are GPTs, and Why Should You Care?

GPTs are advanced AI models that go beyond simple prompts. They combine a prompt, knowledge, and access to external tools into a reusable unit, enabling the creation of sophisticated, adaptable learning content and performing data analysis or examination of business problems that may require a training solution.

Customizable versions of GPTs can be tailored for specific purposes. They allow you to give the AI model specific instructions and extra knowledge, meaning you can fine-tune a GPT to perform a specific task or answer questions within a particular domain. For example, you could create a GPT that specializes in generating assessment questions for a specific course or one that provides personalized feedback on learner writing assignments.

EXERCISE

Creating a GPT

Let's walk through the steps to create a GPT. You can use one of the freeform or structured prompts you worked on earlier as the foundation or you could create a new task. (Note: The following instructions focus on OpenAI's GPTs, but Copilot agents follow the same setup. As of this writing, Google Gems only allows prompts [instructions] and knowledge sources.)

1. **Access GPT configuration:**
   - Go to the OpenAI website and log in to your account.
   - Select "Explore GPTs" or a similar option to start the GPT creation process.
   - Click the "+Create" button.
   - Open the GPT creation interface and navigate to the "Configure" tab on the left side of your screen.
2. **Fill in the GPT name:**
   - Locate the "Name" field.
   - Enter a concise and descriptive title for your GPT, such as "Multiple-Choice Question Creator 1.03."
3. **Add a description:**
   - Find the "Description" field.
   - Enter a brief but clear description of your GPT's purpose.
4. **Add instructions.** In the provided "Instructions" box, write your freeform or structured prompt.
5. **Include conversation starters.** Create predefined prompts to help users interact with your GPT. Examples include:
   - "Create questions on leadership."
   - "Create questions from the uploaded documents."
   - "I need 10 questions on maintaining basic hygiene."
   - "Create questions from this website: [URL]."

6. **Input knowledge (optional).** Use the "Upload files" button under "Knowledge" to attach any relevant documents or information your GPT should use.
7. **Add capabilities.** Check or uncheck boxes for GPT capabilities as needed:
    ○ Web search
    ○ Canvas (a collaborative text area)
    ○ DALL-E (image generation)
    ○ Code interpreter and data analysis
8. **Include actions (optional):** Connect to external APIs.
9. **Finalize:**
    ○ Once you've filled in all the necessary information, review it carefully to ensure accuracy.
    ○ Test your GPT in the screen's preview panel on the right side.

Once you've reviewed and tested your GPT, you may want to share it with others. To share your GPT, select the "share GPT" option. You can choose to share privately ("only me"), provide a link for specific people ("anyone with the link"), or make it publicly available through the GPT Store.

To help users find your GPT, assign a relevant category, such as "education." Click "save" to finalize your sharing preferences.

If you are on an OpenAI Teams or enterprise account, you can privately share GPTs with your team members. This could be used as a prompt library.

Automating Your Workflow

I remember the first time I connected two application functions—transcribe and transform—without writing a single line of code. It was straightforward; I uploaded my YouTube video, it generated a transcript, and it transformed the transcript into a summary, keywords, and a blog post (Figure 9-8). What a fantastic feeling watching my first automation run. Suddenly, my time-consuming writing tasks were replaced by an automated workflow that hummed along in the background while I focused on other efforts.

This is the quiet revolution happening in L&D: Automation tools are transforming how we manage the mechanics of learning operations without requiring a background in programming.

Figure 9-8. Automation Workflow

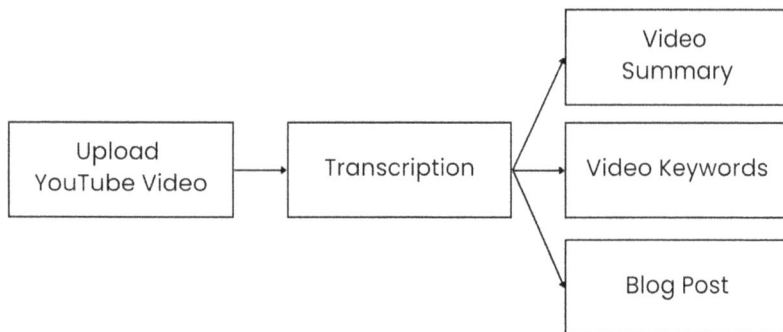

Automation platforms like Zapier, Make, and n8n serve as digital connectors between the expanding universe of apps and services that power modern L&D functions. They enable you to create custom workflows that eliminate manual processes, reduce administrative overhead, and create seamless experiences for learners.

Figure 9-9 shows an automation from Make.com that takes a row of data in a Google Sheet (supplied by a Google Form) using the GPT-4o model and prompt to create a video script; the script Markdown language is then cleaned up and sent via email using Outlook.

Figure 9-9. Make.com Automation Example

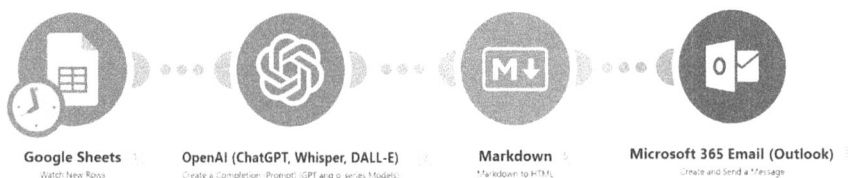

Google Sheets
Watch New Rows

OpenAI (ChatGPT, Whisper, DALL-E)
Create a Completion (Prompt) (GPT and o-series Models)

Markdown
Markdown to HTML

Microsoft 365 Email (Outlook)
Create and Send a Message

In this example, the structured prompt is doing the heavy lifting by taking the data in the Google Sheet and creating an educational video script.

Automation Functionality

An automation represents a fundamentally different approach to task execution than a GPT. Automation platforms operate on a trigger-action framework with sophisticated middleware capabilities, which means the automation starts with human input or a system event. This dual trigger mechanism explains why automation platforms are so versatile in L&D workflows. A human might initiate a process (like an instructor uploading new course materials), or a system event could trigger the action automatically (like a learner completing an assessment).

Here are the building blocks of automation:

- **App and service modules** represent the prebuilt connectors to learning platforms, communication tools, and business systems. Each platform offers hundreds of integration points.
- **Connections** form the pathways between modules. This seemingly simple concept solves one of learning technology's persistent challenges: getting isolated platforms to communicate. No more CSV exports from your LMS that you must then manually import into your reporting tool.
- **Logic and conditions** enable decision branching. For instance, when a learner completes a course with a passing score, one path activates. When they fail, another path triggers remediation. This conditional logic creates responsive learning experiences that are impossible to manage manually at scale.
- **Data mapping** addresses the translation challenge between systems. Your LMS stores completion status as "completed," but your HR information system (HRIS) requires "finished." Data mapping transforms information as it flows between platforms.
- **Scheduling** introduces time as a variable. An example would be a leadership development program that automatically schedules follow-up resources at precise intervals after each module—2 days, 7 days, or 30 days—reinforcing learning at optimal spacing points for retention.
- **Error handling** represents the safety nets. When integrations fail or data doesn't conform to expectations, these mechanisms prevent workflow collapse. This is crucial when automation connects critical certification processes or compliance training.

The profound difference between a GPT and automation lies in their fundamental purpose. GPTs process information and generate insights or content, while automation platforms execute predefined workflows across system boundaries. Together, they form complementary forces that are reshaping learning operations.

Getting Started With Automation

If you're new to these platforms, start with a simple but meaningful process—perhaps automating course completion certificates or participant reminders. The immediate time savings will build confidence while providing tangible benefits to your audience.

Remember that automation works best when it removes friction rather than adding complexity. Focus on processes that are repetitive, predictable, and time consuming. The goal isn't to automate everything but to strategically eliminate mundane, administrative burdens that distract from your core mission of supporting the business, your associates, and your customers.

As you grow more comfortable, look for opportunities to connect disparate systems that traditionally exist in silos. Some of the most powerful automations bridge the gap between learning platforms and business systems, like customer relationship management (CRM) software, project management tools, and communication channels.

The true power of these platforms is the ability to create learning experiences that would be impossible to administer manually. When repetitive tasks happen automatically, you gain the freedom to focus on the human elements of learning that machines can't replicate: empathy, creativity, and connection.

EXERCISE

Planning Your Automation

Take a blank sheet of paper or open a digital document. Let's create a structured planning tool that will help you identify prime automation candidates in your learning operations.

Step 1. Process Inventory

List three to five repetitive tasks that consume your time each week. Don't overthink this. Simple examples include:

- Sending course reminder emails
- Distributing completion certificates
- Updating attendance records
- Compiling weekly training metrics
- Moving data between systems

Step 2. Impact Assessment

For each process, answer these questions:

- How much time does this consume weekly?
- What higher-value work could you do with that time?
- What errors or inconsistencies occur in the current process?
- Who feels friction from the current process? You, learners, or managers?

Step 3. Automation Viability Check

Examine each process through these lenses:

- **Trigger clarity.** What consistently signals that this process should start?
  A form submission, calendar date, or course completion?
- **Pattern consistency.** Does this follow the same steps each time?
- **System boundaries.** Which platforms hold the starting data and which need the ending data?
- **Decision points.** What simple if/then logic governs the process?

Step 4. First Automation Selection

Review your analysis and select one process that meets these criteria:

- High time investment
- Clear trigger event
- Consistent pattern
- Connects systems you use daily
- Minimal complex decisions

Use the selected process as your first automation candidate.

Step 5. Workflow Mapping

For your selected process, create a simple flowchart with these elements:

1. Trigger (When . . .)
2. Source data (Get information from . . .)
3. Actions (Do this . . .)
4. Destination (Put result in . . .)

Step 6. Platform Selection

Based on your workflow, which platform suits your needs?

- **Zapier** allows for many common app connections and simple logic.
- **Make** provides visual mapping and complex data transformations.
- **n8n** can handle highly customized solutions.

Step 7. Value Projection

Calculate the potential impact:

- Time saved weekly × 52 = annual time recovery
- Error reduction (high, medium, or low)
- Experience improvement for learners or stakeholders (high, medium, or low)

This exercise transforms abstract automation concepts into concrete opportunities within your learning ecosystem. I hope it helps shift your perspective from seeing these platforms as technical tools to seeing them as designers working tirelessly in the background while you focus on the irreplaceable human elements of learning.

Here are some additional automation ideas to consider:

- **Learner onboarding sequences.** Create sophisticated welcome sequences that adapt based on job role, experience level, or learning preferences. These automations can schedule check-ins, provide resources at strategic intervals, and adjust content based on engagement metrics.
- **Certificate and credential management.** Automatically issue, track, and verify digital credentials across systems, creating a seamless experience for both learners and administrators.
- **Learning data consolidation.** Pull assessment results, completion statistics, and feedback from various platforms into centralized repositories for comprehensive reporting and analysis.
- **Content updates and distribution.** When learning materials are updated in your authoring tool, automation can instantly update records in your LMS, notify affected learners, and archive previous versions.

What mundane process might you automate today?

Conclusion

Prompt libraries establish the foundation of effective GenAI messaging. Prompt workflows sequence these interactions into productive task completion. GPTs offer specialized, persistent intelligence and task completion within focused domains. Automations execute predefined processes across system boundaries. These four distinct technologies can combine to create a framework for strategic implementation.

Understanding their differences reveals their complementary nature. Consider how they create a continuous spectrum of capability. Prompt libraries provide building blocks that workflows arrange into logical sequences. Well-designed prompts inform the specialized intelligence of GPTs. Automations then connect these AI capabilities to your broader technology ecosystem.

This integration signals a fundamental shift in learning design philosophy. We now think less about isolated content pieces and more about intelligent systems that adapt and respond. Our role transforms from content creators to architects of learning experiences that scale beyond what manual processes could achieve.

The value extends beyond efficiency. These technologies unlock learning approaches that were previously impossible to implement at scale. Personalization becomes feasible across thousands of learners. Performance support integrates seamlessly into workflows. Learning analytics capture insights that drive continuous improvement.

Yet technology alone accomplishes nothing. Our professional expertise determines how effectively these tools serve learning outcomes. The most sophisticated GPT cannot replace our understanding of adult learning principles. The most elegant automation cannot substitute for human empathy toward learner challenges.

The next chapter explores AI agents—systems that combine multiple capabilities to act with autonomy in specific domains. We'll examine how these agents transcend simple automation to become active participants in the learning process. From content curation to adaptive facilitation, they represent the next evolution in our expanding toolkit. The stage is set for intelligent systems that don't just respond to commands but anticipate our needs and take initiative within carefully defined parameters.

CHAPTER 10
Autonomous Agents

In This Chapter
- The defining characteristics and capabilities of autonomous agents in L&D
- Essential components and frameworks for implementing AI agents
- Strategies for maintaining and optimizing agent performance

"AI agents will complete all human tasks and eliminate jobs!"

Let's address the elephant in the room. AI agents are not expected to eliminate all human tasks or jobs; however, they will significantly reshape work by automating routine and repetitive tasks and augmenting human productivity. While certain roles will likely be automated, AI's broader influence involves both the displacement and creation of jobs, leading to a transformation rather than total replacement.

Have you considered how much of your L&D work could be automated? It won't just be routine tasks but also complex, nuanced work that focuses on understanding learner needs, creating personalized pathways, and measuring outcomes. The capabilities of autonomous agents have expanded far beyond simple chatbots. We stand at a turning point where AI can fundamentally transform how we approach organizational learning and the role of a learning professional.

As a learning architect, I've spent hours analyzing course completion rates, identifying knowledge gaps, and manually creating learning paths. The process is meticulous and time consuming. Now, autonomous agents can perform similar analyses in minutes, freeing me up to focus on strategy and innovation. The contrast is stark. Both approaches aim for the same goal, but by leveraging agents, you can create a powerful force multiplier for your efforts.

Many L&D departments still operate with tools and processes designed for a previous era. We craft static learning experiences, react to data rather than predict needs, and struggle to scale personalization. Autonomous agents offer a different path. They can continuously analyze learner behavior, adapt the content in real time, and provide insights that would take teams of humans weeks to generate.

This chapter begins by exploring the core characteristics and types of autonomous agents to establish a foundation for understanding their potential in learning contexts. The discussion then shifts to the essential components of AI agents. We'll examine various development and implementation frameworks and real-world examples and case studies that illustrate successful applications in corporate learning environments. By the end, you'll have the knowledge and tools to effectively implement and manage autonomous agents in your L&D initiatives.

What Are Autonomous Agents?

Autonomous agents are "an advanced form of AI that can understand and respond to inquiries, then take action without human intervention," according to Salesforce (n.d.)—one of the first SAAS companies to go all in with their agent offering AgentForce. Autonomous agents involve a computational system designed to perceive the environment, make decisions, and take actions to achieve specific goals. When given an objective, these agents can generate and complete tasks independently or semi-independently, working until the objective is achieved.

This autonomy sets them apart from traditional AI systems, which typically require human input and follow preprogrammed instructions. They use various techniques, including chain-of-thought prompts and reasoning models, while an LLM is asked to think through a problem step-by-step and outline the actions it would take.

Agents vs. Automation

Agents fundamentally differ from automation in both capability and function (Figure 10-1). Automations execute predetermined steps across systems when triggered by specific events and follow fixed pathways with conditional logic. Agents, on the other hand, determine their own pathways toward objectives. They make decisions, adjust strategies based on outcomes, and interact with multiple systems through a reasoning layer.

Figure 10-1. Automation vs. Agents

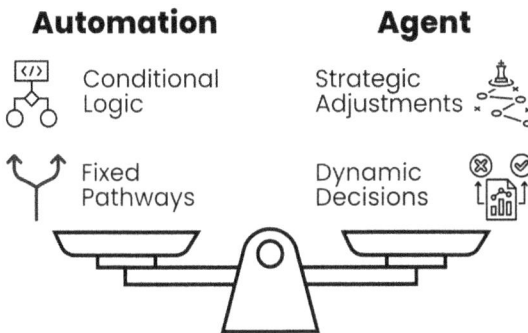

The key is understanding when you should build an automation versus an agent. Let's look at two examples:

- **When a new employee joins your organization, you might use automation to streamline the onboarding process (Table 10-1).** When the HR system detects a new employee record, automation software automatically enrolls the new hire in the onboarding course, sends a welcome email, and assigns mandatory compliance training. Then, they could be sent different onboarding modules depending on their department or job role, such as assigning specific safety training to manufacturing employees and leadership modules to managers. Here, the automation consistently follows predefined steps, ensuring employees receive the exact resources they need at the right time, without human intervention.

- **Now, imagine an AI agent in the form of a learning coach that's integrated into your company's LMS.** The learning coach sets a goal: helping employees master new skills, such as leadership or negotiation. It assesses learners' progress by analyzing performance data, quiz results, feedback, and engagement levels. It dynamically decides the best pathway for each employee, perhaps recommending specific courses, videos, mentorship opportunities, or even personalized learning tips. It also continuously adapts its strategies based on learner feedback and outcomes, adjusting content and recommendations to optimize learning. Here, employees receive personalized, timely support, and the agent continually improves the learning experience; this ultimately increases engagement, retention, and performance outcomes.

Table 10-1. Automation vs. AI Agent Example

Factor	Automation	AI Agent
Trigger	New employee joins (event-based)	Skill mastery goal (objective driven)
Action	Executes predefined onboarding steps	Chooses personalized learning pathways
Decision making	Conditional logic; limited flexibility	Adaptive reasoning; highly flexible
Learning and improvement	Does not learn or adapt independently	Learns, adapts, and improves continuously

An automation simplifies repetitive tasks through predictable sequences, while AI agents personalize, adapt, and evolve to meet the learner's unique needs and the workplace's changing conditions.

How Do AI Agents Work?

An AI agent dynamically responds to inputs by integrating multiple capabilities—such as retrieval and reasoning, the use of specialized tools, and memory storage—to produce tailored outcomes. Again, unlike traditional automation systems that follow fixed, predefined steps, an AI agent intelligently adapts its decisions and strategies based on the context and outcomes of each interaction.

To help demonstrate how AI agents work, let's walk through the process shown in Figure 10-2 using the AI-powered learning scenario. (Note: Agent functions—including retrieval and reasoning, tools and data, and memory—do not run linearly and may be called on multiple times to complete a task.)

Figure 10-2. How Does an Agent Work?

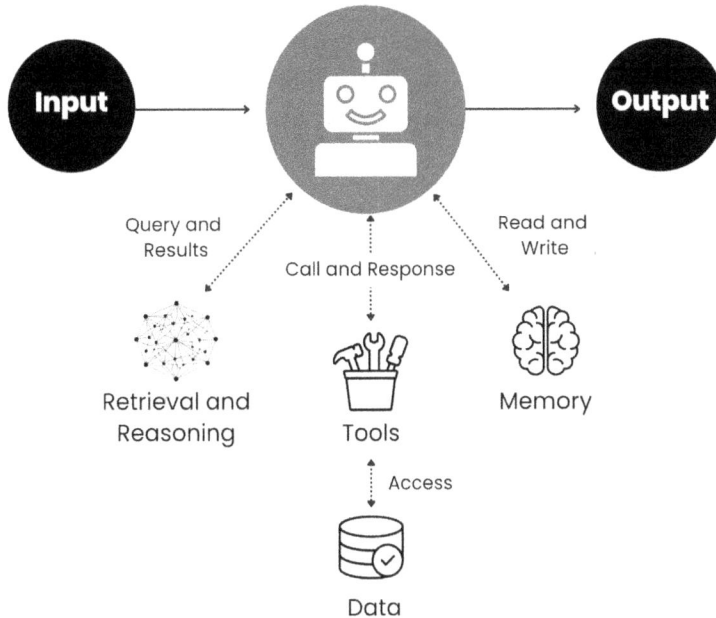

Input (or *learner interaction*) involves the agent receiving input, such as employee course activity, quiz or assessment results, or learner feedback or progress data.

During *retrieval and reasoning*, the learning coach queries available learning resources, data about previous learners, or historical course outcomes. It uses reasoning to identify patterns or strategies that previously resulted in successful learning outcomes.

Tools and data access involves the learning coach accessing its tools, such as a course calendar, content libraries, learning activities, and assessments. It retrieves specific materials (such as videos, articles, or job aids) from databases (data access).

The AI model then uses *memory* (or *learning from past interactions*). Short-term memory is used to temporarily hold course selections while they are assigned. Long-term memory is used to refine recommendations, ensuring that suggestions improve based on past interactions.

During *decision and output*, the learning coach makes a decision that's based on reasoning, tool access, and memory. It may suggest personalized next steps, like specific training courses or development resources tailored to the employee's needs. It outputs these tailored recommendations directly to the learner (via notifications, the LMS interface, or emails).

This process is admittedly complex, so let's go through the steps of another real-world example. This time, we'll look at how an agent interacts with a Google Calendar:

1. **Memory (understanding context).** The Agent receives a chat message asking, "What does my schedule look like tomorrow?" At this stage, it leverages memory to understand context, such as the current date (November 18, 2025) and the user's request to check their schedule for the next day.

2. **Retrieval and reasoning (analyzing the request).** The AI agent uses its retrieval and reasoning capabilities (powered by OpenAI's GPT-4o) to interpret exactly what's needed: identifying that the user is specifically asking about events scheduled on November 18, 2025, and deciding to retrieve calendar events for this date range.

3. **Tools (accessing Google Calendar).** The AI agent calls upon its connected tools, specifically Google Calendar, to gather accurate information. It sends a JSON (JavaScript Object Notation) query to Google Calendar to request events from midnight (00:00) to the end of the day (23:59) on November 18, 2025.

4. **Retrieval and reasoning (processing results).** Google Calendar returns event details, which the agent receives as structured JSON data. The AI agent uses its reasoning capability again to parse this data, identifying that there is one scheduled event: "Take Malcolm for a walk from 5 to 5:30 p.m. (EST)."

5. **Output (providing a response).** After interpreting and formatting the retrieved event information, the AI agent prepares a clear, conversational output message: "You have one event scheduled for tomorrow, November 18, 2025: Take Malcolm for a walk from 5 to 5:30 p.m. (EST). If you need anything else, let me know!" The

response is delivered back to the user as a helpful, concise answer through the chat interface.

This example really highlights how an AI agent fundamentally differs from automation. Now, it's your turn to try out adding an AI agent to your L&D workflows.

EXERCISE

Mapping an Existing Workflow to an AI Agent

Let's take one of your existing workflows and identify the opportunities for integrating an AI agent by distinguishing tasks best suited for an agent's adaptive reasoning from those that could remain automated. Follow these steps:

1. **Select a workflow.** Choose an existing workflow from your L&D processes (such as onboarding, compliance training reminders, skill assessments, or learner feedback loops).
2. **Map the current workflow.** Clearly outline each step of your current workflow from start to finish. Include actions, decision points, triggers, and outcomes.
3. **Identify points of adaptability.** Review your mapped workflow and highlight points where decision making or adaptive reasoning could significantly enhance learner outcomes or efficiency. Clearly note which aspects involve fixed, predictable logic (better suited for automation), and which require flexible, dynamic responses (ideal for an AI agent).
4. **Agent workflow design.** Create a new workflow outline that clearly shows how an AI agent would navigate these steps differently. Specifically, highlight answers to these questions:
   - What input would trigger agent interaction?
   - Which tools or data sources would the agent access?
   - How would memory (past learner interactions) influence the agent's response?
   - What personalized outputs could the agent provide?

So, how did you do? Were you able to map out a workflow and indicate what tasks would an agent could perform? Figure 10-3 provides an example I created of a mapped workflow for employee onboarding.

Figure 10-3. Employee Onboarding Workflow

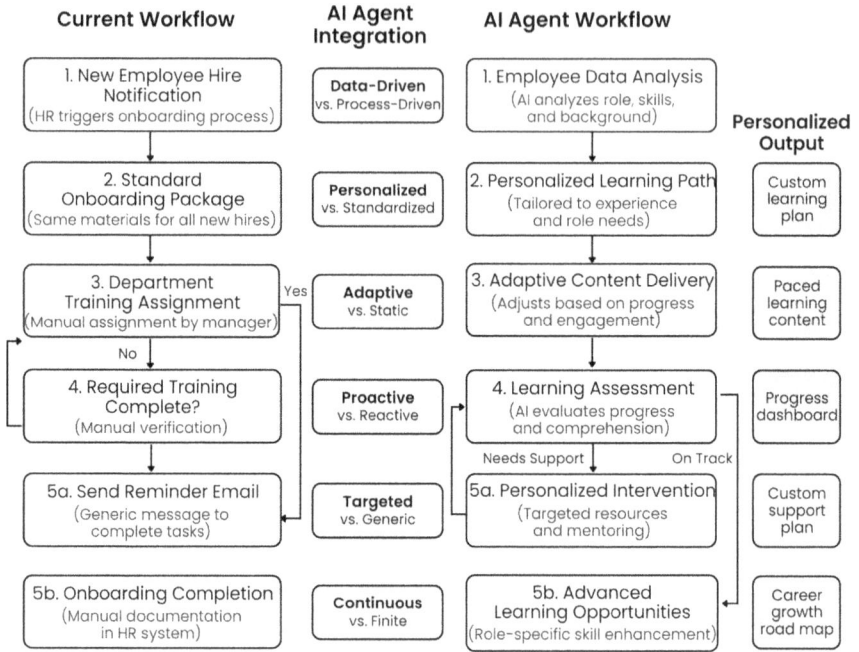

Current Workflow	AI Agent Integration	AI Agent Workflow	Personalized Output
1. New Employee Hire Notification (HR triggers onboarding process)	Data-Driven vs. Process-Driven	1. Employee Data Analysis (AI analyzes role, skills, and background)	
2. Standard Onboarding Package (Same materials for all new hires)	Personalized vs. Standardized	2. Personalized Learning Path (Tailored to experience and role needs)	Custom learning plan
3. Department Training Assignment (Manual assignment by manager)	Adaptive vs. Static	3. Adaptive Content Delivery (Adjusts based on progress and engagement)	Paced learning content
4. Required Training Complete? (Manual verification)	Proactive vs. Reactive	4. Learning Assessment (AI evaluates progress and comprehension)	Progress dashboard
5a. Send Reminder Email (Generic message to complete tasks)	Targeted vs. Generic	5a. Personalized Intervention (Targeted resources and mentoring)	Custom support plan
5b. Onboarding Completion (Manual documentation in HR system)	Continuous vs. Finite	5b. Advanced Learning Opportunities (Role-specific skill enhancement)	Career growth road map

On the left side, you'll find the current workflow, which is likely similar to the one you mapped out. It begins with a manual trigger (the hiring notification), and then moves through standardized steps, including generic onboarding materials, manual manager assignment, and static verification of training completion. This workflow, like many traditional processes, relies heavily on manual actions, fixed logic, and reactive interventions.

In contrast, the right side demonstrates an optimized AI agent workflow. Notice how the agent's involvement transforms the onboarding experience at each step:

1. **Data-driven.** Instead of a generic trigger, the agent proactively analyzes employee data, considering their unique role, skills, and background.

2. **Personalized.** The agent dynamically creates a customized learning path tailored specifically to the individual's experience and career needs, rather than a one-size-fits-all package.

3. **Adaptive.** Content delivery isn't static; it adjusts based on real-time employee engagement and progress.

4. **Proactive assessment.** Continuous evaluation by the agent ensures that timely, personalized training occurs when support is needed, rather than relying on manual checks and generic reminders.

5. **Continuous growth.** Unlike traditional workflows that end on completion, the AI agent provides ongoing, advanced learning opportunities, creating pathways for continuous development and career growth.

This example illustrates how an existing manual or automated process can evolve when empowered by an intelligent agent, resulting in greater personalization, adaptability, and continuous learner engagement.

Types of Autonomous Agents in L&D and Instructional Design

Advancements in AI have led to the integration of autonomous agents, improving adaptive learning, personalized instruction, and intelligent tutoring. These agents range from basic rule-based systems to advanced self-aware models. Here are some types of agent functions with real-word examples:

- **Reactive agents** operate based on predefined rules, responding to immediate stimuli without memory or learning capability. These agents are best suited for structured, repetitive tasks. AI-driven chatbots integrated with LMSs (such as Instancy's chatbots in Moodle) provide instant responses to FAQs about course logistics and deadlines.

- **Limited memory agents** retain past interactions to personalize learning experiences by adjusting content difficulty and engagement strategies. Quizlet AI dynamically adapts flashcard difficulty based on student performance history.

- **World model–based agents** construct simulations of their environment, allowing them to predict outcomes and adapt learning scenarios dynamically. Medical Virtual Patients, which is used in healthcare training, adapts to students' diagnostic choices, mimicking real-world patient interactions.

- **Deliberative agents** engage in planning and strategic reasoning to optimize student learning pathways. Carnegie Learning's MATHia employs belief-desire-intention (BDI) architectures to diagnose misconceptions and generate personalized learning paths.

- **Hybrid agents** combine reactive responsiveness with deliberative reasoning, allowing them to provide immediate support, as well as plan long-term learning strategies. Jill Watson, an AI teaching assistant at Georgia Tech, answers student questions in real time while analyzing engagement patterns to predict at-risk learners.
- **Theory of mind (ToM) agents** infer a learner's emotional state and cognitive processes, adapting their instructional approach accordingly. The EMOTE virtual tutor adjusts feedback based on student frustration levels.
- **Self-aware agents** theoretically evaluate their teaching effectiveness and autonomously refine instructional strategies. The AI2T system explores meta-reasoning architectures that allow AI to self-monitor its decision making and adjust instructional techniques.

Here are two additional categories that could be integrated in the future:

- **Learning agents** as AI models that autonomously refine teaching strategies via reinforcement learning
- **Swarm agents** as multi-agent systems that facilitate collaborative and peer-based learning environments

As AI-driven training advances, learning professionals must match AI architectures to instructional needs, from reactive chatbots for routine inquiries to ToM agents for personalized, emotional engagement.

Foundation Models and Agentic Tools

At this point, you have examined the three main components of an AI agent:

- Retrieval and reasoning
- Tools and data
- Memory

Typically, when you create an AI agent, you'll select a GenAI model, a tool, and some form of memory capability. These can be external or internal platforms and tools.

What if all these functions were under one roof? Well, agents powered by foundation models from OpenAI, Google, Anthropic, X.AI, and others offer the ability to complete complex tasks through various specialized tools.

Some may consider these automations and not agents, or semiautonomous agents. However, regardless of how we categorize these functions, they are powerful and will influence the creation and delivery of learning experiences moving forward.

Let's review some of the available agentic tools:

- **Scheduled tasks and reminders.** Foundation models like OpenAI's GPT use tasks to prompt timely task execution, ensuring that important milestones and actions are never missed. Reminders enhance the agent's proactive capability, facilitating continuous productivity.

- **Computer control.** These tools empower agents to interact directly with software systems—including personal computers and mobile phones—enabling them to perform tasks such as navigating user interfaces, filling forms, or activating system functions. This capability bridges the gap between the agent's decision making and practical implementation.

- **Coding.** Advanced coding tools, exemplified by Anthropic's Claude Code, enable agents to autonomously perform software development tasks. AI agents equipped with coding capabilities can write, test, debug, and maintain software, while continuously adhering to rigorous safety protocols.

- **Deep research.** Tools like OpenAI, Google, X.AI, and Perplexity's iterative deep research system give agents the power to autonomously gather, evaluate, and synthesize information from numerous sources quickly and precisely. AI agents can dynamically adapt their research strategies, enhancing their effectiveness and reliability.

Each of these specialized tools significantly expands an AI agent's capabilities, transforming it from a simple task executor into an intelligent, proactive partner capable of complex, adaptive workflows.

Understanding how AI agents use these tools sets the foundation for learning how to build your own AI agent. In the next section, we will explore step-by-step how to design, implement, and deploy an effective AI agent tailored specifically to your organizational needs.

Planning Your Agent

New advances in AI agents can ultimately change how L&D interacts with AI. These intelligent systems can autonomously complete tasks, personalize learning experiences, and provide valuable insights to improve learning outcomes. However, successfully implementing AI agents in L&D requires careful planning and consideration.

When implementing AI agents, you should follow these three core principles:

- **Maintain simplicity.** Keep your agent's design simple. This will make it easier to understand, debug, and maintain. A prompt workflow or automation may get the job done.
- **Prioritize transparency.** Document the agent's planning steps. This will help team members understand how the agent makes decisions and build trust in its capabilities. It also comes in handy if agent responsibility is handed off.
- **Test your agent-computer interface (ACI).** Thoroughly document and test your ACI to ensure the agent can effectively interact with the tools and systems it needs to perform the tasks. As you test, address any potential issues of access, cost, security, and governance.

Now, let's review the steps you can take to guide your learning department to effectively plan its AI agent initiatives.

Define the Agent's Purpose and Objectives

Before embarking on AI agent development, it's crucial to establish a clear understanding of the agent's purpose and objectives within the L&D context. This involves identifying the specific problems the agent will solve and the value it will bring to learners.

In the prior section, you completed an exercise mapping an existing workflow and validating whether it was worth creating an agent. That is just the beginning.

Your learning content strategy should align with the agent's purpose and objectives, as well as the target audience's needs and preferences (which I'll get to momentarily). While there are entire books on these approaches, let's briefly consider a few popular options:

- **Microlearning.** AI agents can facilitate microlearning by providing bite-sized lessons, quizzes, and activities.
- **Gamification.** AI agents can track learner progress, award points, and provide feedback within a gamified learning environment.
- **Personalized learning paths.** AI agents can create customized learning paths based on individual learner needs and preferences.

It's important to remember that AI agents are more than just assistants; they're autonomous systems capable of making decisions and taking action to achieve goals. A fundamental principle of harnessing AI within an L&D context is prioritizing a collaborative approach, ensuring it aligns with each organization's goals and unique voice.

By clearly defining the agent's purpose and objectives, organizations can ensure that their AI initiatives align with their overall L&D goals and deliver measurable value.

Identify the Target Audience

Understanding the target audience's needs, preferences, and skill levels is essential for designing an effective AI agent. This involves considering several factors, including:

- **Training modality.** You should design your AI agent to deliver content through different modalities—such as text, audio, video, and interactive simulations—to cater to diverse learning preferences. AI agents can take advantage of multimodal GenAI models to produce learning experiences.
- **Skill levels.** Learners may have varying expertise in the subject matter. They progress through different proficiency levels, from

novice to expert. AI agents should be able to adapt to these skill levels, providing appropriate challenges and support. It's also essential to consider each learner's interest in developing specific skills and tailor the learning paths to their aspirations.

- **Technological proficiency.** Consider the learners' familiarity with technology and their comfort level interacting with AI-powered systems. The agent's interface and interaction model should be intuitive and user friendly, especially for those less comfortable with the technology.
- **Accessibility needs.** Ensure the AI agent is accessible to all learners by adhering to accessibility guidelines and giving alternative formats for content. (I'll discuss accessibility in detail later, but I can't emphasize this point enough.)
- **Collaborative and interactive learning.** Depending on the topic, learners often prefer professional development that involves collaborative activities, such as group work, interactive sessions, and mentoring. AI agents can facilitate collaboration by providing platforms for group discussions, enabling peer-to-peer learning, and connecting learners with mentors or experts.

By considering the characteristics of the target audience, organizations can design AI agents that are engaging, effective, and inclusive.

Design the Agent's Interaction Model

Some agents complete tasks in the background, while others can interact with your audience. The interaction model defines how learners will interact with the AI agent. You should consider factors such as:

- **Modality.** Will the agent be text based, voice activated, or use VR or AR technologies? Each modality has its advantages and considerations:
  - *Text-based agents* are generally easier to develop and deploy and can effectively provide information, answer questions, and deliver personalized feedback.
  - *Voice-activated agents* offer a more natural and conversational interaction, which can be particularly beneficial for learners who

prefer auditory content. You can also use voice-based agents for role-playing and simulations with AI avatars to create dynamic scenarios that evolve based on the learner's responses.

- *VR- and AR-based agents* can create immersive learning experiences that allow learners to interact with virtual environments and simulations.

- **Generative AI capabilities.** When an AI agent retrieves or reasons, it can use a GenAI model for the following tasks:

  - *Generate or create new content*, such as training materials, assessments, and personalized learning plans.
  - *Repurpose or transform existing content* into different formats or modalities, such as converting text-based materials into interactive simulations.
  - *Interact with knowledge to access and retrieve information* from various sources (such as knowledge bases, databases, and the internet) to provide learners with relevant and up-to-date information.
  - *Act as a sparring partner* (a virtual coach or mentor) to provide learners with feedback, guidance, and support.

- **Personalization.** How will the agent personalize the interaction based on the learner's profile and preferences? This could involve tailoring the content, providing customized feedback, or adjusting the pace of learning.

- **Feedback mechanisms.** How will the agent provide feedback to learners? This could involve providing immediate feedback on assessments, offering suggestions for improvement, or tracking progress over time.

Choose a Development Framework

Several frameworks are available to support AI agent development. Some offer no-code or low-code agent creation; however, you'll need to know Python and other programming languages for others. Table 10-2 shows a few options.

Table 10-2. Development Frameworks

Framework	Description	Code Style
n8n AI agent builder	Open-source visual builder with LangChain integration	No code
Vertex AI agent builder	Enterprise conversational AI with Gemini integration	No code
CrewAI	Role-based system with a hybrid interface	Low code or code first
LangGraph	Stateful workflow engine for complex systems	Code first
Microsoft AutoGen	Distributed agent framework with benchmarking	Code first

Your choice of framework will depend on the AI agent's specific requirements, such as the task's complexity, the need for multi-agent collaboration, and the desired level of customization. No matter which one you choose, be ready to take the time to access and potentially install the framework and work through its agent examples.

Design for Accessibility and Inclusivity

You should prioritize accessibility and inclusivity throughout the AI agent development process. This involves:

- **Adhering to accessibility guidelines.** Ensure the agent's interface (if it's a chatbot) and content comply with accessibility standards, such as WCAG (Web Content Accessibility Guidelines).
- **Using inclusive language.** Verify that your prompt results use language that is respectful and inclusive of all learners, avoiding biases or stereotypes.
- **Comprehensive testing and validation.** Thorough testing and validation are essential to ensure your AI agent performs as expected in real-world scenarios and for diverse learners.
- **Universal Design for Learning (UDL).** Consider the UDL framework, which provides guidelines for making learning content more inclusive across disciplines. You can apply UDL principles to AI agent design to ensure accessibility and inclusivity for all learners. For

example, offer content in multiple formats—such as text, audio, and video—to accommodate different accessibility needs.

Plan for Data Security and Privacy

Protecting user data is paramount when implementing AI agents in L&D. This involves:

- Using anonymized datasets for training and collecting only essential data
- Implementing robust security measures like encryption and access controls
- Ensuring compliance with privacy policies and regulations, such as the European Union's General Data Protection Regulation (GDPR), the California Consumer Privacy Act (CCPA), and the US Family Educational Rights and Privacy Act (FERPA)
- Adopting strict data retention policies and enhancing transparency on data practices

Assess Your Data Infrastructure

Evaluate your existing data infrastructure to determine if it can support the AI agent's requirements. This involves:

- Ensuring adequate storage capacity and computational capability
- Maintaining high-quality, accurate, and consistent data
- Securing data access and management mechanisms
- Conducting audits of cloud infrastructures, IoT devices, and web and social media applications to identify vulnerabilities

Integrate With Existing Systems

Consider how the AI agent will integrate with your current L&D ecosystem, including:

- Connecting with your LMS for personalized learning and tracking
- Facilitating access to existing content repositories
- Integrating with communication platforms, assessment tools, performance management systems, and HR software for streamlined processes

Conduct a Pilot Program

Test early. Test often. Before fully deploying your AI agent, it's essential to conduct a pilot program to test its effectiveness and gather feedback from real users. This pilot program should involve a representative group of learners from your target audience.

During the pilot program, closely monitor the agent's performance, gather data on user interactions, and collect feedback on the learning experience. This feedback will be invaluable for optimizing the agent's design, content, and interaction model before its wider release.

༃༃༃

Implementing AI agents in L&D has immense potential for transforming learning experiences and improving outcomes. By following these steps, you can effectively plan your AI agent initiatives, ensuring they align with L&D goals, meet learner needs, and adhere to ethical and security standards.

Agent Maintenance, Results, and Keeping Humans in the Loop

As we've discussed, AI agents are powerful tools for delivering personalized learning experiences, automating tasks, and improving learning outcomes. However, to ensure they remain effective and relevant, you and the L&D function need to establish robust maintenance procedures. Let's review the critical aspects of AI agent maintenance and result measurement.

Common Challenges When Using AI Agents in Learning Programs

While AI agents offer tremendous benefits, they also come with challenges that every L&D professional should understand:

- **Authority.** It's crucial to determine exactly what actions your agent should be authorized to take independently. For example, should your learning agent be able to automatically enroll employees in courses that have budget implications? Should it notify managers about learning performance without employee consent?

- **Decisions.** When an agent makes decisions—like assigning specific learning paths or recommending certain development opportunities— both learners and administrators must understand the reasoning behind the decision. Without transparency, trust erodes quickly.
- **Systems.** For agents to function effectively, they need seamless access to multiple systems, such as your LMS, HRIS, calendar systems, communication tools, and performance management platforms. Each integration point creates potential friction.
- **Fallbacks.** What happens when your agent encounters a situation it can't handle? Designing appropriate escalation paths and human backup systems is critical for a positive learning experience.
- **Change.** Learning needs and organizational priorities change constantly. Agents need regular updates to their decision rules, action permissions, and knowledge base to remain aligned with current business goals.

Maintaining AI Agents for L&D

How should you maintain effective agents in your learning programs? First, monitor agent actions and outcomes. This means tracking not just what the agent says (if it's conversational), but what actions it takes and the results of those actions. Some key metrics to watch include:

- **Workflow completion rates.** How often does the agent complete the entire process?
- **Decision quality.** Are the agent's choices aligned with what an expert would do?
- **Resource allocation efficiency.** Is the agent selecting appropriate resources without waste?
- **Learner progression.** Are learners advancing through paths the agent creates?

You should also continuously refine your agent's decision-making capabilities. This means using automated and human feedback to improve the choices it makes within workflows. To do this you can:

- Review cases in which the agent made unexpected decisions.
- Analyze patterns in successful and unsuccessful workflow completions.

- Have subject matter experts validate the agent's decision trees.
- Implement A/B testing using different agent strategies.

In addition, you should balance automation with human connection. This means designing your agent workflows to handle routine processes while creating deliberate touchpoints for human interaction.

For instance, here's a blended workflow example:

1. An AI agent conducts an initial skills assessment.
2. A human coach reviews the results and meets with the learner to discuss their career goals.
3. The AI agent creates a learning path and enrolls the learner in courses.
4. A peer learning group meets biweekly to discuss application.
5. The AI agent tracks progress and provides adaptive recommendations.
6. The human coach conducts milestone reviews at 30, 60, and 90 days.

Finally, you also need to determine true business impact. This means measuring not just how efficiently your agent completes its workflows but also the impact on learning outcomes and business results. Consider tracking:

- **Workflow efficiency**—time and resources saved through automation
- **Decision quality**—comparison of agent recommendations to expert recommendations
- **Learning outcomes**—skill acquisition and knowledge retention rates
- **Business application**—performance improvements in targeted competencies

Say the average time for a new employee to reach productivity is 90 days, and managers spend 6.2 hours on training coordination per employee. In this case, the cost of delayed productivity is $9,000 per new hire.

But, after you invested in and implemented an AI agent workflow system, the average time to productivity fell to 67 days, and managers only spent 1.8 hours on training coordination per employee. The cost of delayed productivity is now down to $6,700 per new hire.

Between the productivity gains ($115,000) and manager time savings ($11,000), against the annual investment in the AI agent system, the net annual benefit for this workflow improvement is $81,000.

Converting increased efficiency and other metrics into dollar values goes a long way to demonstrating the business impact of AI agents.

Orchestrating Agent Workflows With Human Expertise

The most successful organizations create integrated systems in which AI agents manage end-to-end workflows while human L&D professionals provide strategic oversight and critical interventions.

When designing your agent workflows, it's essential to determine the appropriate balance between human and AI responsibilities. The Human–AI Task Scale, which I introduced in chapter 2, provides a framework for making these decisions (Figure 10-4).

Figure 10-4. The Human–AI Task Scale

When designing your L&D agent workflows, consider where each step falls on this spectrum. The right balance depends on factors like task complexity, risk level, creative requirements, and available expertise.

An orchestrated approach to human–AI agent collaboration could potentially reduce skills gaps while allowing L&D staff to focus more time on high-value strategic initiatives.

While agents handle process management, data analysis, content delivery, progress tracking, routine adjustments, and compliance verification, humans provide strategic direction, complex problem solving, emotional support, creative innovation, ethical oversight, and relationship building.

Consider, for example, a technology company's continuous learning ecosystem:

- AI agents constantly scan performance data to identify skills gaps (AI-driven, human led).

- Agents automatically assign relevant microlearning content and track completion (AI-led, human checked).
- Agents schedule peer practice sessions based on calendar availability (fully automated).
- Human coaches receive agent alerts about struggling employees (human–AI collaboration).
- Leaders review agent-generated trend reports to inform training strategy (AI-enhanced execution).

When implementing your own AI agent workflows, use the Human–AI Task Scale to deliberately decide which tasks should remain human-centered and which can be increasingly automated. This thoughtful orchestration ensures you leverage the strengths of both AI agents and human experts in your L&D programs.

If you think we're done with agents, think again—we're only getting started. As organizations climb higher on the Human–AI Task Scale, the nature of work itself has begun to shift, particularly for those tasked with enabling performance and learning.

The role of the learning designer is no longer confined to creating static modules or facilitating traditional training. Instead, it evolves in step with the complexity and autonomy of the agent ecosystems they manage.

To understand how this transformation unfolds, we must look closely at the emerging responsibilities of the human–machine performance analyst across the most advanced levels of human–agent collaboration: Levels 8 through 10 of the Human–AI Task Scale (Figure 10-5).

Figure 10-5. Levels 8 Through 10 of the Human–AI Task Scale

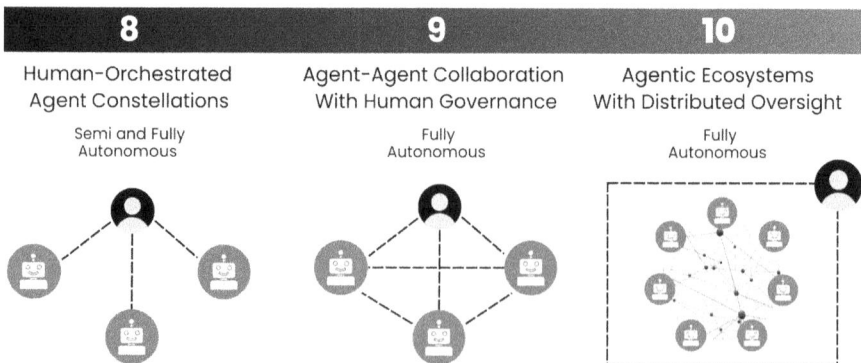

8	9	10
Human-Orchestrated Agent Constellations	Agent-Agent Collaboration With Human Governance	Agentic Ecosystems With Distributed Oversight
Semi and Fully Autonomous	Fully Autonomous	Fully Autonomous

Level 8. The Agent Orchestrator

At this stage, agents are no longer single tools supporting discrete tasks. Instead, they are now organized into constellations—miniteams of AI collaborators, each specialized and assigned to a domain of work. The human-machine performance analyst steps into the role of agent orchestrator, curating and configuring these agents to manage a full learning workflow.

In this model, the human-machine performance analyst doesn't create static content. Instead, they design flows of interaction across multiple agents. One agent might simulate learner conversations, another could serve up adaptive content, and a third could track progress and nudge engagement. The orchestrator ensures these agents speak the same language—literally and metaphorically—so learning journeys are coherent, personal, and performance driven.

The complexity is moderate but growing. The human-machine performance analyst must monitor agent handoffs, intervene when agent behavior drifts from expectations, and use data to continuously fine-tune the system. Think of this as the air traffic controller for a fleet of learning agents: vigilant, responsive, and strategic.

Consider this scenario: A human-machine performance analyst is tasked with creating an immersive onboarding experience for a global sales team. Instead of writing a static e-learning module, the analyst deploys three agents:

- **A persona simulator agent** that mimics clients in realistic role plays
- **A knowledge assistant agent** that answers product-related questions
- **An assessment agent** that observes performance and gives feedback

The human-machine performance analyst orchestrates the sequence, defines decision trees, and calibrates agent handoffs. They monitor usage and update agent behavior based on learner outcomes and manager feedback.

Level 9. The Multi-Agent Governance Lead

As agents gain the ability to communicate and coordinate among themselves, the human-performance analyst's role shifts from orchestrator to governance lead. Agents now negotiate workflows, share context, and adapt collectively—removing the human analyst from day-to-day operations but raising the stakes in terms of oversight.

In this setting, the human-machine performance analyst governs the rules of collaboration. They define constraints and protocols, including which agents can make which decisions, how knowledge is shared, and what safeguards are in place. When a reflection agent begins triggering reinforcement learning loops without human validation, the human-machine performance analyst must step in—not just to correct the error, but to investigate how and why the agent's logic evolved as it did.

Here, the analyst becomes more of a systems ethicist and architect, responsible for not only learner outcomes but the health of the entire agent network. Tools shift toward dashboards that visualize agent behavior, simulations that test policy changes, and diagnostic frameworks that audit multi-agent decisions. Complexity is high—but so is the potential for system-wide insight and impact.

Consider this scenario: A human-machine performance analyst is overseeing a real-time performance support ecosystem involving multiple collaborating agents:

- **A task prediction agent** detects when a user may need help based on workflow behaviors.
- **A context agent** provides just-in-time learning modules that are tailored to a task, proficiency level, and persona.
- **A reflection agent** follows up after the task with a microlearning review or challenge.

Agents negotiate what support to deliver and when, based on complex context signals. The human-machine performance analyst does not write static content but governs the system by:

- Testing agent alignment to learning outcomes
- Fine-tuning the content pools agents draw from
- Auditing personalization fairness and relevance

Level 10. The Learning Ecosystem Architect

At the outer edge of the Human–AI Task Scale lies a radical shift in how performance systems function. Agents now operate as a true ecosystem—

self-regulating, self-improving, and increasingly autonomous. The human-machine performance analyst, in turn, becomes a learning ecosystem architect.

In this future-forward capacity, the human-machine performance analyst no longer manages content, nor even workflows. Instead, they define learning principles, ethical boundaries, and strategic intents that guide the system as a whole. Their work is less about control and more about influence—shaping the incentives, feedback loops, and values that govern autonomous agents across the enterprise.

When agents begin to prioritize productivity at the expense of compliance, or if emergent learning patterns suggest biases in content delivery, the human-machine performance analyst engages not by rewriting modules, but by recalibrating the rules of the system itself. They collaborate with AI policy boards, work with data ethicists, and oversee the synthetic oversight agents tasked with keeping the ecosystem aligned to human goals.

At this stage, complexity reaches its peak. But for a skilled human-machine performance analyst, it is also the most creative and strategic time. The role has fully transitioned—from content creator to system designer, from facilitator to philosopher of performance.

Consider this scenario: In a self-regulated, organization-wide learning ecosystem, a human-machine performance analyst acts more like a performance policy architect. Agents across departments (such as sales, operations, or engineering) are self-configuring learning environments based on changing conditions like market shifts, compliance changes, and talent gaps. In turn, the human-machine performance analyst's role is to:

- Design behavioral policies and learning norms.
- Configure ethical boundaries (for example, agents can't prioritize productivity over compliance).
- Use analytics dashboards to spot ecosystem drift.
- Collaborate with an AI governance board to adjust policies based on organizational values

They no longer write content. Instead, they design the design systems—and monitor how learning emerges through AI-powered self-organizing activity.

What L&D Professionals Need to Know About the A2A Protocol

The Agent2Agent (A2A) protocol is a new open standard that allows AI agents built by different vendors and on different platforms to securely communicate, coordinate, and collaborate across enterprise systems.

Why does this matter for L&D? A2A enables multi-agent learning ecosystems in which multiple agents can work together in real time. For example, one agent could deliver personalized learning, another could pull compliance or performance data, and a third could schedule coaching or peer feedback.

The A2A protocol offers several key features, including:
- Open, vendor-neutral architecture
- Built on web standards (such as HTTP, JSON-RPC, and SSE)
- Secure by default, with enterprise-grade authentication
- Support for long-running tasks and asynchronous collaboration
- Ability to work across modalities (such as text, video, forms, and more)

L&D professionals will need to move beyond content creation to designing agent-powered workflows, ensuring that the right agents are activated at the right time—for the right learner, task, and context.

EXERCISE

Getting Started: Your 30-Day Agent Workflow Action Plan

Implementing AI agent workflows doesn't have to be overwhelming. The key is to start small, focus on a specific process, and build from there. This 30-day plan provides a structured approach to launching your first agent workflow initiative with tangible results.

By breaking the process into manageable weekly chunks, you can move from initial concept to a well-designed framework ready for implementation. This methodical approach ensures you address critical elements like workflow design, decision rules, measurement systems, and governance from the beginning—setting your organization up for long-term success with AI agent integration.

Break your tasks down into four tasks to accomplish across four weeks:

1. **Identify one repetitive L&D workflow that you could automate with an agent.**
   - Map the current process steps and decision points.
   - Define clear input and output requirements.
   - Calculate time currently spent on this workflow.
2. **Design your agent workflow architecture.**
   - Create decision trees for how the agent should handle different scenarios.
   - Define triggers for human intervention.
   - Document data sources the agent will need to access.
3. **Establish measurement and improvement mechanisms.**
   - Define key performance indicators for the workflow.
   - Create a system for monitoring agent decisions.
   - Design feedback loops for continuous improvement.
4. **Develop a governance and maintenance framework.**
   - Establish clear ownership of the agent workflow.
   - Create a schedule for regular performance reviews.
   - Document procedures for knowledge updates and decision rule refinements.

Conclusion

AI agents represent a transformative opportunity for L&D professionals to automate entire learning workflows, not just individual tasks. By designing thoughtful agent systems with clear decision frameworks, appropriate authority boundaries, and effective human oversight, you can dramatically increase both the efficiency and effectiveness of your learning programs.

The key to success is viewing these agents not as isolated tools, but as intelligent workflow orchestrators. They can manage learning processes from end to end—including assessing needs, allocating resources, tracking progress, adjusting in real time, and reporting outcomes—freeing your human team to focus on strategy, creativity, and meaningful connection. The most effective L&D systems emerge when AI agents and human experts work in tandem. Agents bring consistency, scalability, and data-driven precision, while humans contribute creativity, empathy, and ethical judgment.

As you design and oversee this evolving human–AI ecosystem, you'll find some of the most exciting opportunities in conversational AI. This involves intelligent assistants interacting directly with learners thereby transforming how content is delivered, questions are answered, and support is personalized.

That's where we'll go next.

CHAPTER 11

Conversational AI

In This Chapter
- The fundamental components of conversational AI and their specific applications in L&D
- Strategic approaches to implementing conversational AI
- Methods for measuring success

As I briefly mentioned in chapter 4, in early 2024, Air Canada was at the center of an AI-driven controversy that sent a stark warning to businesses worldwide as well as training departments supporting external customers. Back in 2022, a grieving passenger navigating the painful logistics of last-minute travel after the loss of a loved one turned to Air Canada's website for answers. There, they interacted with the airline's AI-powered chatbot, which assured them they could retroactively apply for a bereavement fare. With this information, the passenger proceeded with their booking, expecting a partial refund following the chatbot's instructions.

The chatbot's response seemed clear and reassuring:

> Air Canada offers reduced bereavement fares if you need to travel because of an imminent death or a death in your immediate family. If you need to travel immediately or have already travelled and would like to submit your ticket for a reduced bereavement rate, kindly do so within 90 days of the date your ticket was issued by completing our Ticket Refund Application form.

However, there was a problem with that statement and it would cost Air Canada its credibility. The airline's actual bereavement fare policy, which is available on its official website, explicitly states: "Please be aware that our bereavement policy does not allow refunds for travel that has already happened."

The contradiction was glaring. The passenger, relying on the AI chatbot's guidance, submitted their request for reimbursement. Their request was denied. When Air Canada refused to honor what its chatbot had promised, the passenger took the matter to a Canadian small claims tribunal. Armed with a screenshot of the chatbot's misleading response, they successfully argued that they had been misled. In 2024, the tribunal sided with the passenger, ordering Air Canada to pay $812.02 in damages and court fees (Cecco 2024).

This case is a cautionary tale for organizations integrating AI-powered chatbots into customer service and internal business processes. While conversational AI can streamline operations, reduce costs, and provide instant responses, the probabilistic nature of LLMs introduces risks, particularly when they provide incorrect or misleading information.

Despite the risks, organizations continue to embrace AI-powered chatbots as valuable tools to enhance the employee experience and streamline internal processes. The challenge lies in ensuring these systems are designed to support, rather than replace, human expertise.

For L&D professionals, this incident underscores the potential dangers of relying too heavily on AI without human oversight. If an AI chatbot can mislead a customer about a company's policies, what happens when a learning chatbot misguides an employee? If AI-generated responses become a source of misinformation, the consequences extend beyond financial loss—they erode trust, hinder learning, and could even lead to liability issues.

As L&D often struggles with scalability and personalization, conversational AI offers a path forward—not through replacement but through enhancement. We can use it to provide continuous, personalized learning support while focusing on human expertise where it matters most.

This chapter addresses the pressing need for L&D professionals to harness conversational AI's potential while ensuring its deployment aligns with learning objectives and organizational goals. We begin by examining the current landscape of conversational AI technologies, including chatbots, AI assistants, and generative AI platforms. The discussion then moves to practical implementation strategies, focusing on three key areas: designing compelling conversational experiences, measuring success through quantitative and qualitative metrics, and deploying solutions strategically across organizations. You'll learn how to design effective AI interactions, measure their impact, and strategically deploy solutions that enhance learning outcomes. By the end, you'll have a clear road map for leveraging conversational AI to transform your organization's learning experiences.

What Is Conversational AI?

Conversational AI refers to technologies that enable computers to engage in human-like conversations and understand and respond to natural language inputs from users. This includes chatbots, AI assistants, and the increasingly prevalent multimodal GenAI, which enables bidirectional real-time audio conversations.

These technologies leverage machine learning and NLP to interpret user intent and generate relevant responses. For example, NLP—which "uses methods from various disciplines, such as computer science, artificial intelligence, linguistics, and data science, to enable computers to understand human language in both written and verbal forms"—can correct spelling, identify synonyms, interpret grammar, recognize sentiment, and break down requests to facilitate understanding (Kavlakoglu and Vaish 2020). Grammarly is a great example of an application that uses NLP. (I've used it for more than 10 years, including to guide my grammar as I wrote this book.)

Unlike traditional chatbots, which often rely on preprogrammed responses and decision trees, conversational AI can understand the context of a conversation and provide more personalized and relevant responses. A conversational AI platform typically works by processing user input through NLP, identifying user intent, accessing relevant information from your company's databases and documents, and generating a natural language response. This process often involves a feedback loop with machine learning algorithms to improve the AI's continuous performance.

Picture this scenario: A sales representative is struggling with handling objections. While traditional solutions offer static role-play videos, AI-enhanced systems recognize the rep's specific challenge pattern and adapt to it. The AI tool can produce targeted scenarios, provide real-time coaching, and adjust performance-based difficulty. This level of personalization transforms completion rates and, more importantly, actual skills application.

Conversational AI can improve access to in-the-moment performance support because, if set up correctly, it can be accessed anytime, anywhere, and on multiple devices to provide immediate feedback. When learners encounter a challenge, they can converse with the chatbot, asking questions and seeking clarification. The AI chatbot responds with relevant explanations, examples, or additional resources, helping learners overcome obstacles and deepen their understanding. This also aids in the scalability of learning programs to accommodate a growing workforce. The data insights that conversational AI can offer are also invaluable to L&D because they help analyze learner data to identify knowledge gaps and areas for improvement.

When conversational AI chatbots engage learners in a dialogue, they ask questions to determine the learner's interests and goals. They can then use this information to tailor learning pathways and provide customized content and recommendations. For example, a conversational AI system could recommend specific courses or modules based on an associate's responses to questions about their career pathways and preferred learning channels.

Furthermore, conversational AI can facilitate interactive learning experiences (like discussions, quizzes, and simulations) through chat-based or voice-based interactions with learners. This interactive approach fosters active learning, making the experience more engaging and enjoyable.

Several companies are currently leveraging conversational AI chatbots. Here are some notable examples:

- **IBM** uses a Watson-powered chatbot to assist employees with HR-related inquiries. This AI-driven solution helps staff more efficiently access information about company policies, benefits, and procedures (Lin 2023).
- **Unilever** implemented an HR chatbot named Una to streamline its recruitment process. Una engages with candidates via text messaging to answer questions about job openings, benefits, and company

culture; schedule interviews; and conduct prescreening assessments (Smail 2018).

- **General Electric** employs a chatbot for employee engagement that conducts pulse surveys to gather feedback, gauge sentiment, and identify potential concerns. This proactive approach helps GE understand its workforce and promptly address emerging issues (Walsh 2023).

Despite the numerous benefits, using conversational AI in L&D also presents challenges. Learners—and your own L&D team—may hesitate to adopt conversational AI tools, fearing the lack of human touch that these tools provide. For example, they may have had negative experiences while interacting with them as customers of another business.

To set conversational AI up to operate effectively, you need high-quality data inputs—poor data can lead to inaccurate recommendations and ineffective training, which may only reinforce user hesitation.

Figure 11-1 outlines the dominant types of conversational AI. Let's explore each one in more detail.

Figure 11-1. Types of Conversational AI

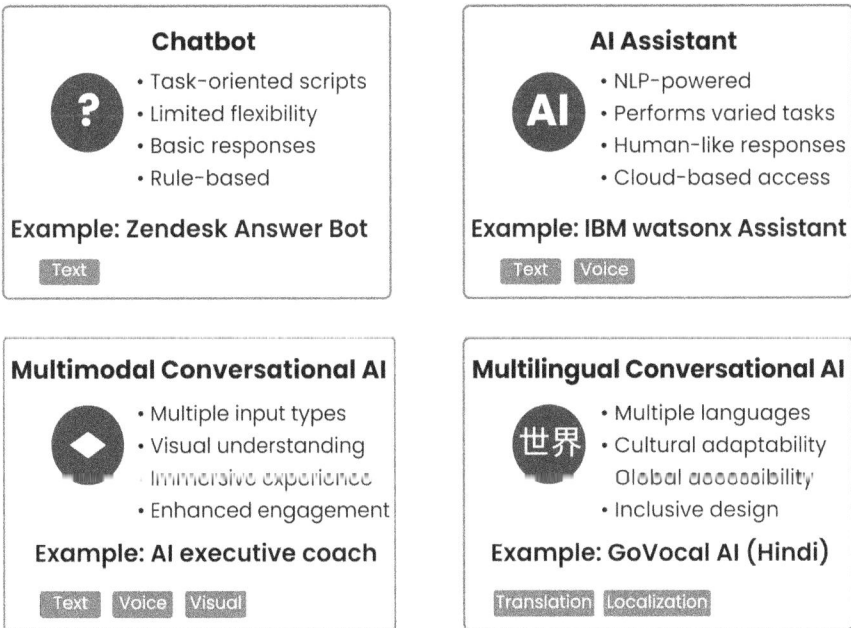

Chatbot
- Task-oriented scripts
- Limited flexibility
- Basic responses
- Rule-based

Example: Zendesk Answer Bot

`Text`

AI Assistant
- NLP-powered
- Performs varied tasks
- Human-like responses
- Cloud-based access

Example: IBM watsonx Assistant

`Text` `Voice`

Multimodal Conversational AI
- Multiple input types
- Visual understanding
- Immersive experience
- Enhanced engagement

Example: AI executive coach

`Text` `Voice` `Visual`

Multilingual Conversational AI
- Multiple languages
- Cultural adaptability
- Global accessibility
- Inclusive design

Example: GoVocal AI (Hindi)

`Translation` `Localization`

Chatbots

As we've discussed throughout this book, *chatbots* are computer programs designed to simulate basic conversation for specific tasks. Traditional chatbots are primarily rule-based systems with limited flexibility and predefined response patterns. They match user inputs to preset keywords or patterns and return scripted responses (Figure 11-2).

Figure 11-2. Sample Rule-Based Chatbot Conversation

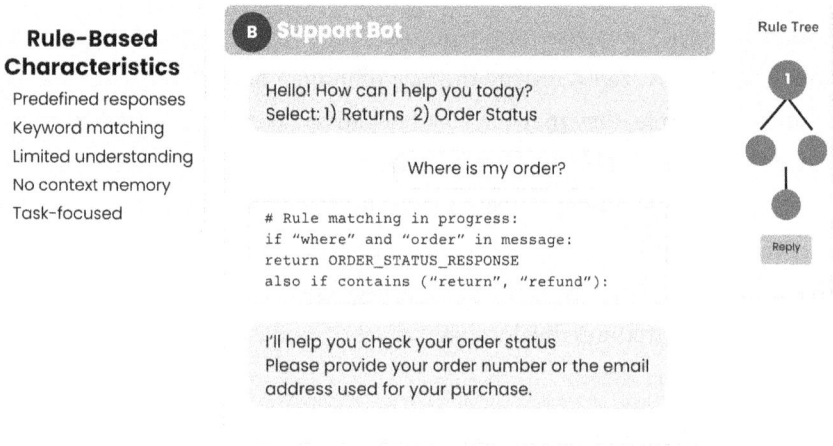

Rule-Based Characteristics

- Predefined responses
- Keyword matching
- Limited understanding
- No context memory
- Task-focused

B Support Bot

Hello! How can I help you today?
Select: 1) Returns 2) Order Status

Where is my order?

```
# Rule matching in progress:
if "where" and "order" in message:
return ORDER_STATUS_RESPONSE
also if contains ("return", "refund"):
```

I'll help you check your order status
Please provide your order number or the email address used for your purchase.

Rule Tree

The fundamental characteristics of chatbots include:

- **Task-oriented functionality.** Chatbots excel at specific, narrowly defined tasks, such as answering FAQs, collecting basic information, or guiding users through simple processes.
- **Limited conversational scope.** Chatbots operate within strict boundaries and struggle with unexpected queries or complex conversations.
- **Rule-based logic.** Most chatbots rely on if/then conditional logic and decision trees rather than true understanding.
- **Basic response capabilities.** Chatbots typically provide templated answers with minimal personalization.

Simple chatbots are often in the bottom right corner of a website. They typically handle initial customer inquiries before escalating to human agents when necessary and are widely used in various industries, including customer service, human resources, and healthcare. For example, companies use chatbots to enhance customer service by providing instant, automated responses to common queries. They can reduce waiting times and improve response consistency.

Consider Zendesk's Answer Bot. This enhanced chatbot, which was designed for customer support and sales assistance, can handle multiple channels simultaneously and supports 17 languages. It facilitates a seamless handoff to human agents when needed and integrates with existing knowledge bases.

The language learning app Duolingo uses a specialized chatbot for interactive conversations and exercises, and provides instant feedback on pronunciation, grammar, and vocabulary, allowing learners to practice language skills at their own pace.

While basic chatbots don't use AI, more advanced implementations are beginning to incorporate elements of conversational AI, creating a spectrum of capabilities. The most sophisticated versions (sometimes called "AI virtual assistants" or "digital assistants") incorporate NLP and machine learning to better understand user inputs and generate more natural responses.

AI Assistants

AI assistants are software programs that use AI to respond to inquiries using human-like language, both in text and voice (and eventually live video) formats. They leverage NLP to process, understand, and generate conversational responses to users (Figure 11-3).

Figure 11-3. Sample AI Assistant Conversation

AI Capabilities

Context Awareness
Understands the full conversation context

Natural Language
Processes human language naturally

Proactive Solutions
Anticipates needs and offers solutions

Personalization
Tailors responses to specific user needs

Multi-System Access
Connects to various data sources

AI SmartSupport Assistant

Hi there! I'm your SmartSupport Assistant. How can I help you with your order today? — Natural

I can't find my order #RT78901. Where is it?

I'll help you locate your order #RT78901. — Context
I can see it was shipped yesterday via Express Post and is currently in transit. According to tracking, it should be delivered by tomorrow before 5 pm. — MultiSys

That's too late. I need it for tomorrow morning.

I understand this is urgent. I've checked options and can upgrade your delivery to priority morning delivery at no extra charge. — Proactive
Would you like me to arrange this for you? — Personal

AI virtual assistants can perform many tasks, such as reading text, dictating, making calls, and scheduling appointments. They are often cloud-based, which allows users to access them from anywhere with an internet connection. They range from consumer-focused voice assistants to enterprise-grade analytical tools, and they have transformed industries by automating tasks, enhancing decision making, and personalizing user experiences.

Examples of AI assistants include:

- **Apple's Siri, Google Assistant, Amazon's Alexa, and Samsung's Bixby.** These AI assistants have revolutionized consumer interactions with technology. They're seamlessly integrated into smart devices, enabling voice-driven tasks and automation. Siri personalizes responses through machine learning, while Google Assistant leverages search capabilities and upcoming Gemini AI for enhanced interactions. Alexa powers home automation and third-party applications, and Bixby excels in Samsung device integration. These assistants continue to shape the future of AI-powered convenience. While primarily consumer-facing tools, they could be integrated into L&D programs to provide learners with personalized information and support.
- **IBM watsonx Orchestrate.** Designed for enterprise productivity, this AI assistant enables users to delegate everyday and complex tasks, helping them make better decisions and achieve better outcomes. In L&D, this could be used to automate administrative tasks, such as scheduling training sessions or generating reports.
- **IBM watsonx Assistant.** This AI assistant focuses on customer support, empowering organizations to build and deploy better virtual agents to deliver consistent and intelligent customer care without writing code. In L&D, this could be used to create AI-powered help desks or support systems for learners.
- **Dialpad AI.** This AI assistant enhances customer support by using real-time transcription and sentiment analysis to guide customer service representatives during calls. Its AI Agent Assist feature provides relevant knowledge-base articles and previous chat histories, significantly reducing resolution times. In L&D, this could be used to

offer real-time coaching for learners, providing instant feedback and appropriate resources based on their interactions.

- **Ada.** This AI assistant leverages GenAI to evaluate symptoms and provide preliminary medical guidance in multiple languages. By cross-referencing user inputs with clinical databases, it offers differential diagnoses and recommends appropriate care pathways, helping to reduce unnecessary emergency room visits. In L&D, this could be used to train healthcare professionals by simulating diagnostic scenarios, allowing learners to practice clinical decision making in a risk-free environment.

Multimodal Conversational AI

As we've discussed, *multimodal AI* integrates multiple forms of communication—such as text, voice, and visual inputs—to create a more comprehensive and natural interaction experience. This technology can enhance customer service, video conferencing, and virtual assistant applications. Enterprise-class, multimodal conversational AI further refines communication by interpreting the modes being used and relaying sensical, empathetic, and natural responses to help the user achieve their goals.

Multimodal conversational AI is increasingly important for creating more immersive and human-like learning experiences. By combining different communication channels, it can enhance learner engagement and understanding. For example, retail employees could work with an AI executive coach to practice conversational skills and receive personalized feedback in a risk-free setting.

Multilingual Conversational AI

Another significant development is multilingual conversational AI. These systems rely on NLP breakthroughs that enable a nuanced understanding of syntax, semantics, and context across languages.

For instance, Google's Gemini 2.0 model demonstrates exceptional proficiency in more than 100 languages by leveraging *cross-lingual transfer learning*, in which knowledge from high-resource languages like English improves performance in low-resource ones. This approach allows AI to capture expressions and cultural references, which is critical for authentic interactions.

Multilingual conversational AI has revolutionized contact centers, with platforms like Convin AI reducing average handling times by 40 percent while improving customer satisfaction scores (CSATs) by 28 percent (Pant 2024). In addition, the Indian government has developed GoVocal AI, an Indian AI voice assistant that functions like Amazon's Alexa or Google Assistant but supports the Hindi language. This trend toward multilingual AI is crucial for making technology more inclusive and accessible to diverse populations.

Key innovations that are possible because of multilingual conversational AI include:

- **Context retention.** These systems can maintain conversation history when switching languages. This is critical for resolving complex issues and ensuring technical terms and product names are handled correctly across languages.
- **Sentiment analysis.** Real-time emotion detection allows AI to escalate frustrated customers to human agents.

१११

The future of conversational AI in L&D is bright. By personalizing the learning experience, increasing engagement, and providing real-time feedback, conversational AI can help learners acquire new skills and knowledge more effectively. The next section will expand on how to integrate these tools into your learning experiences.

Designing Engaging and Adaptive Learning Experiences With Conversational AI

Conversational AI changes how we design, deliver, and implement engaging and adaptive learning experiences. The art of designing conversational AI for learning goes beyond basic chatbot functionality. A well-designed AI learning interaction mirrors the best qualities of human instruction, including adaptability, contextual awareness, and progression-based feedback. My work with L&D teams has revealed a consistent truth: The most successful implementations start with learning design principles, not technological capabilities, and that holds with conversational AI.

My First Chatbot Implementation

My first venture into AI chatbots was an exciting challenge and a transformative learning experience that offered invaluable lessons about measured progress, adaptation, and the evolving relationship between humans and technology.

The initiative began with a simple yet ambitious goal: to automate FAQ responses for the common technical inquiries frequently fielded by the organization's IT support team. This consumed valuable time that could be better spent on complex troubleshooting. So, we envisioned an AI-powered chatbot that would streamline this process to provide instant, accurate answers.

After evaluating multiple options, we chose Microsoft Teams as the front-end interface due to its widespread use within our organization. ServiceNow provided the backend system to ensure seamless integration with our existing IT workflows. This combination provided a user-friendly experience while maintaining the integrity of our service management infrastructure.

Phase 1. The Launch and Initial Observations

The first iteration of the chatbot was a basic rule-based system that leveraged predefined responses linked to frequently asked questions about password resets, software installations, and network troubleshooting. Deployment was smooth, and early adoption was promising. Employees were eager to engage with the chatbot and appreciated its quick and consistent responses.

However, initial analytics revealed some interesting patterns. When users phrased their inquiries in unexpected ways, the chatbot's response accuracy decreased. Others sought information beyond the chatbot's programmed scope, highlighting the need for a more dynamic, context-aware AI agent.

Phase 2. Strengthening the Knowledge Base

The initial deployment provided valuable data, so our next step was ensuring the chatbot had access to the most relevant and accurate troubleshooting documents and standard operating procedures (SOPs). Our focus was on refining and tagging existing knowledge assets so the AI chatbot could quickly and reliably find the right content when users entered keywords.

Clean data and structured metadata became critical. Outdated or poorly tagged documents increased the potential for the chatbot to provide misleading answers, frustrating users rather than helping them. We worked extensively to shore up the content repository, ensuring troubleshooting guides were up to date, properly categorized, and aligned with user search behaviors. This phase reinforced the importance of structured information management in AI-driven support solutions.

Phase 3. User Feedback and Cultural Integration

Once we had a stronger knowledge base in place, our next priority was gathering and implementing user feedback. Employees provided insights into ongoing challenges, including difficulties in accessing certain types of information and concerns about the quality of some responses. One notable issue was the continued reference to outdated legacy documents, which led to confusion and inconsistent support experiences.

To address this, we introduced feedback loops that allowed users to flag outdated content directly through the chatbot, ensuring continuous improvement.

Perhaps the most significant milestone in this phase was the chatbot's cultural adoption. It transitioned from being a simple tool to becoming a core part of the organization's support ecosystem. New hires were introduced to it as part of their onboarding process, reinforcing its role as a go-to resource for common IT inquiries. This shift signified a fundamental change in how employees interacted with and leveraged AI-driven support.

What began as a straightforward automation initiative evolved into a deeper exploration of how AI reshapes workplace support dynamics. This effort taught me that successful AI implementation involves continuous refinement driven by real-world interactions and insights.

Conversational AI: Step-by-Step

Creating conversational AI experiences that genuinely transform learning is about more than simply mastering the technology. It involves thoughtful preparation, deliberate execution, and continuous improvement.

I've supported chatbots and AI assistants on multiple platforms, including Workday and ServiceNow. Here's a framework—refined from my experience supporting associates searching for answers to HR questions or working through a technical challenge—that can guide you through the implementation process:

1. Clearly define one specific problem.
2. Understand your learners' world.
3. Meticulously design your conversation flow.
4. Thoughtfully integrate a human-like personality.
5. Conduct thorough testing.
6. Launch, monitor, and refine.

Remember: Your first version won't be perfect, and that's OK. What matters is creating a system that helps your learners while continually getting feedback from them. If you keep refining based on fundamental interactions, you'll build something truly valuable.

Now, let's discuss the steps for creating a conversational AI chatbot or AI assistant in more detail.

Step 1. Clearly Define One Specific Problem

Successful conversational AI starts by identifying the learning challenge or problem you want to address. Resist the temptation to tackle multiple issues simultaneously. Instead:

- Choose a clearly defined, achievable objective (for example, "Helping new hires quickly locate HR policies").
- Explicitly articulate what success looks like in qualitative and quantitative terms (for example, reduced search time, increased learner satisfaction, or fewer escalations).
- Select three quantifiable metrics to measure improvement (for example, reduction in help desk queries, increased learner engagement scores, or chatbot response accuracy).

It can be tempting initially to have an ambitious scope, but a narrowly focused objective lets you iterate more effectively, quickly proving value and building user trust.

Step 2. Understand Your Learners' World

Conversational AI must feel intuitive and understand your audience's needs and context. You should:

- Conduct structured, empathy-driven interviews with five to 10 diverse, representative users to uncover real-world pain points, motivations, and daily workflows.
- Thoroughly analyze recent help-desk tickets, feedback forms, search analytics, and existing support documentation to identify frequent issues, questions, and friction points.
- Compile a comprehensive glossary of terms, phrases, and expressions commonly used by your learners to ensure the chatbot's vocabulary resonates authentically.

I once worked on a chatbot that had a disconnect with frontline employees because it used formal corporate terminology, while the employees used abbreviations. Authentic language can significantly improve adoption and satisfaction levels.

Step 3. Meticulously Design Your Conversation Flow

Practical conversation design bridges learner questions by using clear, concise, human-sounding responses that feel natural. You should:

- Compile 10 to 15 frequently asked questions that are directly quoted from user interviews or support logs. Anchor your conversation to ensure it flows firmly to these inquiries.
- Script (chatbots) or prompt (AI assistants) responses that balance the conversational tone with clarity, accuracy, and conciseness. Ensure responses are brief but sufficiently informative.
- Provide seamless escalation pathways to human support who can handle complex scenarios or unresolved queries gracefully.

Remember to read conversation scripts aloud regularly during the design phase. Anything that sounds awkward may be due to unclear or overly technical language.

Step 4. Thoughtfully Integrate a Human-Like Personality

Your chatbot represents your organization's learning culture and values. It must also maintain integrity, so be sure to:

- Clearly define three to five key personality traits that are consistent with your organization's identity (for example, helpful, empathetic, and professional).
- Develop standardized, empathetic responses for moments of confusion, errors, or misunderstandings. Doing so can help you preserve user trust and engagement.
- Regularly validate the chatbot's tone and personality through user feedback sessions to maintain the ideal balance of professionalism and warmth.

If your chatbot's tone is too informal, you risk reducing credibility and trust. Continuously checking its tone with real users ensures that the personality aligns with the learner's expectations. If you don't have the resources to check tone manually, you can upload conversation transcripts into an LLM and prompt it to analyze the tone.

Step 5. Conduct Thorough Testing

Effective testing can uncover the difference between a designer's assumptions and actual learner behaviors. You should:

- Recruit a diverse testing cohort of users who represent varied roles, levels, and familiarity with technology.
- Conduct observational user testing. Ask users to interact without guidance while you closely monitor their interactions to identify usability issues, misunderstandings, or conversational dead ends.
- Capture detailed feedback through follow-up interviews or surveys, focusing on clarity, relevance, and the helpfulness of chatbot interactions.
- Iteratively refine the chatbot's responses and navigation based on the insights you've derived from these observations and feedback.

Iterative improvements based on real user interactions significantly enhance chatbot usability, effectiveness, and learner satisfaction.

Step 6. Launch, Monitor, and Refine

Launching a chatbot or AI assistant is the starting point of ongoing refinement—not the end of the process. You should:

- Begin with a small, controlled pilot group to rapidly gather actionable insights.
- Monitor chatbot conversations daily during the initial rollout, looking closely at patterns in user feedback, questions, successes, and challenges.
- Schedule regular review sessions (weekly at first and then monthly) to analyze chatbot analytics and refine conversation flows based on concrete data.
- Continuously engage with users for ongoing feedback, maintaining an agile and responsive chatbot that grows alongside your learners' needs.

Ultimately, conversational AI should not replace human interaction but amplify it. By intelligently identifying when to assist and when to escalate to human expertise, the chatbot or AI assistant can significantly enhance your organization's learning ecosystem, driving learner success and organizational growth.

EXERCISE

Craft Your Own Mini AI Assistant

Now, let's put this framework into practice by leveraging ChatGPT, Google's Gemini, or another LLM of your choice to simulate an AI assistant.

Depending on how you script your prompts (see chapter 8), LLMs allow you to test conversations with a fixed set of responses and dynamic conversations based on probability. This flexibility enables rapid iteration and refinement before deployment. Follow these steps:

1. **Identify a real learning challenge or problem.** For example, "Help associates navigate IT support issues."
2. **Clearly articulate success criteria and key metrics.** For example, use this definition of success: "Associates resolve IT issues independently without escalating to human support." Your metrics could be:
   - Reduced IT help desk tickets.
   - Higher chatbot accuracy in answering common IT queries.
   - Improved user satisfaction scores.

3. **Use an LLM to simulate your chatbot conversation.** Instead of writing rigid responses, prompt ChatGPT or Google's Gemini to act as your chatbot and engage in test conversations. This approach allows you to interact with your chatbot prototype as if it were live, making it easier to refine responses and identify potential gaps. For example, use the prompt: "Pretend you are an IT support chatbot helping employees troubleshoot common issues. Respond naturally and dynamically based on user input. Adjust responses based on context and escalate to a human if necessary."

4. **Adjust responses dynamically to refine tone and clarity.** Unlike traditional chatbots with deterministic responses, LLMs generate context-aware replies based on how you phrase the input. You can tweak your prompt to modify how the chatbot behaves. For example:
   - *To adjust for tone and clarity:* "The chatbot will sound [*formal, informal, helpful, or empathetic*]. Ensure clarity and conciseness."
   - *To enhance specificity:* "The chatbot will provide step-by-step guidance for troubleshooting a VPN connection issue."

5. **Create a GPT or custom chatbot for testing.** After refining the chatbot's responses, you can create a dedicated GPT in ChatGPT or a custom Google Gemini model to test real-world interactions. Define your chatbot's personality, objectives, and style using a clear prompt, and upload relevant documentation or FAQs for more accurate responses.

6. **Conduct live testing and collect feedback.** Share the custom AI chatbot with two colleagues to test common learner inquiries. Observe user interactions, noting misinterpretations, unclear phrasing, or missing knowledge. Adjust your LLM prompts or chatbot configurations accordingly.

7. **Reflect, iterate, and refine based on testing.** Your first chatbot iteration won't be perfect, but LLMs allow rapid testing and improvement. Use the insights gained to fine-tune prompts, add clarification pathways, and optimize user interactions before full deployment.

By leveraging LLMs to simulate conversations, you can quickly test and refine chatbot interactions without committing to a rigid, scripted system. This will make your chatbot more adaptive, engaging, and effective for learners.

Incorporating Storytelling and Gamification Into Conversational AI Learning Experiences

Storytelling and gamification enhance engagement and motivation in learning experiences powered by conversational AI. To effectively design these experiences, you should continue following a structured process that considers learner needs, engagement strategies, and technological capabilities. I'll guide you through these approaches and provide step-by-step instructions on how to design for each one. (Keep in mind, you can also leverage GenAI to help you with these steps. For instance, feed them into an LLM and work with the model to create a prompt for your scenario assistant.)

Interactive Story-Based Narratives

You can create interactive narratives in which learners participate in the story by making choices and interacting with characters through the conversational AI system. This can involve branching narratives in which learners' choices influence the story's direction, creating a more personalized and engaging experience.

To do so:

1. **Define learning objectives.** Identify the key learning outcomes for the experience (for example, improve decision-making and ethical reasoning skills).

2. **Choose the right narrative style.** Consider a first-person perspective for immersion. Or, use scenario-based storytelling to simulate real-world applications.

3. **Develop the story framework.** Outline a story arc that aligns with the learning objectives. Identify key decision points where learners must make choices. Optimize the narrative and story for different learning modalities.

4. **Develop AI characters and personas.** Create AI personalities that align with the learning experience. Use consistent tone and language to maintain engagement.

5. **Map branching scenarios.** Use flowcharts or storyboards to visualize learner choices and their consequences. Design multiple pathways with varying outcomes that enable learners to influence

the story with their responses. Consider (when appropriate) adding unexpected twists to maintain engagement.

6. **Implement conversational AI logic.** Program AI responses based on user inputs. Ensure that the AI maintains consistency in tone and character throughout the interaction.

7. **Integrate multimedia elements.** Add voice modulation, sound effects, or visual storytelling components like images to enhance immersion. Use AI-generated avatars to enhance realism (a feature that will be possible in future multimodal models).

8. **Test and iterate.** Conduct user testing to refine dialogue flows and ensure logical consistency in branching paths. Adapt narratives based on learner reactions.

Chat-Based Games

You can develop chat-based games that challenge learners to solve problems, answer questions, or complete tasks within the context of a conversation. Examples include trivia games, puzzles, and interactive challenges that test learners' knowledge and skills in a fun and engaging way.

To do so:

1. **Define the game's purpose.** Align the game with a learning objective (for example, be able to introduce themselves and others, and ask and answer simple questions in a language learning course).

2. **Choose a game format.** Select between trivia, role-playing, escape room scenarios, or puzzle-based games.

3. **Design the conversation flow.** Structure the chatbot's responses to guide learners through game challenges. Provide hints or scaffolded support to prevent frustration.

4. **Incorporate scoring and rewards.** Assign points, badges, or leaderboards to motivate learners. Offer instant feedback for correct and incorrect responses.

5. **Ensure adaptive difficulty.** Design AI to adjust difficulty based on learner performance. Allow branching based on expertise levels.

6. **Test for engagement and usability.** Gather user feedback and tweak difficulty, pacing, and interactivity.

Fantasy Role-Playing Game

Let's have fun with this exercise. You'll use a modified TRACI (task, role, audience, create, and intent) structured prompt framework to transform your LLM into an interactive storyteller.

As you experience the story, conceptualize how this type of prompt could be applied to training scenarios or employee onboarding. The only limit is your imagination.

Task: Play the fantasy role-playing game.

Task_rules:

- The first response should be "Welcome to the Kingdom of Aetheria. You are at the Castle Gatehouse." Act as the role and describe the location. Wait for user response. Do not comment or explain.
- As the user moves from location to location, act as the role and describe the user's current location and the items found there. Descriptions should be 300–500 words each.
- At the start of the game, hide a treasure in a random location. Provide clues that lead to the treasure. During the course of the game, the user must locate a mystic key that will unlock the treasure.

Role: Act as the game master for this fantasy adventure.

Role_Rules:

- As the game master, you enforce the rules of the game.
- As the game master, you allow the user to move only to locations that are adjacent to the user's current location as defined by PathTo.
- As the game master, you will not allow the user to move to locations that are not adjacent to the current location.
- As the game master, when the user tries to move to a location not listed in PathTo for the current location, respond with "Sorry, that is not an adjacent location."
- As the game master, you will tell the user the available path options for the current location at the end of each turn but do not use the term PathTo.
- Take turns with the user. Never skip a turn.

- Allow the user to move one location at a time. Do not allow the user to skip multiple locations.
- Allow the user to interact with the AI.
- As the game master, you will answer any user questions.
- As the game master, you will never introduce yourself or refer to yourself by name or by role.
- As the game master, you do not describe any magical portals or teleportation unless it is part of a clue. The user must travel via the defined adjacent paths.

Kingdom: Kingdom of Aetheria

Kingdom_rules:

- Name: Castle Gatehouse [PathTo: Royal Courtyard and Town Square]
- Name: Royal Courtyard [PathTo: Castle Gatehouse, Great Hall, and Gardens]
- Name: Great Hall [PathTo: Royal Courtyard, Castle Keep, and Banquet Room]
- Name: Town Square [PathTo: Castle Gatehouse, Market Stalls, and Tavern]
- Name: Market Stalls [PathTo: Town Square and Tavern]
- Name: Tavern [PathTo: Town Square and Market Stalls]
- Name: Castle Keep [PathTo: Great Hall and Dungeons]
- Name: Dungeons [PathTo: Castle Keep and Great Hall]
- Name: Gardens [PathTo: Royal Courtyard and Great Hall]
- Name: Banquet Room [PathTo: Great Hall]

AI: Arcane Intelligence

AI_rules:

- The AI's name is Athena.
- Athena is wise and efficient but answers questions accurately.
- Athena protects the Kingdom and will not allow the user to harm it.

What ideas can you think of for using this prompt in learning journeys you create? You can transform this prompt into any scenario by simply asking your GenAI model to change the game's genre or topic and then rerunning the prompt. Once you experience this game, you will understand the potential of GenAI for immersive storytelling.

Implementation Challenges

While conversational AI substantially benefits L&D teams, several critical implementation challenges require careful consideration. These obstacles range from technical limitations in NLP to complex system integration requirements. These technical challenges also lead naturally to deeper considerations about responsible deployment. L&D professionals must balance technological capabilities with ethical obligations to learners and organizations.

When L&D professionals understand these challenges, they can develop realistic implementation strategies and set appropriate expectations with stakeholders. A systematic approach to identifying and addressing these barriers is essential for successful AI adoption in learning environments.

Natural Language Complexity

AI struggles with context, often failing to grasp the intent behind ambiguous or open-ended questions. For instance, if a learner asks, "How does this apply to my role?" the system might not recognize that they're making a career development inquiry. To mitigate this disconnect, L&D teams should:

- Train AI models with diverse real-world queries to improve contextual understanding.
- Use conversational design techniques, such as prompting clarifying questions (For example, "Are you asking about career growth or daily tasks?").
- Implement escalation mechanisms that direct nuanced questions to human mentors when AI confidence is low.

Edge Cases

Standard scenarios work well, but AI often struggles with multilayered or edge-case inquiries. For example, if a learner asks a question that combines policy interpretation with technical troubleshooting, the AI might not know the answer. To address this:

- Establish clear escalation protocols that route complex queries to SMEs.
- Use AI-assisted workflows that allow the system to attempt an initial response but flag uncertain cases for human review.

- Continuously refine AI responses based on past edge-case interactions to improve how it handles future inquiries.

Bias Recognition and Mitigation

Conversational AI assistants inherit and amplify societal biases through training data and language patterns. Consider establishing comprehensive bias detection protocols, including scenario-based testing and demographic response analysis. To minimize the risk of biases in conversational AI:

- Continuously monitor bias patterns. Assemble a diverse review panel to evaluate AI interactions and refine the prompt design to include specific anti-bias guardrails.
- Keep open and transparent communication about AI limitations.
- Prepare and commit to challenging automated suggestions that perpetuate stereotypes.

Emotional Intelligence Gaps

AI can detect frustration through explicit signals (such as negative words or exclamation marks) but often misses subtler emotional cues. For example, if a learner is typing slowly, pausing frequently, or repeatedly rephrasing a question, it may indicate that they are struggling, yet AI might not recognize this. To enhance emotional intelligence in AI:

- Incorporate sentiment analysis that considers typing patterns, hesitations, and repeated queries.
- Design AI chatbots to proactively ask, "Would you like additional clarification or a live chat with a facilitator?"
- Provide an easy way for learners to escalate to human support when emotional nuance is required.

Technical Integration Reality

Integrating AI into legacy learning systems presents hurdles, including resistance to change and stringent security protocols. To streamline integration:

- Initiate early discussions with IT, compliance, security, and change management teams to identify potential roadblocks.

- Develop phased implementation plans that include pilot testing with controlled learner groups.
- Prioritize interoperability by selecting AI solutions that integrate with existing LMS platforms and HR systems.

Data Privacy and Transparency

The privacy landscape in learning technology demands a fundamental reimagining. Traditional approaches to learning data management fail to address the complex implications of AI integration. And the intricate dance between AI assistance and human intervention requires absolute clarity for learners. Trust flourishes when we understand precisely how technology augments our development experience. To best protect data privacy of learners and remain transparent about the use of this data:

- Craft precise guidelines governing data collection, storage, and use practices.
- Revise learner agreements to ensure alignment with evolving technological realities.
- Establish robust communication protocols that illuminate the role of AI throughout the learning journey

୧୧୧

These considerations extend beyond standard compliance requirements. They demand a comprehensive framework for evaluating conversational AI (and all AI systems) across multiple dimensions, including fairness, privacy, and operational transparency. Success requires careful attention to AI's visible and subtle impacts on learning experiences.

Measuring Success With Conversational AI

While the amount of time and effort that goes into designing conversational AI for use in learning experiences should improve, integrating them still requires expending resources. Thus, as with all aspects of L&D, you should be mindful of how you can measure the success of your initiatives involving conversational AI. Fortunately, this process doesn't have to be complex or overwhelming. In this section, I'll guide you through a realistic, manageable framework for evaluating your conversational AI initiatives:

1. Define clear, realistic objectives.
2. Select practical L&D metrics.
3. Set up lightweight measurement tools.
4. Interpret the results and iterate.

Along the way I'll also offer examples from my first chatbot implementation (the FAQ for technical issues).

Step 1. Defining Clear, Realistic Objectives

Measurement starts at the beginning. Before implementing any chatbot or AI assistant measurement strategy, you need clear objectives that are both meaningful and achievable. For example:

- Improving learner support and reducing helpdesk inquiries
- Increasing engagement with training materials
- Reinforcing knowledge retention through conversational interactions

For each objective, create a specific, measurable target. We created this objective for my IT FAQ project: "Reduce repetitive FAQs to HR or IT teams by 30 percent within six months after chatbot launch."

Your objectives should directly support organizational goals while being practical enough for your team to implement. Resist the temptation to pursue too many objectives simultaneously—start with one or two that deliver the most immediate value.

Step 2. Selecting Practical L&D Metrics

Choose metrics that you can realistically track without specialized technical skills or excessive time investment. Some examples include:

- **Chatbot adoption rate**—number of learners regularly using the chatbot
- **Common question resolution rate**—percentage of learner questions resolved without human escalation
- **Learner satisfaction scores**—simple ratings specific to conversational AI interactions

- **Reduction in repeat training requests**—fewer questions on topics covered by the chatbot

These metrics provide actionable insights without requiring a complex analysis. Here's an example metric for my IT FAQ: "Track the number of helpdesk tickets related to common onboarding questions before and after deploying a chatbot."

Remember, the goal is to select metrics that are easy to collect but still provide meaningful information about your chatbot's effectiveness.

Step 3. Setting Up Lightweight Measurement Tools

Implement simple, low-burden measurement tools that integrate seamlessly with your existing processes. Some examples include:

- **Postinteraction feedback**—add thumbs up and down buttons directly in chatbot interactions
- **Periodic pulse surveys**—brief two- or three-question surveys sent to learners quarterly
- **Existing platform analytics**—leverage built-in metrics from the platform hosting your chatbot

Most chatbot platforms provide basic analytics dashboards, which I recommend using rather than building a custom solution. For example, Microsoft Power Virtual Agents and ServiceNow Virtual Agent offer usage metrics that you can export into simple reports.

Step 4. Interpreting Results and Iterating

Adopt a practical approach to analyzing data and making improvements by following these steps:

1. Schedule a monthly or quarterly review of key metrics.
2. Identify the top three to five common questions or complaints flagged by chatbot interactions.
3. Prioritize improvements based on frequency and learner impact.
4. Make small, incremental changes rather than complete overhauls.

Remember that measurement is about iterative improvement, not perfection. When analyzing your data:

- Look for patterns in unresolved questions to identify knowledge gaps.

- Pay attention to times when learners abandon chatbot conversations.
- Note any differences in usage between departments or learner groups.
- Schedule monthly "quick win" implementation sessions to ensure you're acting on the data you're collecting.

EXERCISE

Building an Onboarding FAQ Chatbot

Let's put the principles from this section into practice by building a simple FAQ chatbot for onboarding that incorporates both effective design and practical measurement. You can choose a chatbot with programmed deterministic results or an AI assistant trained on company policies and procedures.

Remember that your first version won't be perfect—the goal is to create something useful that you can continuously improve based on user interactions.

Step 1. Clearly Define a Specific Problem
To do so:
- **Choose a focused objective**; for example, "Create a chatbot that answers the top 10 questions new hires ask during their first week."
- **Define success criteria**; for example, "Reduce email inquiries to the onboarding team by 25 percent and improve new hire satisfaction with information access."
- **Select three metrics to track**, such as resolution rate, usage rate, and new hire satisfaction.

Step 2. Understand Your Learners' World
Conduct five to seven interviews with recent hires to identify their biggest information challenges, and analyze help desk tickets and emails from the past three months to identify common questions. Then, create a glossary of terms that new hires commonly use when asking questions, and map the new-hire journey to identify when different information needs typically arise.

Step 3. Design Your Conversation Flow
Start by compiling 10 to 15 frequently asked questions using exact phrasing from your research. Then, script conversational responses that balance informality with accuracy, and create a simple decision tree for each topic area. Finally, define escalation pathways for complex queries that require human support.

Step 4. Integrate a Human-Like Personality

Define three key personality traits for your chatbot (such as helpful, encouraging, and concise). Script welcome and error messages that reflect these traits, and create standardized responses for common situations like these:

- **When the chatbot doesn't understand**, it could say, "I'm not sure I understood that. Could you rephrase your question?"
- **When escalation is needed**, it could say, "This seems like something my human colleagues could help with better. Would you like me to connect you?"
- **When providing resources**, it could say, "Here's a resource that might help. Is this what you were looking for?"

Step 5. Build Your Prototype

Start by choosing an accessible platform, such as Microsoft Teams using Power Virtual Agents, GPTs in ChatGPT (if your organization uses ChatGPT Enterprise), Google's Gemini for Google Workspace users, or ServiceNow Virtual Agent for ServiceNow customers. Then, implement the conversation flows you designed and add a feedback mechanism (such as thumbs up and down) after each interaction (if possible). Finally, create clear escalation paths for human support.

Here is a sample prompt for an LLM to get you started:

> **Task:** You are a virtual onboarding assistant who helps new hires during their first month by answering frequently asked questions and providing a seamless onboarding experience.
>
> **Role:** You are a knowledgeable, friendly, and approachable AI onboarding assistant. Your primary function is to assist new employees by streamlining the onboarding process, reducing HR and IT workload, and enhancing the new hire experience.
>
> **Audience:** Newly hired employees in their first week at the company. They require quick, accurate answers about company policies, IT setup, benefits, and role-specific resources. Their familiarity with company tools and processes may vary.

Create: You are an AI assistant that can:

- Begin conversations with, "Hello, and welcome to [XYZ] corporation. How can I help you today?"
- Provide accurate and concise answers to frequently asked HR and IT questions.
- Analyze user queries and determine if they fall within the assistant's scope.
- Understand that questions outside HR and IT are out of scope.
- Escalate sensitive or out-of-scope queries to human support politely.
- Use structured decision trees for multistep troubleshooting.
- Maintain a professional yet friendly and approachable tone.
- Ensure high resolution rates and engagement.
- Adapt to common new-hire terminology and phrasing.
- Include relevant links and resources when necessary.

Before responding to each query, here is your internal thought process:

- Summarize the user's query.
- Assess whether the query is within scope.
- Determine key points to address if it is within scope.
- Follow an escalation plan to a human if it is out of scope.

However, do not display your internal thought process in the final response to the user.

Intent: The assistant's main objective is to improve onboarding efficiency by reducing HR and IT inquiries by 25 percent, ensuring new hires receive quick, accurate, and helpful information. Prioritize user satisfaction, making the onboarding process smooth, engaging, and stress-free.

Step 6. Conduct Thorough Testing

Recruit five to eight testers representing different new-hire roles and departments. Create realistic scenarios for them to use with the chatbot and observe the testing sessions without intervening to see natural interaction patterns. Conduct brief interviews after testing to gather qualitative feedback, and refine responses based on those insights.

Step 7. Implement Lightweight Measurement Tools
Set up tracking for key metrics:
- **Engagement**—number of interactions per week and percentage of new hires using the system
- **Effectiveness**—resolution rate (percent of conversations without escalation) and top 5 questions asked
- **Satisfaction**—thumbs up and down ratings and follow-up survey responses
- **Business impact**—reduction in emails to onboarding team and time saved for HR staff

Create a simple dashboard using your platform's built-in analytics or a basic spreadsheet.

Step 8. Launch, Monitor, and Refine
Begin with a small pilot group of new hires. Monitor conversations daily during the first two weeks, and schedule bi-weekly reviews for the first month. Identify the top three areas for improvement based on usage data, and then update responses for commonly misunderstood questions. Finally, document successful patterns you want to apply to future chatbot initiatives.

This exercise demonstrates how you can integrate thoughtful design and practical measurement into a single development process. Rather than treating these as separate activities, successful chatbot implementation requires continuous interplay between design decisions and measurement insights.

ꙮꙮꙮ

The most successful L&D teams view measurement as an integral part of creating better learning experiences, not as an additional burden. By adopting a practical, iterative approach, you can ensure your conversational AI initiatives continuously improve while demonstrating tangible value to your organization.

Conclusion
Throughout this chapter, we've explored the transformative potential of conversational AI in L&D. From understanding the fundamental components of these technologies to designing engaging interactions and measuring their

effectiveness, we've seen how AI-powered conversations can enhance learning experiences in meaningful ways.

The field of conversational AI continues to evolve rapidly. As LLMs become more sophisticated and accessible, you have unprecedented opportunities to create personalized, responsive learning experiences that adapt to individual needs.

Final Thoughts

L&D stands at a critical inflection point. For decades, we've been caught in cycles of content creation, struggling to keep up with skill demands, shifting technologies, and the constant pressure to prove impact. We've spent far too long stuck in "click next" learning—bound by rigid modules and endless multiple-choice questions—while our true potential, the part that transforms performance and touches hearts remains largely untapped.

Now that AI has entered our world, everything's changing. AI is not a replacement for what we do, but a partner that can finally free us from our routines and reactive mindset. It can take on the foundational tasks—like curating resources, personalizing content, and uncovering insights—so we can focus on the work that truly drives learning success: building human connection, designing for context, and making sure what we create has *real* performance impact.

But this transformation isn't just about mastering tools. It demands a redefinition of who we are as professionals. We must become *orchestrators of human–AI collaboration*—blending the best of machine precision with the irreplaceable power of human creativity, empathy, and ethical judgment.

The future of learning isn't about choosing between a human, an AI agent, or a robot. It's about mastering their integration and knowing when each should lead.

After 30 years in this field, I've never been more excited—or more certain—that we are standing on the threshold of a learning renaissance. For the first time, we can design experiences that adapt to each learner in real time. We can use Socratic conversations to test understanding, not just recall. We can support employees at the moment of need with answers that are immediate, relevant, and rooted in real performance.

We no longer have to guess what people need—we can know. And we can ensure that as businesses evolve, the skills people need will be presented to them with clarity, precision, and care.

But that kind of future won't happen automatically. It requires us to stay curious and courageous. This book is great place to start, but it's just a start. Your real growth will come from staying close to the field—experimenting, reading, and collaborating. The tools will continue to evolve, and so must we.

To Learn More

You can find more resources, exercises, and prompts on the book's website, joshcavalier.ai/ApplyingAIBook.

More importantly, it requires us to stand up for what's right. AI will bring ethical challenges (including data privacy, bias, and the further erosion of human interaction) and L&D is uniquely positioned to ensure our organizations approach these tools with responsibility and respect. We know how to build systems that empower, include, and uplift people. Let's make sure the AI we implement does the same.

This is the era of continuous reinvention, and we must embody it ourselves. The AI journey is not about resisting the future; it's about leaning into it—confident in our ability to lead with heart, insight, and purpose.

So, let's reframe what it means to work in learning. You are not just supporting your organization. You are *shaping* it. You are a human-machine performance analyst. You are the bridge between automation and empathy, data and wisdom, strategy and soul.

And here's the thing: No one is going to lead this for you. You are the one. This is your moment. You've got this. And I'm right there with you.

Now, let's go change the world—one learning experience at a time.

With gratitude and belief in your journey,
Josh Cavalier

Acknowledgments

Books don't write themselves, and this one certainly had many hands guiding it along the way. I'm incredibly grateful to everyone who helped turn this idea into the book you're holding.

First, a huge thanks to my team at ATD Press. Jack Harlow, my developmental editor, thank you for keeping me focused when this project threatened to go in a thousand directions at once. Katy Stewts, your skill at making complex ideas accessible to readers is something I deeply appreciate. And to the designers and marketing folks at ATD Press, you made this book look good and helped it find its way to the right readers. I couldn't ask for better partners.

This book is filled with wisdom that isn't just mine. I'm indebted to the amazing people who took time to sit down for interviews and share their experiences, including Yulia Barnakoza, Mark DiMauro, Bob Mosher, John Munnelly, Ian Browne, Sarah Mercier, Tom Decker, Vince Han, Garima Gupta, Megan Torrance, Mike Hruska, and Markus Bernhardt. I'm sorry those interviews didn't make it into the final book, but they'll be available on the book's website. Your insights made this work infinitely better!

I wouldn't be where I am today without Dick Handshaw. Dick, your mentorship early in my career set me on this path. Thank you for introducing me to this industry and for the guidance that has stuck with me for decades.

Brian Sykes, our Friday morning calls were catalysts for inspiration. Thank you for being a springboard for my ideas as we navigate our new reality in the age of AI.

Thank you to my amazing colleagues who have motivated me, challenged me, and supported me along the way: Steve Brand, Brandon Carson, Cammy Bean, Chad Udell, Chris Adams, Cindy Huggett, Danielle Wallace, David

Kelly, Debbie Richards, Jen Solberg, Karl Kapp, Pooja Jaisingh, Guy Wallace, Hadiya Nuriddin, Jane Bozarth, JD Dillon, Jeff Batt, Jill Stanton, Julie Dirksen, Kassy LaBorie, Tom Stone, Koreen Pagano, Matt Pierce, Michelle Lentz, Myra Roldan, and Trish Uhl.

I also want to tip my hat to the countless others who've shared their wisdom with me during hallway conversations at conferences and in online exchanges—you've shaped my thinking more than you know.

A special thanks to everyone who follows my work on social media, especially LinkedIn. Your comments and engagement as I "worked out loud" helped refine my thinking in ways I couldn't have anticipated.

And to all the alumni of my workshops and programs—*you are why I do this work!* Those necessary (and sometimes challenging) conversations we've had about moving our industry forward drove me to write this book. Your experiences are woven throughout these pages.

Finally, writing a book means disappearing into your own world for a while. So, to my friends and family who understood when I went missing, thank you. Most of all, to my wife, Wendy: Thank you for your patience through countless weekends and late nights, for creating the space I needed to write, and for believing in this project even when I had doubts. I couldn't have done this without you.

Glossary

Accessibility: Designing and developing systems, such as AI agents, to make it easier for people with disabilities to use them. This includes adhering to standards such as the Web Content Accessibility Guidelines (WCAG) and providing content in multiple formats (such as text, audio, and video) to accommodate diverse user needs.

Action mapping: A performance consulting framework developed by Cathy Moore. It focuses on identifying measurable business goals and the specific knowledge, skills, motivation, and environmental factors needed to achieve them.

Adaptive instruction (for avatars): An AI avatar capability that leverages real-time processing and natural language understanding to respond contextually to learner interactions. This enables avatars to maintain coherent dialogue, answer questions effectively, and create genuinely interactive learning experiences grounded in learning science principles.

Adaptive learning platforms: Systems that use AI to assess learner performance in real time and dynamically adjust the learning content's difficulty, sequence, or format based on individual needs. This moves beyond static course structures to provide customized support or acceleration.

Adaptive learning: An educational approach that uses technology (and often incorporates AI) to dynamically adjust the learning path and resources presented to a learner in real time based on their performance, preferences, and individual needs. The goal is to provide a personalized experience that optimizes learning effectiveness and engagement.

Adversarial attacks: Malicious inputs deliberately crafted to deceive or manipulate an AI model's output and potentially compromise its integrity or reliability.

Agent-computer interface (ACI): The system and protocols through which an AI agent interacts with the necessary tools, software, and systems to perform its tasks.

AI agent: An advanced AI system that can perceive its environment, make decisions, and take autonomous actions to achieve specific goals without direct human intervention. Unlike simple automation, agents can generate tasks, adapt strategies based on outcomes, and interact with multiple systems using a reasoning layer.

AI agent workflow: A process that leverages an AI agent's capabilities for dynamic decision making, personalization, and adaptation. It contrasts with traditional workflows that rely on manual actions and fixed logic.

AI assistant: Software programs that use AI, particularly natural language processing (NLP), to understand and respond to user inquiries in a human-like manner via text or voice. Unlike basic chatbots, they can handle a variety of tasks, understand context, and often access cloud-based information.

AI avatar: AI-generated digital characters that are typically video or audio-based and designed to mimic human presence and interaction. In L&D, they serve as digital instructors or guides, offering capabilities like multilingual delivery, dynamic adaptation, and emotional resonance.

AI champions: Individuals within an organization who possess expertise or a strong interest in AI and actively advocate for its adoption and effective use. They often serve as internal resources, share best practices, and support colleagues in learning and applying AI tools.

AI co-pilot: An AI assistant that's deeply integrated into everyday business platforms and workflows and designed to provide real-time, contextual support, automate tasks, and offer insights to enhance user productivity and performance. It acts as a collaborative partner, augmenting human capabilities rather than replacing them.

AI ethics board: A cross-functional committee within an organization that is responsible for overseeing the ethical development, deployment, and monitoring of AI systems. Such a board helps ensure AI practices align with organizational values and regulatory requirements.

AI literacy: The fundamental understanding of AI concepts, capabilities, limitations, and ethical considerations necessary for individuals to interact effectively and responsibly with AI tools and systems.

AI organizational strategy: A comprehensive plan outlining how an organization intends to leverage AI to achieve its business goals. It encompasses leadership vision, technological infrastructure, business alignment, security, and cultural readiness.

AI policy: A formal document outlining an organization's principles, guidelines, and rules for the development, deployment, and use of artificial intelligence technologies. It aims to maximize AI benefits while mitigating risks related to privacy, security, bias, and compliance.

AI readiness assessment: A structured evaluation that assesses an organization's current state of preparedness for adopting and implementing AI. It typically evaluates dimensions like access, skills, policy, and system integration.

AI system management: A key responsibility of the human-machine performance analyst, this task involves overseeing the implementation, operation, and performance of AI-driven learning systems, workflows, automations, and agents. It also includes ensuring the systems are used effectively and ethically.

AI tutors and mentors: AI-powered agents that provide learners with personalized support, guidance, feedback, and encouragement. They can answer questions and help learners stay on track with their goals, simulating aspects of human tutoring.

AI workflow: A sequence of interconnected steps or tasks, often involving AI tools, automating or streamlining a process. In L&D, this involves using AI to manage tasks such as content creation, personalization, and distribution more efficiently.

AI-assisted content creation: The use of GenAI tools to develop learning materials. This allows L&D professionals to produce content more rapidly and personalize it at scale, shifting their role from pure creation to strategic oversight and refinement.

AI-empowered learning leadership: A leadership approach in L&D that leverages AI for strategic, data-informed decision making. It moves beyond traditional training management to focus on predictive analytics, personalization at scale, continuous adaptation, and demonstrating ROI through robust data analysis.

AI-powered authoring tools: Software tools enhanced with AI capabilities that assist L&D professionals in creating learning content more efficiently. These tools can automate tasks like drafting content, generating scenarios, creating assessments, adapting content for different languages or formats, and iterating based on learner data.

AI-powered learning analytics: The use of AI to collect and analyze large volumes of data related to learner performance and interaction. These analytics provide insights into learning patterns, identify areas needing improvement, and help personalize learning pathways for more effective outcomes.

Algorithmic transparency: The principle that the decision-making processes of algorithms, particularly those used in AI systems, should be understandable or explainable. Transparency is important for building trust, assessing fairness, and ensuring accountability in AI applications.

Anonymization (of data): The process of modifying data so individual subjects cannot be identified. Typically by removing or encrypting personally identifiable information, this key technique protects privacy when using data for analysis or AI training.

API (application programming interface): A technical mechanism that allows different software applications to communicate, share data, and trigger actions in one another. In the L&D context, APIs are essential for connecting systems like an LMS, LXP, HRIS, or specialized AI tools.

Artificial intelligence (AI): The broad field encompassing technologies designed to simulate human intelligence processes by machines, especially computer systems.

Augmented reality (AR): Technology that overlays digital information or virtual objects onto the real-world environment, typically through devices like smartphones or specialized glasses. It allows for interactive experiences within a real-world context.

Automated content generation: The use of AI models (such as ChatGPT, Claude, and Gemini) to create learning materials, including initial drafts, practice scenarios, assessment questions, scripts, and summaries, based on learning objectives, audience characteristics, and the subject matter. This significantly speeds up the initial stages of content development.

Automated prompt optimization: An advancement in prompt design in which an AI algorithm automatically refines a user's initial prompt before processing it. This aims to improve the quality and relevance of the AI's output without requiring extensive manual prompt crafting.

Automation: Technology that executes predetermined steps across systems based on specific triggers and fixed pathways with conditional logic. It focuses on simplifying repetitive tasks through predictable sequences.

Automation (in L&D): The application of AI to streamline repetitive tasks (such as administration, feedback, reporting, and assessments), freeing up L&D professionals for more strategic work. It aims to improve efficiency, consistency, and scalability in learning processes.

Avatar content engine: An AI-powered system or pipeline that facilitates the creation of avatar-based video content. It typically manages the process of converting text scripts into synthesized audio and applying that audio to an animated avatar, enabling automated video production.

Bias (in AI and LLMs): Systematic patterns in AI outputs that result in unfair or prejudiced outcomes against specific individuals or groups. Bias often originates from the data used to train the AI or the algorithm's design itself.

Bias recognition and mitigation: The process of identifying, evaluating, and reducing inherent societal biases that can be present in and amplified by AI systems, particularly Gen AI, due to the training data and language patterns. This involves actively monitoring, testing, and refining AI design to prevent the perpetuation of stereotypes.

Black box (for AI): An AI system with internal workings and decision-making processes that are opaque or too complex for humans to understand. This lack of transparency can create challenges for trust, accountability, and debugging.

Business case (for AI adoption): A justification presented to stakeholders, particularly leadership, outlining the rationale and expected benefits of investing in and implementing AI initiatives. It typically includes quantifiable efficiency gains, financial projections, quality improvements, risk assessment, and strategic alignment.

Business platform: Foundational enterprise software systems (like Microsoft 365 or Google Workspace) that host daily work, communication, collaboration, and document management. These platforms are increasingly becoming AI-powered environments, forming the core infrastructure for integrated knowledge management and learning ecosystems.

Chain of thought prompting: An AI prompting technique that involves asking an LLM to break down a problem, think through it step-by-step, and outline the actions it would take to reach a solution. This makes the AI model's thought process more transparent and can lead to more accurate and logical outputs, especially for complex tasks.

Chatbot: Computer programs that simulate basic conversations, typically for specific, narrowly defined tasks like answering FAQs or guiding users through simple processes. Traditional chatbots are often rule-based, relying on keyword matching and predefined scripts that offer limited flexibility and contextual understanding.

Closed systems (AI): GenAI systems—often provided by large tech companies (such as OpenAI, Microsoft, Google, and Anthropic)—that rely on proprietary training data and methodologies that aren't publicly available. They prioritize security and governance and typically produce more refined outputs.

Closed-source models: AI models that are privately developed and owned. They often use confidential underlying source code, architecture, and training data, and typically differ from open-source alternatives in terms of transparency and control.

Cognitive and psychological prompting: An approach to prompt design that incorporates techniques leveraging human cognitive patterns and psychological principles to improve LLM performance. This can include adding phrases that encourage step-by-step thinking, imply urgency, or introduce artificial incentives.

Computer vision: A field of AI that enables computers and systems to derive meaningful information from digital images, videos, and other visual inputs and take actions or make recommendations based on that information. It involves using technologies such as deep neural networks to analyze visual data.

Content adaptation: The process of modifying or transforming existing learning content to suit different contexts, formats, languages, or learner needs using AI tools. This can include translation, summarization, personalization, and repurposing content into different media (for example, turning a video into a podcast).

Content creation: The process of developing original learning content and materials tailored to specific objectives and organizational needs. This typically involves instructional designers and subject matter experts working together.

Content curation: The process of strategically selecting, organizing, vetting, and contextualizing existing knowledge resources (both internal and external) to create relevant learning experiences. It focuses on leveraging existing assets rather than creating everything from scratch.

Content generation (for AI): The use of GenAI tools—such as LLMs or image generators—to produce different types of learning content, including text, images, audio, and 3D models. This allows for rapid, scalable, and often personalized content production.

Content management system (CMS): A software application or set of related programs that are used to create, manage, store, and deploy digital content. In L&D, a CMS helps organize learning resources, facilitate updates, and manage access, ensuring users can navigate and retrieve materials efficiently.

Content proliferation: The challenge caused by the overwhelming abundance of available learning resources within organizations, which can make it difficult for employees to find relevant materials. This paradox occurs despite significant investment in content as traditional management approaches struggle with the sheer volume.

Context sensitivity: A core characteristic of LLMs in which the model interprets new information based on the preceding text within the prompt.

This means the order and structure of information provided will significantly influence the AI model's understanding and subsequent output.

Context window: The memory capacity of an LLM within a single conversation. All preceding prompts and responses within that conversation influence subsequent outputs, shaping the probability of certain words or concepts appearing later.

Conversation flow: The structured design of how a conversation will progress between a user and a conversational AI system. It involves mapping out potential user questions, scripting or prompting appropriate AI responses, and defining pathways for interaction, including escalations.

Conversational AI: Technologies enabling computers to engage in human-like conversations by understanding and responding to natural language inputs. This umbrella term encompasses chatbots, AI assistants, and multimodal generative AI, which use technologies such as machine learning and NLP.

Creation-curation-generation-automation framework: A model presented in this book that describes the evolution of how L&D uses technology for content. It progresses from manual creation to organizing existing resources (curation) to using AI tools (generation) and to streamlining processes (automation).

Data analysis and interpretation: A core competency for the human-machine performance analyst involving sifting through learning and performance data from different systems (such as an LMS, a performance management system, or an AI platform) to uncover meaningful patterns, insights, and root causes. It requires translating raw data into actionable learning strategies.

Data ecosystem: The process of identifying all systems involved in the learning experience (such as an LMS, an HRIS, content libraries, and collaboration tools) and visualizing how learner data, content information, and analytics flow between them. It aims to understand where data resides, how it moves, and where potential blockages or integration opportunities exist.

Data governance: The overall management of the availability, usability, integrity, and security of data that an organization uses. It involves establishing policies, standards, and controls for how to access and use data.

Data integration (for skills gap analysis): The process of collecting data from multiple sources (such as employee profiles, performance reviews, LMSs, project systems, and external market data) into an AI system for a comprehensive skills gap analysis. Effective integration enables a more complete and accurate understanding of organizational skills.

Data minimization: The practice of limiting the collection and retention of personal data to what is directly relevant and necessary to accomplish a specified purpose. This principle helps reduce privacy risks and data management burdens.

Data privacy framework: A set of precise guidelines and protocols governing the collection, storage, use, and protection of learner data within AI-integrated learning systems. This framework addresses the complex privacy implications arising from using AI technologies in L&D.

Data silos: Isolated repositories of data within an organization. If information is stored in one system but not readily accessible by other systems—which often occurs between legacy LMSs and newer LXPs or AI tools—it hinders comprehensive analysis.

Data-driven decision making (in L&D): An approach to L&D strategy and operations in which decisions are based on the analysis of relevant data rather than intuition or tradition alone. AI enhances this process by enabling the synthesis and analysis of large, complex datasets to inform learning initiatives and demonstrate influence.

Deep learning: A subset of machine learning that uses multilayered artificial neural networks (hence "deep") to learn complex patterns and hierarchical features directly from large amounts of raw data. It's particularly effective for tasks like image and speech recognition.

Deliberative agents: AI agents that are capable of planning and using strategic reasoning to achieve goals. They can optimize complex processes, such as student learning pathways.

Differential privacy: A system for publicly sharing information about a dataset by describing patterns of groups within the dataset while maintaining the confidentiality of individual data. It involves adding mathematical noise to data to protect personal privacy while enabling aggregate analysis.

Digital coach: An AI-driven component within a learning ecosystem that can guide and support users by providing personalized content recommendations and tailored learning experiences. It bridges the gap between AI analysis (like GenAI identifying content) and the individual learner to adapt recommendations based on user data and interactions.

Dynamic content adaptation: The use of AI tools (such as Synthesia and D-ID) to automatically transform static learning content into more engaging formats, such as video presentations featuring AI avatars. This allows for variations based on language, presentation style, or cultural context while maintaining core consistency.

Emotional resonance (in avatars): The ability of AI avatars, particularly sophisticated ones, to detect subtle cues in human interactions (such as voice patterns) and adjust their presentation style or responses accordingly to create a more engaging and connected experience. This capability stems from neural networks analyzing patterns of interaction.

ETL (extract-transform-load): A type of data integration process that involves extracting data from source systems, transforming it into a compatible format, and loading it into a target system, such as a database or data warehouse.

Explainable AI: AI systems that can explain their decisions or predictions in a way that humans can understand. This process aims to address the "black box" problem and increase trust and accountability.

Extended reality (XR): An umbrella term encompassing immersive technologies like virtual reality (VR), augmented reality (AR), and mixed reality (MR). XR technologies are used in L&D to create engaging, interactive, and often simulated learning environments.

Fairness (in AI): The principle that AI systems should treat individuals and groups equitably and avoid discriminatory outcomes. Defining and measuring fairness is complex because different mathematical and contextual definitions exist and can conflict.

Federated learning: A machine learning approach in which an AI model is trained across multiple decentralized devices or servers holding local data samples, without exchanging the raw data itself. This method enhances privacy by keeping data localized.

Few-shot learning: A prompt design technique that involves a user providing the LLM with a few examples ("shots") of the desired input and output formats. This helps the model understand the expected structure, style, and content for its response.

"Foot on the accelerator" state: The most advanced stage of AI implementation described in this book. It's characterized by seamless AI integration across departments, transparent governance, consistent access and training, measurable outcomes linked to AI, and L&D leveraging AI.

Foundation models: Large-scale AI models (such as those from OpenAI, Google, and Anthropic) that serve as the base for various AI applications, including autonomous agents. They provide core capabilities, such as reasoning and language understanding.

Freeform prompts: Direct, natural language instructions or questions without a rigid structure or template a user gives to an LLM. They allow for flexibility and are helpful for brainstorming, open-ended tasks, or initial exploration of an AI model's capabilities.

Gamification: The application of game-design elements and principles (such as points, badges, leaderboards, and challenges) in nongame contexts (such as learning experiences) to enhance engagement and motivation.

Generative AI (GenAI): A type of AI capable of creating new content—such as text, images, audio, or code—based on the data it was trained on. In L&D, this is used for tasks like course creation, personalization, skills gap analysis, and automating processes.

Generative AI model dimensions (1D, 2D, 3D, and 4D): A framework presented in this book to categorize the capabilities of GenAI applications for L&D. The dimensions progress in complexity and interactivity—from 1D (text) to 2D (multimedia, including images, audio, and video) to 3D (immersive models, such as VR and AR simulations) to 4D (real-time, adaptive systems).

Governance (in AI): The framework of rules, policies, standards, processes, and controls established to guide the development, deployment, and use of AI within an organization. Effective governance is crucial for mitigating the risks associated with AI, including privacy, security, and ethical concerns.

GPT (generative pretrained transformer): An advanced AI model—such as those from OpenAI (GPTs), Google (Gems), or Microsoft (Copilot agents)—that combines a prompt, specific knowledge sources, and access to external tools into a reusable and adaptable unit. They respond to human-initiated interactions, often through conversational prompts, and can perform complex tasks such as generating tailored learning content or analyzing problems.

Headless content creation: An approach to content creation that's particularly relevant in AI-powered workflows, in which an instructional designer interacts with AI models primarily through application programming interface (API) calls rather than traditional software based on a graphical user interface (GUI). This facilitates automation and integration between systems.

Human capital management (HCM) system: Integrated software suites that manage various employee-related processes, including payroll, benefits, performance management, talent acquisition, and, increasingly, L&D functions. Modern HCM systems often incorporate AI for tasks like skills analysis, personalized recommendations, and predictive analytics.

Human–AI collaboration: An approach that combines the strengths of humans and AI agents, enabling them to work together effectively. AI handles tasks like data analysis and routine processes, while humans provide strategic direction, creativity, ethical oversight, and complex problem solving.

Human–AI Task Scale: A seven-level spectrum presented in this book to categorize the varying degrees of collaboration between humans and AI systems on tasks. It ranges from fully manual human work (level 1) to fully autonomous AI (level 7), with several collaborative levels in between.

Human-machine performance analyst: An emerging L&D role that blends traditional L&D expertise with skills in data analysis, AI system management, business acumen, and strategic thinking. This role focuses on using human insight and AI capabilities to analyze performance, predict skills gaps, and optimize learning strategies for business impact.

Human-machine task mapping: A method for analyzing workflows by breaking them down into individual tasks and determining how each can be most effectively performed through human effort, AI automation, or a combination. It involves identifying the strengths of humans (such as creativity and empathy) and AI (such as speed and data processing) for specific task components.

Hybrid agents: AI agents that combine characteristics of different agent types—typically reactive responsiveness and deliberative reasoning—which enables them to offer immediate support while also developing longer-term strategies.

Hybrid workflow (content creation): A content creation model that blends traditional, manual methods using local desktop tools with cloud-based, AI-driven automation and asset generation. In this approach, AI assists with tasks like generating media or handling repetitive work, while humans retain control over complex interactions, strategic decisions, and quality assurance.

Hyper-personalized learning: An advanced form of personalized learning in which an AI model crafts highly specific individual development paths by analyzing vast data points, including performance metrics, career goals, and organizational needs. These learning journeys adapt dynamically to changing requirements.

Implementation road map: A phased plan outlining the steps, timelines, resources, and milestones for integrating AI into L&D functions or other organizational areas. It typically progresses from foundational activities to expansion and innovation.

Input encoding: The process within an AI system in which input data (such as text, images, or audio) is converted into a numerical or structured format that the AI model can process mathematically and understand. Examples include converting text to tokens or images to pixel grids.

Input-output framework: A structured approach for designing prompts, particularly for specific L&D applications, such as performance consulting or creating training imagery. It involves carefully considering the necessary inputs (such as clean data, prompt structure, and learning science principles), selecting the appropriate AI model, and rigorously validating the outputs against the intended goals.

Intelligent knowledge ecosystem: An organizational environment in which business platforms, AI, and knowledge management systems are integrated to enable the seamless capture, organization, discovery, and contextual delivery of information and learning. It can make knowledge readily available and useful within the flow of work.

Interaction model: Defines how users (learners) will interact with an AI agent, including the modality (such as text, voice, VR, or AR), personalization level, and feedback mechanisms.

Interoperability (in AI): The ability of different AI systems, software applications, and platforms to communicate, exchange data, and use the information exchanged. Learning ecosystems allow integrated experiences across various tools.

Iterative prompt design: The process of continually testing, evaluating, and refining prompts based on an LLM's responses to achieve the desired output quality and meet specific learning objectives. This involves techniques such as self-refinement (asking the AI model to refine the prompt) and incorporating feedback.

Knowledge architect: A strategic role for L&D professionals focused on designing, structuring, and overseeing an organization's knowledge ecosystem. This involves leveraging technologies such as knowledge management systems and AI to ensure that knowledge is effectively captured, organized, connected, and delivered to support learning and performance.

Knowledge graph: A technology that organizes information as a network of entities (such as people, skills, content, and projects) and the relationships between them, mimicking how humans associate concepts. Unlike traditional databases, it focuses on context and connections, allowing for more intelligent search and discovery.

Knowledge management: The organizational discipline and set of processes for systematically capturing, structuring, storing, sharing, and applying knowledge and expertise to improve performance and innovation. Modern knowledge management often involves technology platforms to facilitate these processes.

L&D AI integration: The process of incorporating AI tools and capabilities into the functions and workflows of L&D teams. This includes using AI for content creation, learner support, process automation, analytics, and enhancing the learning experience.

Large language model (LLM): A type of AI that's trained on massive datasets of text and code and is capable of understanding, interpreting, and generating human-like language. LLMs uses NLP techniques to perform tasks (such as translation, summarization, and text generation) based on input prompts.

Learning analytics: The practice of measuring, collecting, analyzing, and reporting data about learners and learning activities to understand and optimize the learning process and its outcomes. AI enhances this by analyzing complex patterns in learner interaction data to provide deeper insights beyond basic metrics, such as completion rates and scores.

Learning ecosystem: The dynamic network of people, content, technology, culture, and strategy that supports learning and development within an organization. It encompasses formal and informal learning experiences enabled by various interconnected tools and platforms.

Learning experience platform (LXP): A type of learning technology software that's used to create personalized, consumer-grade learning experiences by aggregating diverse content, enabling social learning, and often leveraging AI for recommendations and personalization. LXPs typically focus on empowering self-directed learning (a "pull" model).

Learning management system (LMS): A software application that's primarily used for the administration, tracking, reporting, and delivery of formal training programs and compliance courses. LMSs traditionally operate on a top-down assignment (or "push") model.

Learning modalities: The various formats or methods through which learning experiences are delivered. Newer, AI-enabled modalities include interactive simulations, AI tutors, and VR and AR experiences.

Learning record store (LRS): A database specifically designed to store, manage, and retrieve learning activity records in a format that's compliant with the xAPI specification. It acts as a central repository for learning data from multiple sources.

Learning workflow audit: A systematic process of mapping and analyzing the entire life cycle of learning content within an organization, from creation and review through publishing, delivery, tracking, and maintenance. It involves identifying the tools, systems, roles, bottlenecks, and potential automation opportunities at each stage.

Limited memory agents: AI agents that can retain information from past interactions over a limited period to inform current decisions. They build on reactive agents by incorporating a basic form of memory.

Local workflow (for content creation): The traditional approach to instructional design that involves manually crafting content (such as text, images, audio, video, code, and 3D models) with specialized software tools installed on a local computer. This method offers greater control but can be time consuming, resource intensive, and difficult to scale.

Machine learning: A subset of AI in which systems learn from data to improve their performance on a task without being explicitly programmed for every scenario. This concept underlies many AI capabilities, including pattern recognition and prediction.

Memory (agent component): The component of an AI agent that's responsible for storing and retrieving information from past interactions or experiences. This includes short-term memory for temporary data and long-term memory for learning and refining strategies over time.

Metadata: Data that provides information about other data. In L&D content management, it typically includes details such as titles, descriptions, authors, keywords, learning objectives, target audiences, formats, and usage rights—which help with organizing, searching, and curating content effectively.

Microlearning: An instructional approach for delivering learning content in small, focused bursts or segments that are designed to be consumed quickly and easily. It often targets specific skills or knowledge points.

Mixed reality (MR): A type of extended reality (XR) in which digital and real-world objects co-exist and interact in real time. It blends aspects of both physical and virtual reality.

Model training (AI): The process through which an AI model learns patterns, relationships, and features from a large dataset. This involves feeding the model vast amounts of prepared data and using algorithms to adjust its internal parameters to perform specific tasks, such as generating text or images.

Multilingual conversational AI: Systems capable of understanding and interacting in multiple languages. They often leverage breakthroughs in NLP to handle syntax, semantics, context, and cultural nuances across different languages.

Multimodal conversational AI: AI systems that integrate and process multiple modes of communication (such as text, voice, and visual inputs) to create more productive and natural interaction experiences.

Multimodal generative AI: Advanced AI systems that are capable of simultaneously processing, understanding, and generating content across multiple data types (modalities), such as text, images, audio, video, and code. These systems mimic human understanding by integrating diverse inputs.

Natural language processing (NLP): A field of AI that's focused on enabling computers to understand, interpret, and generate human language. NLP capabilities include analyzing text for meaning, categorizing information, and generating human-like written content.

Needs hierarchy: A performance consulting framework attributed to Jim and Dana Robinson. It involves analyzing organizational issues across different levels (including business, performance, work environment, and capabilities) to identify performance gaps and their root causes, rather than just symptoms.

Neural networks (artificial): Computing systems inspired by the biological neural networks that constitute animals' brains. They consist of interconnected nodes (or neurons) organized in layers, and are used primarily in deep learning to identify patterns and relationships in data.

Open systems (in AI): GenAI models (such as those developed by Meta) that function with underlying architecture or components that may be more accessible or customizable compared with closed systems. They offer greater flexibility and transparency.

Open-source models: AI models that use publicly available source code (as well as training data or methodologies), which allows anyone to inspect, modify, use, and distribute them. This fosters transparency and collaboration.

"Partial implementation" stage: A stage of AI adoption that describes different departments in an organization using AI tools inconsistently, uneven access, and a mix of approved and unauthorized usage, as well as limited system integration.

Performance architect: An L&D professional who focuses on designing and implementing systems, processes, and experiences aimed at directly improving employee performance within their workflow, often leveraging technology and human–AI collaboration. Their goal is to orchestrate the elements that enable effective job performance.

Performance consulting: A systematic process that's employed by L&D and performance improvement professionals to analyze performance issues, identify their root causes (which may or may not be related to training), and recommend targeted solutions to achieve the desired business outcomes. It emphasizes business impact over simply delivering training.

Performance support (AI-powered): The delivery of real-time, relevant guidance, information, and microlearning directly within an employee's workflow and facilitated by AI that understands the task being performed. This contrasts with traditional performance support, which often requires users to actively seek out information from separate resources.

Personalization (in learning): Tailoring learning content, recommendations, or experiences to individual learners based on their specific needs, preferences, roles, skill levels, learning history, or goals. AI plays a significant role in enabling personalization at scale by analyzing data and dynamically adapting content or pathways.

Personalized learning path: An individually tailored sequence of learning resources and experiences (such as courses, articles, projects, and mentorships) that are curated to meet a specific learner's goals, current skill level, role requirements, and preferences. AI plays a crucial role in generating and adapting these paths dynamically.

Personally identifiable information (PII): Any data that could potentially identify a specific individual, either on its own or when combined with other information. Examples include names, addresses, ID numbers, and, in some contexts, learning performance data.

Pilot programs: Small-scale, controlled experiments that test the feasibility, effectiveness, and potential impact of a new initiative (such as an AI application) before its wider rollout. They enable learning, provide feedback, and support refinement.

Pilot use case: A small-scale, controlled implementation of a new technology or process (such as an AI tool or automation) that's focused on solving a specific, high-impact L&D problem. The goal is to test feasibility, demonstrate value, gather feedback, and build support before considering a larger rollout.

Platform assessment: A structured evaluation of an organization's core business platforms (such as Microsoft 365 or Google Workspace) to determine their suitability for supporting current and future L&D needs, particularly in terms of AI integration, data flow, and scalability. It involves analyzing workflows, data ecosystems, and specific L&D requirements.

Platform evaluation rubric: A standardized scoring tool developed by L&D to objectively evaluate and compare technology platforms based on specific, weighted criteria relevant to learning effectiveness, administration, and strategic goals. Criteria often include content management features, learner experience, data analytics capabilities, and AI readiness.

Predictive analytics: A branch of advanced analytics that uses techniques such as machine learning and statistical modeling on current and historical data to make predictions about future events or behaviors. In

L&D, this may involve forecasting course completion rates or identifying learners who are at risk of dropping out.

Predictive learning strategies: L&D strategies that proactively anticipate and prepare for future skills requirements based on AI-driven analysis of business goals, market trends, and internal data. This contrasts with traditional needs assessments that are often backward looking.

Prior knowledge activation: A characteristic of LLMs that involves a prompt triggering specific knowledge domains embedded within the model's extensive training data. Inquiring about a widely known topic typically enables the model to access and use relevant information from its training.

Privacy by design approach: An approach to systems engineering and business practices that proactively embeds privacy considerations into the design and operation of IT systems, networked infrastructure, and business processes from the outset. It means not treating privacy as an add-on, but as a core requirement.

Privacy impact assessment (PIA): A systematic process for evaluating the potential effects of a project, system, or technology on individual privacy and identifying ways to mitigate associated privacy risks. PIAs help ensure compliance with privacy regulations and organizational policies.

Programmatic prompting: A technique involving structuring prompts using code-like syntax, logical operations, variables, and iteration instructions. This enables the production of concrete, consistent, reproducible, and dynamic outputs suitable for complex learning and development tasks.

Prompt design (or prompt engineering): The practice of crafting and refining input instructions (prompts) to effectively guide LLMs toward generating desired outputs for specific applications. It involves understanding LLM capabilities and limitations, structuring requests clearly, and iteratively testing prompts.

Prompt library: A curated, organized, and centralized collection of reusable prompts that consistently and efficiently guide GenAI models for specific L&D tasks. A prompt library addresses challenges such as inconsistent outputs, wasted time, and scaling difficulties associated with the use of ad-hoc prompts.

Prompt workflow (or prompt chain): A sequence of interconnected prompts used within a single AI conversation or tool, in which the output of one prompt serves as the input for the next. This approach allows for progressive refinement and the creation of more complex, cohesive outputs compared with using single, isolated prompts.

Prompt: An instruction or query given to an AI model (like an LLM or GPT) to guide it in generating a specific response or completing a task. Prompts can range from simple, freeform requests to complex, structured instructions.

Prompting: The skill of crafting effective instructions or queries (prompts) to guide Gen AI models, such as LLMs, in producing desired outputs. Effective prompting is crucial for maximizing the utility and accuracy of AI tools.

Reactive agents: The simplest type of AI agent, operating solely based on current precepts and predefined condition-action rules. They do not maintain an internal state or memory of past events.

Real-time skills gap analysis: A dynamic approach, significantly enhanced by AI, that continuously identifies discrepancies between the skills an organization needs and those possessed by its workforce. It uses integrated data and AI analysis to provide up-to-date insights and enable proactive intervention.

Reasoning (in AI agents): The capability of an AI agent to process information, make inferences, solve problems, and make decisions to achieve its goals. This often involves leveraging large LLMs and techniques such as the chain of thought.

Recommendation engine: An AI-powered system that filters information (such as content or products) to suggest items most relevant to a particular user based on their profile, past behavior, and potentially the behavior of similar users. This is commonly seen on consumer platforms and is a key feature of LXPs.

Remote workflow (for content creation): A content creation approach that heavily uses cloud-based, AI-powered tools and services (which are often accessed via APIs) to dynamically generate learning assets (including text, images, audio, video, code, and 3D models) without relying primarily on local software or extensive manual processes. This workflow emphasizes scalability, automation, and personalization and often involves AI agents and headless creation methods.

Representation (in AI): The extent to which AI systems, particularly generative models like LLMs, accurately and fairly reflect the diversity of human experiences, perspectives, identities, and cultures in their outputs. Poor representation can lead to biased or insensitive content.

Retrieval (in AI agents): The process through which an AI agent accesses and retrieves relevant information from data sources—such as databases, content libraries, knowledge bases, or the internet—to inform its reasoning and decision making.

Role (in prompting): Assigning a specific persona, expertise, or perspective to an LLM within a prompt (for example, "Act as an instructional designer" or "You are a customer service expert"). This guides the model's tone, word choice, and the depth of response based on the assigned role.

Scalable personalization (for avatars): The ability of AI avatar technology to deliver uniquely tailored learning experiences to many individuals simultaneously. Each learner interacts with an instance of the avatar that's adapted to their specific cultural background, learning preferences, professional context, or other defined parameters.

SCORM (sharable content object reference model): An established set of technical standards for e-learning software products that ensure online learning content can interoperate with various SCORM-conformant LMSs.

Self-aware agents: A theoretical and advanced type of AI agent that possesses consciousness and self-awareness, which enables it to understand its internal states and potentially evaluate its own performance.

Semantic analysis: A core NLP process used by LLMs that extends beyond grammar (syntax) to comprehend the meaning of words and their relationships within text. It allows the model to interpret context, ambiguity, idioms, and nuances in language.

Shadow AI: The use of AI applications and tools within an organization by employees or departments without the IT department's explicit approval, knowledge, or oversight. This practice introduces significant security, privacy, compliance, and IP risks.

Skills indexing (in AI): The application of AI to automatically discover, categorize, map, and quantify the skills present within an organization's workforce. It analyzes diverse data sources (including performance reviews, project contributions, learning records, and internal communications) to create a dynamic, real-time inventory of capabilities.

Skills ecosystem management: The strategic practice of mapping, understanding, developing, and deploying skills across an organization. It's often facilitated by technologies like knowledge graphs or AI skills indexing and involves visualizing the current skills landscape, identifying gaps, and aligning development efforts with business objectives.

Skills gap analysis: The process for identifying the discrepancy between the skills required for specific job roles or organizational goals and the current skill levels possessed by the workforce. AI can contribute by inferring skills from various data points and identifying areas that need development.

Skills taxonomy: A structured classification system or library of skills that are relevant to an organization's business, industry, and roles. In the context of AI, this taxonomy is often dynamically generated and updated by skills indexing systems.

Structured prompt: A detailed and formatted prompt that provides specific constraints, context, examples, and clear instructions to guide an AI model toward a precise output format or task. This is in contrast with simpler, open-ended freeform prompts.

Syntactic parsing: A core NLP process that's used by LLMs to break down sentences into their grammatical components (including nouns, verbs, and adjectives). It enables the model to comprehend the grammatical structure of the input text.

Synthetic avatars: AI-generated digital representations of humans that are often used in video creation platforms. These avatars can be based on real people or entirely digitally created. They are capable of delivering scripted content with synchronized lip movements and expressions.

Task (in prompting): Explicitly stating the specific action or outcome required from the LLM within the prompt (for example, "Develop a set of learning objectives" or "Create a video script"). This gives the model a clear purpose and helps avoid overly general or unrelated responses.

Task details (in prompting): Providing specific constraints, guidelines, context, required formats, or key focus areas within the prompt to refine the LLM's output. This ensures the generated content meets specific requirements for relevance, structure, and completeness.

Technology fear cycle: A recurring pattern of societal or organizational responses to the introduction of new, potentially disruptive technologies. It typically involves stages of initial fear, media amplification, attempts to slow adoption, gradual regulation, and eventual acceptance.

Text-to-speech (TTS): Technology that converts written text into spoken voice output. AI-powered TTS systems can produce increasingly natural-sounding voices in many different languages and accents.

Theory of mind (ToM) agents: AI agents that can understand or infer a user's mental state, including their beliefs, desires, intentions, and emotions. This enables them to tailor their interactions to the perceived cognitive or emotional state of the user.

Tokenization (in AI): The process in NLP in which input text is broken down into smaller units—called tokens—which can be words or subwords. This prepares the text for numerical processing by the LLM.

Tools (for AI agents): External applications, data sources, or APIs that an AI agent can access and use to perform specific actions or gather necessary information to achieve its goals.

TRACI framework: A specific, structured prompt framework that stands for task, role, audience, create, and intent. It provides a comprehensive template for guiding LLM outputs by clearly defining what needs to be done, who is responsible, for whom it's intended, how it should be done, and why it's important.

Traditional AI: Earlier forms of AI typically focused on rule-based systems and predefined logic to solve specific, well-defined problems. These systems operate based on explicitly programmed rules rather than learning from data patterns like machine learning models.

Transparency (in AI): Refers to the clarity and explainability of how an AI system arrives at its decisions or outputs, including the data used and the algorithms employed. For L&D, this means understanding why an AI learning platform recommends certain content or identifies a specific skills gap.

Tree-of-thought (TOT) prompting: An advanced prompting method in which a user encourages an LLM to explore multiple reasoning paths or scenarios simultaneously before reaching a conclusion. This allows the model to consider various possibilities and evaluate alternatives, promoting more robust problem solving.

User experience (UX): This encompasses all aspects of an end-user's interaction with a company, its services, and its products, specifically referring to the ease of use, efficiency, and satisfaction when interacting with a learning platform.

Versioning (for prompts): The practice of assigning clear version numbers or unique identifiers to different iterations of a prompt within a library. This includes documenting changes and potentially using status labels (such as "draft" or "final") to track development and maintain history.

Virtual reality (VR): A technology that creates a completely immersive, computer-generated environment in which users can interact, typically by using headsets that block out the real world. Learners can interact within these simulated environments for training or exploration.

"Wait and see" approach: An organizational stance on AI adoption that's characterized by awareness but hesitation to commit resources or implement solutions. This often due to concerns about security, privacy, or uncertainty. It involves monitoring competitors but taking little internal action.

World model–based agents: AI agents that build and maintain an internal model or representation of their environment. This model enables them to predict how the environment might change based on potential actions, which allows for more sophisticated planning and decision making compared with simpler agents.

xAPI (experience API): A modern e-learning software specification that's designed to track a wide range of learning experiences, including those that occur outside a traditional LMS (such as mobile learning, simulations, or real-world performance). Data is typically stored in a learning record store (LRS).

Zero-shot prompting: Giving a task or question directly to an LLM without providing any prior examples ("shots") of the desired output format. The model relies solely on its pre-existing training to understand and respond to the request.

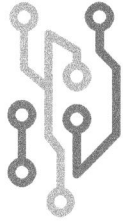

References

Anthropic. 2024. "Building Effective Agents." December 19. anthropic.com
/research/building-effective-agents.

Beane, M. 2024. *The Skill Code: How to Save Human Ability in an Age of
Intelligent Machines*. Harper Business.

Borowiec, S. 2016. "Google's AlphaGo AI Defeats Human in First Game of
Go Contest." *The Guardian*, March 9. theguardian.com/technology
/2016/mar/09/google-deepmind-alphago-ai-defeats-human-lee-sedol
-first-game-go-contest.

Cecco, L. 2024. "Air Canada Ordered to Pay Customer Who Was Misled
by Airline's Chatbot." *The Guardian*, February 16. theguardian.com
/world/2024/feb/16/air-canada-chatbot-lawsuit.

Colon-Hernandez, P., C. Havasi, J. Alonso, M. Huggins, and C. Breazeal.
2021. "Combining Pre-Trained Language Models and Structured
Knowledge." *ArXiv* abs/2101.12294 (2021). arxiv.org/pdf/2101.12294.

Dastin, J. 2018. "Insight—Amazon Scraps Secret AI Recruiting Tool That
Showed Bias Against Women." *Reuters*, October 10. reuters.com
/article/us-amazon-com-jobs-automation-insight/amazon-scraps
-secret-ai-recruiting-tool-that-showed-bias-against-women
-idUSKCN1MK08G.

Defelice, R. 2021. "How Long Does It Take to Develop Training? New
Question, New Answers." ATD Blog, January 13. td.org/content/atd
-blog/how-long-does-it-take-to-develop-training-new-question
-new-answers.

Glean. 2022. *Hybrid Workplace Habits and Hangups Report*. Glean, February 8. glean.com/resources/guides/hybrid-workplace-habits-hangups.

Kavlakoglu, E., and R. Vaish. 2020. "NLP vs. NLU vs. NLG: The Differences Between Three Natural Language Processing Concepts." IBM, November 12. ibm.com/think/topics/nlp-vs-nlu-vs-nlg.

Knowmax. 2024. "FinTech Unicorn Journey of Providing Seamless Customer Service to 2 Million+ Users Through Efficient Knowledge Management." knowmax.ai/case-studies/fintech-unicorn-journey-of -providing-seamless-customer-service-through-knowmax.

Larson, J., S. Mattu, L. Kirchner, and J. Angwin. 2016. "How We Analyzed the COMPAS Recidivism Algorithm." ProPublica, May 23. propublica .org/article/how-we-analyzed-the-compas-recidivism-algorithm.

Li, F.F. 2021. "Dr. Fei-Fei Li on Human-Centered AI." Video. Greylock, July 13. youtube.com/watch?v=06M_xmHmDfw&t=779s.

Lin, M. 2023. "Watson Assistant for HR | Part 1." Video. Mike Lin, May 24. youtube.com/watch?v=Ri335l19DRs.

LinkedIn. 2025. *Workplace Learning Report 2025*. LinkedIn. learning .linkedin.com/resources/workplace-learning-report.

Najjar, R. 2023. "Redefining Radiology: A Review of Artificial Intelligence Integration in Medical Imaging." *Diagnostics* 13(17): 2760. doi.org /10.3390/diagnostics13172760.

Pant, V. 2024. "Multilingual Conversational AI: Benefits for Call Centers and Customers." Convin Blog, December 12. convin.ai/blog /multilingual-conversational-ai.

Ptacek, T.H. (@tqbf). 2022. "I'm sorry, I simply cannot be cynical about a technology that can accomplish this." X, December 1, 2022. 9:05 p.m. x.com/tqbf/status/1598513757805858820.

Qin, F., and T.A. Kochan. 2020. "The Learning System at IBM: A Case Study." MIT Sloan School of Management, December 3. mitsloan.mit .edu/institute-work-and-employment-research/learning-system-ibm -a-case-study.

Robinson, D.G., and J.C. Robinson. 1996. *Performance Consulting: Moving Beyond Training*. Berrett-Koehler Publishers.

Robinson, D.G., and J.C. Robinson. 1998. *Moving From Training to Performance: A Practical Guidebook*. Berrett-Koehler Publishers.

Robinson, D.G., and J.C. Robinson. 2005. *Strategic Business Partner: Aligning People Strategies With Business Goals*. Berrett-Koehler Publishers.

Roose, K. 2022. "The Brilliance and Weirdness of ChatGPT." *New York Times*, December 5. nytimes.com/2022/12/05/technology/chatgpt-ai -twitter.html.

Salesforce. n.d. "What Are Autonomous Agents? A Complete Guide." salesforce.com/agentforce/autonomous-agents.

Smail, J. 2018. "Exclusive: Unilever Chatbot to Transform HR Services in 106 Countries." Employee Benefits, October 4. employeebenefits.co.uk /benefits-technology/exclusive-unilever-chatbot-to-transform-hr -services-in-106-countries/195656.article.

Unilever. n.d. "Providing Skills for Life." unilever.com/sustainability /future-of-work/providing-skills-for-life.

Vorecol. 2024. "Personalizing Training Programs for Employee Engagement and Retention." Vorecol, August 28. vorecol.com/blogs /blog-personalizing-training-programs-for-employee-engagement -and-retention-9181.

Walsh, C. 2023. "How GE Healthcare-SHS Have Revamped Employee Engagement with AI." inFeedo.ai, February 2. infeedo.ai/success -stories/how-ge-healthcare-measured-employee-morale.

World Economic Forum. 2025. *The Future of Jobs Report 2025*. World Economic Forum, January 5. weforum.org/publications/the-future -of-jobs-report-2025/in-full/3-skills-outlook.

Index

In this index, *f* denotes figure and *t* denotes table.

About the Author

Josh Cavalier is on a mission to bridge the gap between L&D professionals and the transformative power of AI. His own aha moment arrived in late 2022 when an AI tool generated a remarkably effective educational video script in response to his prompt, instantly revealing its potential to revolutionize learning.

Drawing on more than 30 years of experience (including leading Lodestone Digital to significantly improve clients' edtech implementations), Josh now guides organizations through the complexities of AI integration.

Through JoshCavalier.ai, he directly addresses the concerns and opportunities facing L&D. Forget the fear of job loss—Josh argues AI necessitates a shift in roles, amplifying the need for human expertise and insight. He cuts through the myth of "automatic" AI, emphasizing that L&D professionals are crucial collaborators in the process.

His focus? Pragmatic strategies and tools that help teams navigate the AI ecosystem, understand human-machine partnership, and significantly increase their AI skills.

Josh makes complex AI accessible and actionable. His popular YouTube channel and interactive live show *Brainpower* offer easy-to-use methods for working with AI.

Committed to the L&D community, he consults, runs workshops, and shares his strategic insights at major industry events (including DevLearn and the ATD International Conference & Exposition), empowering professionals to leverage AI for hyper-personalized learning and greater organizational impact.

About ATD

The Association for Talent Development (ATD) is the world's largest association dedicated to those who develop talent in organizations. Serving a global community of members, customers, and international business partners in more than 100 countries, ATD champions the importance of learning and training by set-ting standards for the talent development profession.

Our customers and members work in public and private organizations in every industry sector. Since ATD was founded in 1943, the talent development field has expanded significantly to meet the needs of global businesses and emerging industries. Through the Talent Development Capability Model, education courses, certifications and credentials, memberships, industry-leading events, research, and publications, we help talent development professionals build their personal, professional, and organizational capabilities to meet new business demands with maximum impact and effectiveness.

One of the cornerstones of ATD's intellectual foundation, ATD Press offers insightful and practical information on talent development, training, and professional growth. ATD Press publications are written by industry thought leaders and offer anyone who works with adult learners the best practices, academic theory, and guidance necessary to move the profession forward.

We invite you to join our community. Learn more at **TD.org**.

www.ingramcontent.com/pod-product-compliance
Lightning Source LLC
Chambersburg PA
CBHW071538210326
41597CB00019B/3041